THE REALLY USEFUL A – Z OF
Pregnancy and Birth

About the author:

Harriet Griffey originally trained as a nurse, and worked on the Paediatric Unit of the Middlesex Hospital, London before working for many years in book publishing. As Editorial Director at Macdonald Optima, she specialized in health books but gave up publishing and subsequently worked for numerous independent television companies as researcher and writer. This included working on many of the BBC's Learning Zone programmes for the Royal College of Nursing, and a number of other independent productions including Channel 4's *Dispatches* and the BBC's *The Business*. She co-authored *Give Your Child a Better Start* with Professor Mike Howe, and continues to work as a freelance researcher, writer and editor. Harriet Griffey has two children and lives in London.

THE REALLY USEFUL A – Z OF

Pregnancy and Birth

Harriet Griffey

Thorsons
An Imprint of HarperCollins*Publishers*

Thorsons
An Imprint of HarperCollins*Publishers*
77–85 Fulham Palace Road,
Hammersmith, London W6 8JB

1160 Battery Street,
San Francisco, California 94111–1213

Published by Thorsons 1996

10 9 8 7 6 5 4 3 2 1

A catalogue record for this book
is available from the British Library

ISBN 0 7225 3175 3

Text illustrations by Peter Cox

Printed and bound in Great Britain by
Caledonian International Book Manufacturing Ltd, Glasgow

For my parents, Angela and Alec Strahan

CONTENTS

Acknowledgements ix

Foreword xi

Introduction xv

A – Z of Pregnancy and Birth 1

Useful Addresses 290

Further Reading 300

ACKNOWLEDGEMENTS

Numerous people have supported and contributed to the
writing of this book, and in a variety of ways, although the
final responsibility for its content must remain with me.
Among those who have provided valuable help are Liz
McCormick; David Fielder; Dr Ann Szarewski DRCOG, for
reading and commenting on the manuscript; Deborah Hughes,
midwife, who was so helpful and whose contribution has
been invaluable; Melanie Every, Professional Development
Officer for Complementary Therapies, Royal College of
Midwives; Hedwig Verdonk, osteopath; Julia Anastasiou,
reflexologist; Sister Lucy Turner, Queen Charlotte's and
Chelsea Hospital; Caroline Flint, Independent Midwife and
President of the Royal College of Midwives; Mandy Kerr,
midwife and aromatherapist; Alistair Scott of Country
Computers; and my editor at Thorsons, Erica Smith.

Particular thanks are due to Janet Tame, for caring for
my younger son while I wrote this book. And to both my
sons, Josh and Robbie, without whom not only would my
interest in pregnancy and birth have remained theoretical,
but, though this book might have been completed sooner,
my life would have been the poorer.

FOREWORD

In 1993, the UK Department of Health published a report called *Changing Childbirth*. It stated that 'The woman and her baby should be at the centre of all planning and provision of maternity care'. This may hardly seem revolutionary, but in reality it meant that a subtle and necessary shift had taken place. After many years, during which time having a baby became increasingly seen as an activity fraught with danger, it was now deemed possible for women to give birth, rather than to be delivered of their babies. It was formally recognized by the health profession that this was a process in which a woman was actively involved, rather than passively standing – or to be more accurate, lying with her feet in stirrups – on the sidelines.

At the same time, a growing awareness of how the woman was feeling, and how this would affect her new baby, was emerging. Why was this so important? I believe it is because if a woman is allowed to take responsibility for the new life she gives birth to, and is then given confidence in caring for her newborn baby, her entry to motherhood gives her confidence rather than detracting from it.

The woman who has been able to make her own decisions, who has felt in control, feels more confident than the woman who has been organized and controlled.

I have found this to be true in both my personal and professional life. As a midwife, I have been 'with women' (the literal meaning of the Anglo-Saxon word *midwife*), supporting their labour and pain, sharing their exhilaration and their joy. As a woman I have felt the empowering experience of feeling totally in control of the birth of my first baby. Despite the pain I experienced the most empowering experience of my life and a wonderful start in the relationship between me and my firstborn. I also know that for women to make decisions about their care during pregnancy and birth, they need information.

In addition to that given to women by their midwives, there is now plenty of written information available to pregnant women. Some written by women, some by men, some by doctors, and some sponsored by babymilk manufacturers ... Here is a book written by a woman, a mother, an ex-nurse and someone who obviously wanted to know more about all sorts of information and care when pregnant. In compiling a book which brings together both orthodox and complementary healthcare information, she has provided a book which enables women to benefit from the best of both worlds when pregnant and giving birth.

The emergent use of complementary therapies, and in particular during pregnancy and birth has been of interest to the Royal College of Midwives for some time, and many midwives now have additional training and expertise in the use of a wide range of complementary therapies – homoeopathy, acupuncture and aromatherapy, for example – which enhances their professional practice. This is entirely appropriate, and it is also appropriate that training and registration should be monitored to ensure best practice.

The Royal College of Midwives is actively supporting this, in line with its support of women's choice and of woman-centred maternity care.

Given this growing interest, a book which combines information about both orthodox and complementary approaches to a subject that couldn't be more woman-centred makes a welcome contribution to current literature. Harriet Griffey has managed to cover pregnancy and birth comprehensively while taking the 'crankiness' out of alternative approaches and providing accessible, up-to-date information of value to any woman having a baby.

Caroline Flint
Independent Midwife and President of the Royal College
of Midwives

INTRODUCTION

The aim of this book is to provide a comprehensive
overview of information useful to women during pregnancy
and birth. More important, the aim is to include all the
alternative and complementary approaches that are
particularly relevant during pregnancy and labour –
alongside the general information found in most books.

Even though pregnancy is a tremendously exciting and
important time in any woman's life, it is unique to each
woman – you don't stop being the individual woman you
were before you got pregnant! The circumstances in which
each of us is pregnant are also completely individual.

For those who are first-time pregnant mothers it is
an exceptional time and, without the demands of other
children, a time that can be particularly enjoyable if it
isn't fraught with unanswered questions and anxieties.
But being pregnant for the first time isn't a finite state. It
represents a transition into motherhood; because of this it
is completely different from any subsequent pregnancy.

Each woman will become a mother in her own way,
influenced by numerous relatives, friends, health
professionals, magazine articles and even books.

One of the aims of this book is to provide information so that a woman can make informed choices about the type of pregnancy and labour she experiences, and about how she wants to start her new life as a mother.

Another aim is to provide a more holistic perspective of pregnancy and birth, and one where a full range of information about coping with the ups and downs of pregnancy is included: the orthodox approach alongside the complementary, rather than as mutually exclusive. This becomes particularly relevant when dealing with some of the common problems associated with pregnancy. You won't find much about dealing with morning sickness in a book written by a male obstetrician!

Finally, the aim was to look at all that was useful to know from whatever relevant source – gleaning it from medical textbooks, alternative health manuals, professional expertise, midwives' dictionaries, personal experience – and try to find the most accessible format for it. I wanted to write the book I looked for, among the many I bought when I was pregnant, and one that would be really useful for this particular stage of a woman's life.

Aa

Active Birth

Giving birth is a physically demanding and strenuous activity – which can come as a bit of a shock to many first-time mothers! In the same way that it is sensible to prepare physically before a skiing holiday or running a marathon, so it is beneficial to prepare physically before giving birth.

To a certain extent, active birth refers to a state of mind as much as to a woman's physical activity during labour and birth. Rather than letting her baby's birth happen to her, the woman participates fully in the process, responding to the impact of her labour as naturally as she can. Exercising during pregnancy can increase a woman's strength, suppleness and stamina; breathing exercises can help her to release tension and reduce the pain of labour.

Most women are encouraged by their midwives to work actively with their bodies during labour and birth. During labour and the birth itself, active birth means that a woman is free to adopt any position that aids this process. There are several different possible positions for labour and delivery; some actually speed up or delay labour.

Many women giving birth find it a painful process in spite of any preparations they have made. In this case there is no point refusing pain relief. While a certain amount of pain in childbirth is natural, if women are to be guided by their own bodies they must also feel free not to be pressurized into accepting pain when they don't wish to. Pain relief can make it possible for many women to enjoy giving birth to their babies. Active birth means being actively involved in all aspects of labour, and this can mean actively deciding on pain relief when necessary.

Compare **Lamaze Method, Leboyer Method, Natural Childbirth**

See also **Breathing Exercises, Exercise, Pain, Pain Relief, Position, Psychoprophylaxis**

Acupressure

Acupressure involves firm massage at certain points of the body. These points are the same as those used in acupuncture, but pressure rather than needles is applied.

In the same way that we instinctively massage our temples when we have a tension headache, acupressure is thought to stimulate and improve the body's own healing power. Initially, consulting an acupressure therapist is the best way of learning more and enjoying acupressure's therapeutic effects. There are several different schools of acupressure, including shiatsu.

Self-administered acupressure can be an extremely useful way of relieving some of the minor symptoms of pregnancy experienced by some women. For example, wearing acupressure wrist bands can help with the nausea and vomiting suffered by many women in the first three months of pregnancy.

An acupressure therapist will be able to advise and instruct on those self-help techniques that will be helpful in pregnancy and which are tailored to an individual woman's needs. Learning more from a qualified practitioner is worthwhile because there may be other ailments, unrelated to pregnancy, that would benefit from treatment.

Compare **Acupuncture, Complementary Therapies**
See also **Morning Sickness, Shiatsu**

Acupuncture

Acupuncture is designed to correct any imbalances in the body which may give rise to disease or illness. By inserting needles at specific acupuncture points along energy channels within the body, called meridians, energy channels can be unblocked or stimulated in order to have an effect on a particular symptom or part of the body (*see Figure 1*). The Chinese call this flow of energy, or life force, 'Qi' (pronounced 'chee').

Traditional Chinese medicine describes the body's balance in terms of yin and yang. The yin force represents traditional female qualities, peacefulness and calm, while the yang force represents traditional male qualities of aggression and stimulation. Any therapeutic treatment does, however, treat the individual holistically, taking into account a full emotional and physical picture. This picture cannot be reduced to terms of diagnosis and treatment.

In pregnancy acupuncture has many applications and is particularly effective and safe for a number of troublesome complaints. It is often recommended in conjunction with another therapy – an osteopath might recommend a short course to help in treating long-standing low back pain, or a homoeopath may recommend it as part of an individual treatment programme for morning sickness, headaches or insomnia.

There are now a number of doctors and midwives who have an additional training and qualification in

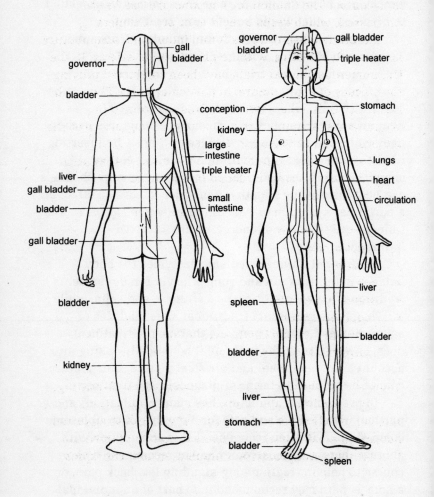

Acupuncture meridian points

acupuncture. There may be one at your local health centre. Unless you know of an acupuncturist locally, your best bet is to contact The Council for Acupuncture (*see Useful Addresses*), which keeps a register of practitioners.

Certainly when it works for an individual, acupuncture is extremely effective, with no negative side-effects. In the UK, numerous clinical trials have been conducted proving the efficacy of acupuncture, in particular at the Plymouth Maternity Unit, where two midwives are trained in acupuncture. Acupuncture is also part of the service at the Maternity Unit at Warwick Hospital.

The following 'minor' ailments – although they seem anything *but* if you suffer from them – are helped particularly well by acupuncture:

- *morning sickness*
- *constipation*
- *backache*
- *piles*
- *breech presentation*
- *inducing labour*
- *pain relief during labour and delivery*
- *insufficient milk production.*

You may find the idea of acupuncture needles off-putting, but if you are in pain or continually vomiting, you may find this is the only source of effective relief. The needles used nowadays are disposable, so there is no risk of infection.

Compare **Acupressure, Complementary Therapies**

Afterbirth

During the third stage of labour the afterbirth, or placenta, is delivered.

See also **Labour, Placenta, Third Stage**

Afterpains

After delivery, the womb, or uterus, contracts eventually to its pre-pregnancy size. Afterpains occur as a result of these contractions and can be mild or quite painful, much as period pains can vary. They are usually stronger after subsequent pregnancies, as the uterus returns to its former shape.

These pains can also be quite strong during breastfeeding as the baby's sucking stimulates the uterus to contract. This is one of the benefits of breastfeeding, as it is thought that it helps the uterus return to normal more quickly, which may be worth bearing in mind if the pains are bad enough to put you off breastfeeding altogether. Any pain will decrease over the first few days. Try taking paracetamol, as you would for period pains, to help. Additionally, consult a homoeopath. Homoeopath Miranda Castro (*see Further Reading*) recommends the remedy *Magnesia phosphorica*.

Afterpains, with lessening severity, can continue for several days after the birth; for some time after that the contractions may remain noticeable (especially during breastfeeding). Mention them to your midwife if they concern you, as she may want to check that your uterus isn't trying to expel any large blood clots. Try consciously relaxing and breathing through them if they are bad in the first few days, as you did during your labour contractions.

See also **Homoeopathy**, **Involution**, **Pain Relief**

AIDS

AIDS (acquired immune deficiency syndrome) can occur following infection by the human immunodeficiency virus (HIV). During pregnancy women who have been infected with HIV, but who haven't yet shown any symptoms of AIDS, may develop symptoms. HIV is also an infection that can cross the placenta and affect the growing baby.

See also **HIV**

Alcohol

Alcohol, like numerous other drugs, can cross the placenta. While it is recognized that drinking alcohol before and during pregnancy can put an unborn baby at risk, the amount of alcohol which might cause harm, and when during pregnancy it is most dangerous to drink, are not fully known.

Many women find that they go off alcohol completely, especially during the first three months, which solves this particular problem for them. For women who drink regularly and for those who regularly have an alcohol 'binge' things are more problematic, as in both these instances it is probably advisable to stop completely when pregnant.

Some women decide to give up altogether, just to be on the safe side, whereas others find the occasional glass of wine, sherry or beer quite medicinal – this is unlikely to do much harm if you are generally in good health. Spirits are probably best avoided as they are a much more concentrated form of alcohol. One suggestion is to avoid alcohol altogether in the first three months, then restrict any intake to one or two glasses of wine or beer a week. There remain people (health professionals among them) who positively recommend the occasional glass of stout for its iron content!

Alexander Technique

The Alexander technique is a method of movement that improves an individual's posture, correcting faults that can prevent the body working to its best capacity. It is also a technique that can alleviate many symptoms ranging from back pain to respiratory disorders, exhaustion to irritable bowel syndrome, headaches to high blood-pressure.

Posture is never more important than during pregnancy, when your body has to accommodate extra weight, and all at the front. This can give rise to a lot of extra stress and strain, which in turn is aggravated by poor posture.

Whether you want to improve your general posture to help your body cope better with pregnancy, or want to find a way to alleviate some specific symptom while you are pregnant, you will need to find a qualified teacher. Once you have learned the technique, you can practise alone – although it is useful to see a teacher regularly in order to make sure you continue to improve.

To find a qualified teacher, contact the Society of Teachers of the Alexander Technique (*see Useful Addresses*).

Compare **Complementary Therapies**

See also **Posture**

Allergies

While it is possible to have an allergy to almost anything, it is unlikely that you will develop any particular allergies during pregnancy. What may be a complication is that, if you do have an allergy for which you use orthodox treatments, you may have to check out their suitability during pregnancy.

Allergic symptoms occur when your body's cells produce chemicals (called histamines) in response to the antibodies that are produced in reaction to whatever substance you're sensitive, or allergic, to.

Because an allergic response is part of the body's immune system, and because during pregnancy your immune system is partly suppressed in order to prevent rejection of the unborn baby, some women with allergies find these seem to get worse. In addition, if your defences are low, allergies may seem worse. This is another good reason to care adequately for your general health when pregnant, making sure your diet is nutritious and you get enough rest.

Compare **Diet, Immune System**

Alpha Fetoprotein (AFP) Test

This is one of a number of blood tests offered routinely to pregnant women. In many places AFP testing has been superseded by the 'triple' test, which screens not only for AFP levels but also for levels of two other substances in the mother's blood.

The concentration of AFP can be most accurately assessed between 16 and 18 weeks of pregnancy. For this reason, the test is always given in conjunction with, or preceded by, an ultrasound scan.

The reasons why the AFP level in the blood may be high include:

- *a false-positive result (approximately 1:7)*
- *the pregnancy is more advanced than previously thought*
- *multiple pregnancy*
- *spinal tube defect, such as Spina Bifida*
- *Turner's Syndrome (very rare)*
- *death of the baby.*

A low level of AFP might suggest:

- *the pregnancy is less advanced than previously thought*
- *a possible chance of Down's Syndrome.*

It will be apparent why it is useful to have an ultrasound scan in conjunction with this test. For example, the scan will immediately confirm or disprove a number of the reasons listed above, and will also provide additional information about, say, the likelihood of a neural tube defect should the AFP level be raised.

If, for any reason, the test indicates a possibility that something is wrong but isn't conclusive, further testing, for example amniocentesis, will probably be recommended. But before any further testing is offered, the blood test will be repeated and checked; in many cases this will be enough to confirm that all is well.

Any test can be refused when offered. Some women just do not want to know until they deliver. Most women, however, are reassured by the usual outcome of this test – that as far as can be told from the test, everything is fine.

Another important aspect of testing is that, should any form of abnormality or defect be detected, however slight, it enables the mother and her partner to prepare for the birth of their baby in the full knowledge of the baby's condition. Parents may need support and counselling, though a negative result should not mean automatic termination.

Compare **Amniocentesis**, **Antenatal Testing**, **Bart's Test**, **Triple Test**, **Ultrasound**

Amniocentesis

Amniocentesis involves taking a sample of amniotic fluid from within the womb by inserting a specially designed needle through the abdominal wall (*see Figure 2*). Ultrasound scanning, done immediately before or at the same time as amniocentesis, has made this procedure as safe as possible. It is possible for the doctor to find a suitable pool of fluid within the uterus, completely avoiding both the baby and the placenta.

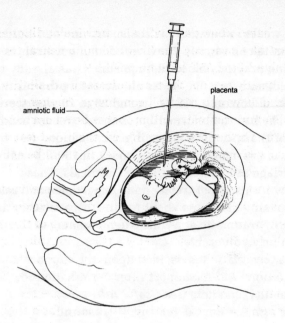

amniotic fluid

placenta

Amniocentesis

The reasons why amniocentesis might be offered include:

- *suspicion of abnormality following either AFP testing or 'triple' test*
- *suspicion of abnormality following ultrasound scanning*
- *family history of congenital illnesses, for example muscular dystrophy*
- *family history of fetal abnormality*
- *following an illness in the mother that could affect the baby*
- *maternal age (37 or over), depending on the results of blood tests.*

One of the problems with amniocentesis is timing. The optimum time for having an amniocentesis is between 16 and 18 weeks, when there is sufficient amniotic fluid from which to take a sample. However, if amniocentesis is offered following previous blood testing, which has already been repeated, and then five weeks elapse before the results come through, a woman could be around 23 to 25 weeks pregnant before she has the information on which to base a decision. If one of the options is a possible termination, the pressure of time is enormous. There is also a 1 in 150/200 risk of miscarriage associated with amniocentesis. These considerations are of tremendous importance and relevance when making decisions about testing, because they are inevitably traumatic at a time when parents are feeling particularly vulnerable.

If a termination is decided upon, the support organization SAFTA (Support After Termination for Abnormality) can help (*see Useful Addresses*).

See also **Antenatal Testing**, **Ultrasound**

Amniofiltration

At a small number of hospitals the highly specialized technique of amniofiltration is available. This technique enables the doctor to extract a sample of amniotic fluid from the uterus, remove the fetal cells for analysis, and replace the excess fluid. This technique has the advantage over other tests (such as amniocentesis) in that it can be carried out from the earlier time of 11 to 12 weeks, in spite of the limited amount of amniotic fluid present at this time. It is usually offered only to women who are known to have a definite risk factor for chromosomal abnormalities.

Compare **Antenatal Testing**

Amniotic Fluid

Amniotic fluid, also called liquor, consists mainly – about 99 per cent – of water, but also contains some fetal cells, food substances and waste products. (It is the presence of fetal cells that make diagnosis with amniocentesis possible.) By distending the fetal sac, amniotic fluid makes growth and movement for the baby possible. It also maintains a constant temperature and protects the baby from bumps and possible injury.

From about 10 weeks of pregnancy the baby begins to urinate, which contributes a little to the volume of fluid. Although there is a wide variation, at 38 weeks there is about 1 litre of fluid, which reduces to around 800 ml at delivery. This can seem an enormous amount if your waters break suddenly or you are having an epidural caesarean!

Sometimes a condition known as polyhydramnios can occur, when the level of fluid reaches around 1500 ml. Alternatively, the level can drop to around 300 ml (this is known as oligohydramnios). In both cases this is an indication that there may be something wrong with the baby.

See also **Fetal Development**, **Fetal Sac**

Amniotic Sac

See **Fetal Sac**

Anaemia

Anaemia in pregnancy is uncommon, but if it does occur it is usually one of two types: iron-deficiency anaemia or folic acid-deficiency anaemia. If it does exist anaemia can pose quite a threat to a mother and her unborn child, which is why your blood will always be tested at your first (booking-in) antenatal visit.

During pregnancy a mother's blood volume increases, but not the number of red blood cells. A blood test showing a reduction in the concentration in haemoglobin (the red pigment in red blood cells responsible for carrying oxygen around the body) may (but does not necessarily) indicate anaemia. Women used to be given iron supplements routinely when they were pregnant, usually in combination with folic acid, but this is less common now, although they may be given a supplement if anaemia is suspected or diagnosed.

Symptoms of anaemia include:

- *shortness of breath*
- *tiredness*
- *feeling faint or actually fainting*
- *palpitations*
- *loss of appetite*
- *paleness of skin*
- *headaches.*

Having been tested at the beginning of pregnancy, women are usually re-checked at about 28 weeks because it is better to pick up on any problems before delivery. Anaemia in late pregnancy can pose a threat to both the mother's and baby's health, but if picked up can be treated.

Red meat remains the most comprehensive source of iron. It is perfectly possible to compensate for meat with a wide range of vegetable sources of iron, but it is particularly important for women who choose a non-meat diet to ensure that it is adequately balanced for their needs in pregnancy. Folic acid is available in leafy green vegetables such as broccoli and spinach, as long as they are not over-cooked. Avocado pears and mushrooms are two other sources of folic acid.

When iron or folic acid supplements are necessary, these will be prescribed by your doctor. Some women find

that iron supplements cause side-effects that are difficult to
tolerate – constipation, for example. As there are a number
of different types of supplements available it may be
possible to find the one best suited to you. Refer back to
your midwife rather than just discontinuing any
supplement, because anaemia during pregnancy needs to be
treated effectively.

Compare **Folic Acid**, **Iron**
See also **Diet**, **Haemoglobin**

Analgesia

Analgesia is the medical term for pain-relief without loss of
consciousness – not to be confused with anaesthesia, which
produces a loss of sensation either generally, with a loss of
consciousness, or locally. Analgesia ranges from
paracetamol for a headache to an epidural during delivery.

You may be asked to state (for example on a birth plan)
which analgesia you would like during labour. This is
difficult because, until you give birth, you won't know what
you will or won't want. It's best to keep your options open,
but it is also important to understand how particular
analgesics work and when they are useful, and how long
they take to become effective. Talk all this through with
your midwife beforehand, and save any final decision until
your labour and delivery.

If you are adamant that you won't have any analgesia
during the labour and birth, you may feel disappointed with
yourself if you end up needing something when the time
comes. Remember, it is the birth of your child and you and
your baby are the most important people in the room. So if
you need pain relief, feel free to ask for it.

One consideration in your choice of analgesia during
labour and delivery may be your own feelings about what
your labour should include. If you want to feel actively in

control, managing and coping with the pain of contractions and delivery in your own way, this can be immensely satisfying. And it is, for some women, very much the point of experiencing childbirth. While some birth partners, and midwives, may find it difficult to witness someone else's evident pain, the experience of pain is entirely individual, as should be any decision about pain relief.

One further consideration about your choice of analgesia is the effect it may have on your baby. TENS has no effect on the baby, while entonox (gas and air) is cleared from the baby's system when he or she takes a first breath. Both pethidine and the anaesthetic used with an epidural cross the placenta and take some time to wear off after delivery. This may cause the baby to be a bit jittery, sleepy or unresponsive, or difficult to comfort.

Compare **Birth Plan**, **Natural Childbirth**

See also **Acupuncture**, **Entonox**, **Epidural**, **Hypnotherapy**, **Pain Relief**, **Pethidine**, **Psychoprophylaxis**, **Pudendal Block**, **TENS**

Antenatal Care

The aim of antenatal care is to ensure the delivery of a healthy baby. Monitoring a mother's health, and that of her unborn baby, throughout pregnancy means that a number of problems can be detected and treated before they cause a complication. For example, if you know that you have a placenta praevia, you can plan for a Caesarean section rather than have to make an emergency decision at the time of delivery.

Following confirmation of pregnancy, referral is made for antenatal care. This can happen in a variety of ways; for most women who are not considered high-risk for any reason, care is shared between the GP practice and the hospital. Given that most pregnant women are healthy, being seen by their GP and midwife at the local health centre usually provides more than adequate care.

The pattern of care goes something like this:

- *at around 6 weeks: confirmation of pregnancy by doctor, referral for antenatal care;*
- *between 8 and 12 weeks: first antenatal or 'booking-in' visit;*
- *visits every four weeks until 32 weeks;*
- *visits every two weeks until the birth.*

This makes for a total of about 10 visits if the pregnancy goes to term.

The first or booking-in visit is an opportunity to record some basic information relevant to a mother's health and, by extension, her baby's. This includes:

- *height;*
- *weight;*
- *blood-pressure;*
- *urine test;*
- *blood tests for ABO blood group, Rhesus type, haemoglobin (Hb) value;*
- *personal health history;*
- *family health history (including that of the baby's father);*
- *details of previous obstetric history.*

This booking-in visit is also an opportunity for your midwife to give you some up-to-date advice about your diet, smoking, any infections, etc. during early pregnancy. Your named midwife will prove an invaluable resource should you have any queries or worries. You will be able to talk through the availability and suitability of various options about where to give birth in your area, and to discuss how you would like your baby's birth to be.

Your antenatal care will also include the offer of a number of antenatal tests for possible problems, plus ultrasound scanning. None of these is obligatory; if you feel, for whatever reason, that they are not for you, talk this through with your midwife or doctor.

Subsequent antenatal visits will probably amount to little more than a general health check, if all is well. The worst bit will probably be the long spell in the waiting room beforehand – UK antenatal clinics being notorious for this. (At least you'll also have plenty of time to practise your pelvic floor exercises!) One trick, especially late in pregnancy (and admittedly easier if you come by car) is to bring a footstool along with you, so you can at least keep your feet up while you wait! It can also be much less stressful if you can possibly arrange to leave any older children with someone else while you go for your appointment.

See also **Antenatal Testing**, **Pre-conceptual Care**

Antenatal Testing

While this generally takes the form of screening for birth defects, antenatal testing also includes those for maternal anaemia, Rubella immunity, toxoplasmosis, listeriosis and high blood-pressure. It is perhaps important to make a distinction between those tests that monitor the mother's health and those that monitor the developing baby's health and vitality. The latter may involve some quite difficult decisions, depending upon the results.

Even the seemingly innocuous ultrasound, which most women have as a matter of routine to confirm their dates, can throw up problems. Ultrasound does, after all, present the opportunity to pick up abnormalities or the symptoms of possible abnormalities. It can come as an enormous shock to have a scan at 16 weeks and be told that there is a problem, and that further tests should be considered.

Blood tests for Down's Syndrome and Spina Bifida can only indicate whether or not there is an increased risk (which may indicate the need for further testing by amniocentesis to make a proper diagnosis). An increased risk is just that: an increased risk, not a definite diagnosis. By the same token, if your risk is within the 'normal' range of, say, 1 in 800 (the risk of Down's Syndrome where the mother is 30 years old), this may still be more of a risk than you are comfortable with.

While most women have no qualms about accepting routine antenatal tests offered to monitor the baby's progress, it is perhaps useful to stop and consider fully the implications of any test before going ahead with it. If you have any concerns, take the time to talk them through with your midwife. If there doesn't seem to be time, make an appointment to come back and talk about it. You should never be pressurized into having any tests if you feel ambivalent about knowing about their outcome.

Compare **Alpha Fetoprotein (AFP) Test, Amniocentesis, Bart's Test, Chorionic Villus Sampling, Screening, Triple Test, Ultrasound**

See also **Anaemia, Blood-pressure, Down's Syndrome, Listeriosis, Rubella, Toxoplasmosis**

Anterior Position

In this position the baby's back is facing out, lying inside the curve of the mother's abdomen (*see Figure 11, page 232*).

During the early part of pregnancy the position of the baby doesn't much matter, as he or she moves freely in the uterus. Only towards the end of pregnancy is it important for the midwife to know how the baby is lying.

Compare **Face Presentation, Occipito-Anterior Position, Transverse Lie, Unstable Lie**

See also **Presentation**

Antibiotics

During pregnancy women might find themselves more prone
to infections than usual. This is because there is a change in
a woman's immuno-responsiveness during pregnancy which
helps prevent rejection of a 'foreign body' – the baby.
Because of this it is important to try and be as healthy as
possible, with a good diet and adequate rest. Occasionally,
however, it isn't possible to avoid all infections and your
doctor may recommend a course of antibiotics.

There are some occasions when it is extremely important
to treat maternal infections that could harm the baby – such
as the listeria bacteria. A highly raised temperature in the
mother can also affect her baby. If your doctor does
prescribe antibiotics for an infection, you can be sure that
he or she is prescribing a drug appropriate to your stage of
pregnancy, and one that will not harm your baby.

As at any other time, when taking antibiotics follow
your doctor's instructions and always finish the course. If
for any reason the antibiotics don't seem to be effective, or
upset your health further in any way, consult your doctor
again. Because antibiotics themselves can sometimes make
you feel under the weather, make sure you take extra care of
your diet, and rest more until you feel better. To avoid the
unpleasant side-effect of thrush, which sometimes affects
some women when they take antibiotics, eat lots of live
yoghurt (that is, yoghurt with live culture of acidophilus –
check the label to make sure).

See also **Listeriosis**, **Thrush**

Antibodies

If we are exposed to infection, our immune system produces
antibodies in response. These antibodies remain after the
infection has passed, and enable us to resist subsequent

infections from the same source. For example, if you have had mumps once, you are unlikely to get them again.

Because antibodies are also produced in response to a foreign body, there can be incompatibility between a mother whose blood group is Rhesus negative and her Rhesus-positive baby.

The production of antibodies that gives rise to immunity can also be conferred artificially, through immunization.

Compare **Rhesus Factor**

See also **Breastfeeding**, **Homoeopathy**, **Immunization**, **Passive Immunity**, **Rubella**

Anxiety

However happy and confident you feel about your pregnancy, feelings of anxiety can still surface as part of your response to impending motherhood, whether or not this is your first time. If there is any ambivalence about the pregnancy, or feelings of ill-health in the early stages, then it can be a very stressful and anxious time.

Anxiety can range from a mild feeling of ill-ease to a full-blown panic attack, and even if pregnancy is the 'most normal thing in the world' you can still feel sick and tired and perilously up and down. It may be part of some necessary adaptive process, but it isn't always comfortable, and isn't always taken seriously by doctors, midwives, husbands, partners, family or relatives. Understanding why you feel like this, without being dismissed as emotionally unstable, can help, as can resorting to some nurturing coping strategies. If you can take a positive approach to helping yourself, even if you are feeling pretty negative overall this is a step in the right direction.

First of all, address any physical complaints that might be getting you down. Make sure you are eating properly and getting enough rest. If you feel particularly unwell during the first few months, don't panic – for most women this improves after about 14 weeks. Avoid anyone or anything that exacerbates how you feel – and don't listen to old wives' tales or horror stories about birth, however compelling! Do not dismiss the effect of the change in balance of your pregnancy hormones, progesterone and oestrogen. This change has a very real impact and some women are more susceptible, especially in the first three months, than others.

Compare **Depression, Emotions, Hormones**

See also **Anaemia, Backache, Constipation, Insomnia, Nausea, Thrush**

For ways of coping with feelings of anxiety, *see* **Acupressure, Acupuncture, Aromatherapy, Autogenics, Autosuggestion, Bach Flower Remedies, Biochemic Tissue Salts, Counselling, Herbal Remedies, Homoeopathy, Meditation, Shiatsu, Thick Skin**

Apgar Test

All babies are checked immediately at birth, and again five minutes later, for the following:

- *heart rate*
- *breathing*
- *skin colour*
- *muscle tone*
- *reflex response.*

Each of these is given up to two points, so the maximum 'score' is 10. An Apgar score of seven or over is considered fine; anything below this may require some action on the part of the midwife or doctor; for example, gentle suction may be necessary to clear any mucus from the baby's throat and make breathing easier.

Most mothers hardly notice these checks being made, partly because their baby is absolutely fine and also because an experienced midwife makes the check so automatically it isn't obvious she is doing so. The Apgar score was devised in 1953 and is universally used, and will be recorded in your notes.

Aquanatal Classes

See **Hydrotherapy**

Areola

This is the pigmented area of skin immediately around the nipple. It is important when breastfeeding to ensure that the baby latches on to the areola, not just the nipple, in order to feed satisfactorily. If the baby only sucks on the nipple, milk flow will be poor or non-existent, and the mother will get very sore from her baby's sucking.

See also **Breastfeeding, Breasts**

Arnica

Arnica tablets should form an essential part of your homoeopathic supplies, and you should make sure you have some for the delivery. *Arnica* is useful for both emotional and physical shock, it reduces swelling, controls bleeding and is appropriate when feeling sore and bruised.

Arnica is also available as a cream, lotion or ointment and is effective when applied to bruises. Please note that it should *never* be applied to broken skin, as it will cause a rash.

See also **Homoeopathy, Labour**

Aromatherapy

The use of essential oils derived from plants, in order to utilize their therapeutic effects, is an ancient art gaining in popularity today. Essential oils can be used in a variety of ways, but most commonly through application to the skin in a carrier oil and in conjunction with the benefits of massage.

In the UK aromatherapy has been used primarily in beauty therapy, which has lessened public awareness of its usefulness. However, more recently a lot of research has been done, in particular on its use medicinally as an alternative or to complement orthodox medicine.

The term aromatherapy may soon be replaced by that of aromatology; because of the single European market the use of the word 'therapy' is restricted. In France, Switzerland and Germany, only medically trained doctors can practise therapy – and this includes aromatherapy.

Essential oils can be used singly or two or more can be blended together. They are usually mixed with a carrier oil (such as sweet almond or grapeseed oil). Sesame seed oil can also be used; this has the advantage of washing out of clothing more easily. Undiluted essential oils should not be applied directly to the skin, unless on medical advice.

In addition, oils can be:

- *added to a bath*
- *inhaled*
- *used in a compress*
- *ingested – but only ever on a therapist's advice and under his or her supervision.*

An aromatherapist will blend together those essential oils thought most suitable to an individual and his or her needs. Essential oils should be bought only from reputable oil producers, some of whom supply via mail-order. These include Shirley Price Ltd., Tisserand and Neal's Yard (see *Useful Addresses*). You get what you pay for in terms of quality with essential oils, and a cheaper oil may well have been produced by a less efficient system, or mixed with a cheaper oil, resulting in a less effective product. To ensure you are getting the most pure distillation, ask for the oil by its Latin name.

No oil should be used for more than three weeks without a break. As with any complementary therapy, it is a good idea to find a qualified therapist to consult and advise in the first instance, especially when pregnant, even if you only want to self-treat minor ailments. If you should then need to use aromatherapy more therapeutically, you will already have established a relationship with a therapist you can trust.

It may also be that your midwife, or another in your local health practice, is trained in aromatherapy – more and more nurses and midwives are looking to supplement their professional training with additional training in complementary therapies.

Many oils are not to be used at all during pregnancy, and some are only recommended at specific times, or during labour or afterwards. However, the following provide a useful range, and some, though not recommended for application to the skin, can still be used in a vaporizer to scent the air.

CAMOMILE *(MATRICARIA CHAMOMILLA)*
This is a wonderful essential oil with lots of therapeutic properties, but it is recommended that it is used only in the last three months of pregnancy. It has relaxation properties, and is anti-inflammatory and antibacterial. (Camomile *tea*, while being relaxing, can also act as a urinary antiseptic, so is useful for bladder problems – *see also* **Cystitis**.)

CLARY SAGE *(SALVIA SCLAREA)*

Although this is contra-indicated during pregnancy, *Clary sage* is good to use during labour and delivery. It is relaxing, eases pain and produces a feeling of well-being. While being a member of the sage family, *Clary sage* is gentler and safer for women to use.

GERANIUM *(PELARGONIUM ODORANTISSIMUM)*

Although best avoided in large amounts during pregnancy, *Geranium* has a specific therapeutic effect on oedema, so can be useful for swollen feet and ankles. It is also analgesic, antiseptic, a tonic and (worth noting for summer evenings) insecticidal.

JASMINE *(JASMINUM OFFICINALE)*

Jasmine is completely contra-indicated in pregnancy apart from its very positive therapeutic effect during labour, when it stimulates contractions. It also has the effect of stimulating lactation, and is an antidepressant, so it's particularly useful after delivery.

LAVENDER *(LAVANDULA AUGUSTIFOLIA)*

Again, this is another oil best avoided during the first three months of pregnancy, but is considered safe in small doses thereafter. *Lavender* has an enormous range of therapeutic qualities: it is antiseptic, antidepressant, hypotensive, analgesic, antiemetic, calming – and smells really nice!

MANDARIN/TANGERINE *(CITRUS RETICULATA)*

Unless you are allergic to citrus fruits, this is one oil that can be used safely throughout pregnancy. It is antiseptic, calming, aids digestion and acts as a tonic.

NEROLI _(CITRUS BIGARADIA/C. AURANTIUM)_

This essential oil is produced from orange blossom, and has excellent all-round effects on depression and alleviating anxiety, is relaxing, helps with constipation and wind, and is also a tonic and aid to circulation.

ROSE _(ROSA CENTIFOLIA/R. DAMASCENA)_

This is, in its purest form, a very beautiful and feminine oil – but it is contra-indicated until the last two to three weeks of pregnancy. It really only comes into its own during labour, when it is thought to have a calming and cheering effect and to help the womb's contractions during delivery.

SANDALWOOD _(SANTALUM ALBUM)_

Best known for its aphrodisiac properties, _Sandalwood_ is also antiseptic, diuretic, sedative and a tonic. Although it is safe to use throughout pregnancy, its strong smell may be too much for some women during the first three months.

TEA TREE _(MELALEUCA ALTERNIFOLIA)_

Tea tree oil has a wide range of antiseptic, antifungal and antiviral effects, as well as a stimulating action on the immune system. It is useful in both avoiding and treating infections. Because of its particularly strong, rather medicinal smell, aromatherapists often blend it with one or more other oils.

Essential oils should never be dismissed as just nice smelling, innocuous additions to a massage oil. They have specific therapeutic properties and can be extremely effective, and there are some that definitely shouldn't be used during pregnancy. These include:

Aniseed	Parsleyseed
Basil	Pennyroyal
Bitter almond	Peppermint

Boldo	Plecanthrus
Camphor	Rosemary
Clove	Rue
Cypress	Sage
Fennel	Sassafras
Horseradish	Savin
Hyssop	Savory
Juniper	Tansy
Marjoram	Tarragon
Mugwort	Thuja
Mustard	Thyme
Myrrh	Wintergreen
Nutmeg	Wormseed
Oregano	Wormwood

Some of those listed above are herbs used in everyday cooking; in this form they present no problem to a pregnant woman. The amounts used in cooking are small and unconcentrated.

To find a qualified aromatherapist, contact the Aromatherapy Organisations Council (*see Useful Addresses*).

Compare **Bach Flower Remedies**, **Herbal Remedies**, **Homoeopathy**, **Naturopathy**, **Reflexology**

See also **Massage**

Autogenics

Autogenic training was developed as a way of reaching a relaxed emotional and physical state without the need for hypnosis. An individual is taught to achieve this state through a series of relaxation exercises and the repetition of key phrases unique to him or her. Once learned, the technique can be practised alone.

Autogenics can be very useful in dealing with acute stress and anxiety, for example during delivery, but this depends on how well you have learned to reach a state of relaxation at will. Initially, some sessions with a practitioner will be necessary (see *Useful Addresses*), but once learned you will have a skill for life, not just during pregnancy and birth. And it will be a skill of great use during your years of bringing up children!

Compare **Autosuggestion, Meditation**

Autosuggestion

This is really an extension of autogenic training, or meditation, by taking the ability to reduce stress and tension further through creating a state of autohypnosis. This is done by the repetition of a simple phrase while in a relaxed or meditative state. While this can be very useful during, say, labour and delivery, it requires some commitment beforehand to become practised enough to use effectively.

The practice was devised almost 100 years ago by a French pharmacist called Emile Coué, who recognized the strength of unconscious healing that could be harnessed by an individual. The repeated phrase for which he is most remembered is, 'Every day, in every way, I am getting better and better.'

Although a self-help technique, advice and instruction can be obtained from a medically qualified hypnotherapist (see *Useful Addresses*).

Compare **Autogenics, Hypnotherapy, Meditation**

Bb

Bach Flower Remedies

These remedies are holistic – that is, they are designed to treat the whole person and, in principle, to treat the internal imbalances that cause physical or psychological problems.

There are 38 Bach flower remedies, named after their originator, Dr Edward Bach; there is also the Rescue Remedy (made up of Impatiens, Star of Bethlehem, Cherry Plum, Clematis and Rock Rose) – this is a useful standby in times of shock, injury or trauma.

Bach flower remedies are sometimes used or prescribed in conjunction with other alternative or complementary therapies. The Bach Centre (see *Useful Addresses*) gives rough guidelines for using the remedies, and the emphasis is on self-help and an honest interpretation of personal symptoms. For example, Walnut might be a good remedy during pregnancy as it is designed to assist in adaptation to change.

Other Bach flower remedies which might be useful during pregnancy and/or labour include:

Aspen	*feeling apprehensive for no apparent reason*
Elm	*feelings of overwhelming responsibility*
Larch	*fear of failure, lack of self-confidence*
Olive	*feeling exhausted and drained of energy*
Walnut	*assists in adjusting to transition or change*
Wild chestnut	*persistent anxiety or worry*
Wild oat	*unsure of direction in life.*

Compare **Aromatherapy**, **Herbal Remedies**, **Homoeopathy**, **Naturopathy**

Back

Because the weight gained in pregnancy – around 13.5 kg (2 stone/30 lb) – is carried mainly at the front, your back is under increasing pressure as pregnancy advances. In addition, the pregnancy hormones progesterone and relaxin have a softening effect on the ligaments of the body, including those of the back, making them more elastic in preparation for the birth. If your posture is poor, your abdominal muscles weak and you are careless about lifting and carrying, your back could be at risk.

It's worth paying attention to possible back trouble, partly because, if a problem arises in pregnancy, it's more difficult to deal with just because of being pregnant. Even after the birth, because of continuing hormonal influences back problems can take time to resolve. And your posture while breastfeeding is important, too.

You can protect your back in a number of ways:

* *try to keep your back straight, not just when walking but also when seated*
* *when lifting, keep your back straight, bending at the knees and letting your legs take the strain;*

- *when carrying one or more items, try to distribute the weight evenly; use a small rucksack or carry your shoulder bag across your front rather than on one shoulder;*
- *make sure your bed has a firm mattress, and take care when getting in and out of bed, especially after you've been asleep and your muscles are relaxed.*

See also **Alexander Technique**, **Backache**, **Breastfeeding**, **Posture**

Backache

Always take backache seriously when you are pregnant, even if only to keep it from getting worse. In some cases backache could be due to a kidney infection, so it should always be mentioned to your midwife or doctor, especially if accompanied by symptoms of feverishness and pain on passing water.

If you have a history of backache before becoming pregnant, take extra care and actively choose to do some gentle exercise that will strengthen and protect your back, for example yoga or swimming, and follow the suggestions in the entry on **Back**.

However, some amount of backache is quite common, especially lower backache, during the last three months of pregnancy. This is largely due to musculo-skeletal strain and can arise just from sleeping awkwardly. First steps in dealing with back pain include:

- *rest;*
- *applying heat – heat pad or hot water bottle – to the affected area.*

If the problem is muscular, this should help.

- *follow the above steps with some massage and gentle exercise, and pay particular attention to your posture;*
- *if the pain is severe enough to prevent you relaxing, taking paracetamol in the prescribed dose should help.*

If you experience a particularly bad episode of back pain, or a recurrence of an old complaint, seek help straight away. Osteopathy is very often the most appropriate first resort, and a fully qualified osteopath will be confident about working with a pregnant woman, finding the right level of treatment for your problem in relation to your stage of pregnancy.

Acupuncture can be useful too in alleviating pain and allowing your back to right itself. Very often back pain causes the muscles around the spine to go into spasm, actually contributing to the pain, in an attempt to protect itself. This pain tends to make you stiffen up, again making the pain worse. If you can remove the pain, at least to some extent, this can help the muscles relax enough to help resolve the back problem.

Massage and shiatsu can be enormously helpful in releasing the tension that both causes and contributes to backache. In addition, essential oils (such as *Mandarin*, *Camomile* and, from 24 weeks, *Lavender*) can be used in massage, as a compress or in the bath.

Homoeopathic remedies include:

Kali Carb 12	*when the back feels weak, stiff and exhausted; or when the pain is worse in the early hours of the morning, after lying on the affected side, or from the cold;*
Pulsatilla 12	*low back pain aggravated by fatigue;*
Phos Acid 12	*back pain following delivery.*

See also **Acupuncture, Exercise, Massage, Osteopathy, Shiatsu, Yoga**

Balaskas, Janet

Janet Balaskas is the founder of the International Active Birth Movement. Having originally trained as a National Childbirth Trust teacher, she went on to research childbirth and in particular the tradition of giving birth lying down. It became apparent from her teaching, research and own experience as a mother of four that lying down during labour and delivery works against the natural progress of events. An upright, squatting position not only takes the weight of the baby and uterus off the deep blood vessels, but also allows the pelvic outlet to open to its widest capacity. The development of her work, combining yoga exercises antenatally with a focus on using gravity during labour to aid delivery, culminated in the Active Birth Movement. During the 1990s her work has extended to promoting the safe use of water during labour and delivery. In addition she has published numerous books, including *Active Birth*, *The Active Birth Partner's Handbook* and, with Dr Yehudi Gordon, *The Encyclopedia of Pregnancy and Birth*

See also **Active Birth**, **Position**, **Water Birth**

Bart's Test

This is an antenatal blood test, so called because it was developed at St Bartholomew's Hospital in London. It is now usually referred to as the Triple Test.

A sample of the mother's blood is tested not only for its levels of AFP (alpha-fetoprotein), but also its levels of two other substances, the hormones oestriol and human chorionic gonadotrophin. The optimum time for this test is at 16 weeks and, taking the mother's age into account, increases the possibility of assessing the risk of the baby having Down's Syndrome.

See also **Alpha Fetoprotein (AFP) Test, Antenatal Testing, Down's Syndrome, Triple Test**

Benefits

All pregnant women in the UK are entitled to free prescriptions and free dental care while they are pregnant and for 12 months after giving birth. To claim, you need to get a signed form from your doctor or midwife to send to the Family Health Services Authority, who will then send you an exemption certificate.

CHILD BENEFIT

Every parent in the UK is entitled to claim Child Benefit. Once you have registered your baby's birth, you will need to send the birth certificate with the completed application form (on the back of the Benefit Agency's leaflet FB8; they also provide a pre-paid envelope) to the Child Benefit Centre. They will return the birth certificate to you. Child Benefit currently stands at £10.40 for the first child and £8.45 for any other children per week, and can be paid weekly, monthly or by standing order direct into your bank or building society account.

ONE PARENT BENEFIT

If you are also eligible to claim One Parent Benefit you will need to complete the form found in leaflet CH11.

Women who are in paid employment and have been paying National Insurance contributions are eligible for either Statutory Maternity Pay (SMP) or Maternity Allowance.

SMP

Statutory Maternity Pay is a weekly payment, for up to 18 weeks, available for women who have worked for the same employer for at least 26 weeks by the end of the 15th week *before* the week your baby is due. Although you are entitled to stop work 11 weeks before the week your baby is due, it is up to you when you want to stop work. You won't be paid SMP while still at work; it only comes into operation after you stop work, which could even be the week your baby is due. For the first six weeks of your maternity leave, SMP is 90 per cent of your average pay. After this you receive the basic rate of SMP, which currently stands at £52.50, for a further 12 weeks.

The SMP payment is made by your employers. You have to write to your employer at least three weeks before you stop work to ask for SMP, enclosing your maternity certificate (form MAT B1). This can be obtained from your doctor or midwife when you are six months pregnant.

MATERNITY ALLOWANCE

Maternity Allowance is a weekly payment for women who have paid full-rate National Insurance contributions for at least 26 weeks out of the 66 weeks previous to the week their baby is due, who don't qualify for SMP. They may, for example, be self-employed or have changed jobs or given up work during pregnancy. If this applies to you, you will need form MA1 from your antenatal clinic or Benefits Agency. You will also need a maternity certificate, as above. You may also need form SMP1 from your employers, if you do not qualify for SMP.

FINDING OUT MORE

There may be other benefits that you are eligible to apply for: Incapacity Benefit (formerly Sickness Benefit); Maternity Payment from the Social Fund; Income Support; Family Credit; Housing Benefit; Council Tax Benefit; Free milk and help with fares to and from hospital. Your local Benefit Agency office is your best source of up-to-date information (see your local telephone directory); The

Maternity Alliance (see *Useful Addresses*) can also help.

See also **Maternity Rights**

Biochemic Tissue Salts

These are a range of 12 mineral remedies for quite commonplace ailments which can be useful during pregnancy as an alternative remedy. They have no adverse side-effects unless you are lactose-intolerant (because the tablets are lactose based).

Herbalists, homoeopaths and naturalists often prescribe tissue salts; they are also available from most chemists, usually in their combination form: Combination F is recommended for migraine and nervous headaches, Combination G for backache, lumbago and piles, Combination H for hayfever, Combination J for coughs, colds and chestiness, and Combination S for nausea and stomach upsets.

Compare **Herbal Remedies**, **Homoeopathy**, **Naturopathy**

Birth

When you're pregnant, anticipating the birth at the end of nine months' waiting feels like the end of something, rather than its beginning. In reality it is a transition which, especially for first-time mothers, marks a major change in life.

However, the process of birth is the focus of all those weeks of planning and preparation, and great store is set by the experience of birth both for the mother and her baby. Keep this in perspective, though, because however momentous an event it is just one of many that will occur in your life and that of your child. For most women giving birth is not the most enjoyable aspect of becoming a mother, although the majority say it was worth it in the end!

That said, it is a glorious transition that brings into the world another life, and something that many women find both awe-inspiring and empowering. In addition to the emotional response to birth, it must be remembered that it is a very physical event and for many women will actually be the most physically demanding thing they ever do.

The process of birth is medically divided into three main stages:

THE FIRST STAGE

This lasts from the beginning of labour until the cervix is fully dilated. Labour may begin with the waters breaking; or a 'show' where the plug of mucus that has protected the cervix throughout pregnancy comes away; or with a steady increase in the regularity and intensity of contractions.

Towards the end of their pregnancy, many women have quite frequent bouts of Braxton Hicks contractions which, although they can be quite strong, are irregular and usually more uncomfortable than actually painful. True labour contractions, once they get going, gain in regularity and strength. Whether or not contractions feel painful in the early stages of labour depends on the individual woman. There is quite conclusive evidence, however, that the better informed and prepared a woman is, the more able she will be to cope with her labour and delivery. That is not to say that she won't experience pain, but will be able to resort to tactics that will help her cope. These vary from changing position, using breathing exercises, relaxing in between contractions, and generally managing the labour pains with the help and support of birth partner and midwife. There is also a place for pain relief, which is part of coping with and managing labour pains.

TRANSITION

This is the phase between the first and second stage of labour. Again, the experience of transition – the change in uterine activity from dilating the cervix fully to pushing the baby out – is different for each woman. Some women don't experience it at all, probably because the sequence of events progresses smoothly. For some, however, the urge to push may occur before the cervix is fully dilated, so it's necessary to try and hold back. Should you be someone for whom transition is a very definite process, you will probably want to take heart from the reassurance of your midwife that this signals the approach of the delivery of your baby. Some women find that they feel emotionally and physically overwhelmed at this stage, but once they can begin the more positive process of pushing the baby out, this passes.

THE SECOND STAGE

During this stage, following the dilatation of the cervix, the contractions work to push the baby out. Most women find the urge to push overwhelming, however tired their preceding labour has made them feel. To say that a mother gets an urge to push is, for many, a bit of an understatement! The amount of pushing that it takes to give birth to some babies is enormous, and will demand all your concentration and strength.

Occasionally the baby will need to be helped, perhaps if the mother is very tired or if the baby is particularly big. If some form of intervention is needed (forceps, vacuum extraction, caesarean) the mother and her husband or partner will be consulted. If there's any doubt about the best course forward, the recommendation may be for 'a trial of labour'.

THE THIRD STAGE

Once the baby has been born, and the cord cut, the placenta and membranes (the empty amniotic sac) detach from the wall of the uterus for delivery. This may be with the assistance of the midwife who, by placing her hand gently over the abdomen, can feel when the uterus contracts and can gently pull on the cord to deliver the placenta. If you immediately place your newly born baby to the breast to suckle, this can help strengthen the contractions needed to deliver the placenta. The midwife then checks to be sure that the membranes surrounding the placenta are intact, and that no residual material is left inside which could cause a problem with infection or bleeding.

It is almost universal policy in hospitals for the third stage to be assisted by the administration of Syntometrine. This is something you might want to discuss with your midwife prior to your delivery, and to include in your notes for your birth plan.

The process of birth is different for every woman, but there are similarities and the process follows a basic pattern. The individual nature of birth is worth remembering, though, because you will probably hear a lot about other mothers' deliveries when you are pregnant. There seems to be an unwritten rule about not mentioning the pain to first-time mothers, though as even this is individual, there shouldn't be: the amount of pain you experience, like everything else about your labour and birth, will be unique to you.

See also **Birth Plan**, **Braxton Hicks Contractions**, **Breathing Exercises**, **Caesarean Section**, **Cervix**, **Contractions**, **Pain Relief**, **Position**, **Syntometrine**, **Third Stage**, **Transition**, **Trial of Labour**

Birth Plan

When you are discussing your labour and delivery with your midwife, and thinking about how you would like it to proceed, you may want to make notes in a formal Birth Plan. This can be kept in your medical notes so that whoever is involved in your actual delivery can be properly aware of your wishes. You may feel this is less relevant for you if you are planning a home delivery, or have booked a Domino or GP delivery. In any event a birth plan needs to be based on information about what you do and don't want, so it's worth talking it through with your midwife, doctor or antenatal teacher. But with anything planned in the abstract, bear in mind that babies seem to have their own ideas and can confound even the best-laid plans. You may be planning a water birth in the comfort of your own home, but your baby may be planning an unscheduled arrival a month ahead of time when you are visiting your parents a hundred miles from home, and *then* have the bad manners to adopt a breech position so you end up having a caesarean! This is a worse-case scenario, but in reality your aim – and everyone else's – is to have a safe and successful birth, and preferably not on the hard shoulder of the motorway. So plan for the best, but remain flexible.

Areas you may want to cover in your birth plan include:

- *your birth partner*
- *labour and birth positions*
- *pain relief*
- *use of enemas*
- *episiotomy*
- *use of Syntometrine in the third stage*
- *how your baby is handled immediately after the birth.*

Whatever you decide, bear in mind that giving birth can be a very variable procedure. Also, if you rule out certain things completely you may find it difficult to concede their necessity during birth. For example, if you have a full rectum it may impede the dilatation of the cervix, so an enema, however much you dislike the idea, may help. They are not just recommended for the convenience of your midwife!

If you have been able to talk through all sorts of questions about labour and delivery beforehand, you will know that while *you* know what you want, *your baby* may, at that crucial moment, need something extra or different. Working with the experience of your midwife is beneficial and should make your baby's birth a more rather than less rewarding experience. Ultimately, like a lot of unknown quantities in life, your only solution is to make the best provision you can and then keep an open mind.

See also **Pain Relief**, **Position**

Blood-pressure

Your blood-pressure will be taken and recorded every time you visit the antenatal clinic. The term blood-pressure relates to the pressure exerted by the flow of blood against the walls of the arteries. The two figures in its measurement relate to the two beats of the heart – the systolic (when the heart contracts) and the diastolic (the pressure when the heart is at rest).

The reason why your blood-pressure is monitored regularly while you are pregnant is that it is a good indicator of a number of possible problems. An increase in blood-pressure can be caused by stress and anxiety, or even hurrying to get to the antenatal clinic on time. However, an increase in blood-pressure other than under these conditions might suggest that a pregnant woman is predisposed to a condition known as pre-eclampsia, which needs close monitoring.

Massage and aromatherapy can be extremely useful in lowering blood-pressure, especially if massage is given regularly, as the effects are cumulative. Both *Camomile* and *Lavender* essential oils have properties that lower blood-pressure and have a calming effect.

See also **Antenatal Testing**, **Pre-eclampsia**

Bonding

After the particularly clinical approach of childbirth in the 1950s and early 1960s, there was something of a return to a more mother-and-child-centred approach to birth. This in turn gave rise to the idea that, unless a mother bonded to her baby within the first 10 minutes after the birth, there would be – ominous note – 'problems'. Certainly this idea influenced a lot of key changes that were good: delivering the baby gently onto the mother's abdomen, allowing her to hold and suckle the baby straight away, etc. But for those mothers who, in spite of all this, felt no immediate rush of maternal adoration, there could sometimes be the feeling they hadn't 'bonded' with their baby at all – particularly for those mothers who had to be under necessary anaesthesia, as for a caesarean delivery. It is worth bearing in mind that, if for any reason you and your baby are separated for a period after the birth, research suggests that there is no long-term effect on the relationship.

Bonding is the development of a close emotional tie with another person. For some parents and their child this happens within minutes of birth: they literally 'fall in love' with their baby. For others the process takes longer, as parent and child observe, touch and explore each other. Either way, parents and their babies must be allowed time to get to know each other properly.

Bonding is part of the process of 'primary maternal preoccupation' observed and reflected upon by the paediatrician and child psychiatrist Winnicott, and thought to last for at least six months. This is described as a time of intense involvement a mother has with her infant, and is thought to be biologically determined in order to ensure the baby's survival – one of nature's ways of keeping the species going.

Some mothers feel actively resentful after birth, especially if the labour and delivery have been particularly arduous and painful. To then be asked to care and accept responsibility for this tiny being can seem like adding insult to injury. But in spite of all this, over time and with sensitive help from family and friends and plenty of rest, relaxation and time to get to know their baby, a bond will inevitably be formed. And it is this continued bonding that enables parents to weather the storms of parenthood.

Bottle-feeding

In Westernized countries, bottle-feeding is a safe alternative to breastfeeding, if all the instructions about sterilizing, mixing, storing and giving baby milk formula are followed. However, bottle-feeding doesn't help you utilize some of the fat stores laid down in pregnancy in preparation for breastfeeding, or provide the baby with antibodies, immunity to some illness and protection against allergies, diabetes and heart disease later in life, as does breastfeeding. Nor does it give you added protection against breast cancer. And it isn't available on demand.

That said, the choice is yours. If at all possible, however, you might want to consider breastfeeding your baby for at least the first three to four months, as it is well worth it from both your and your baby's point of view.

Compare **Breastfeeding**

Bowels

Bowels are worth a quick mention because they are affected by the pregnancy hormone progesterone, making them sluggish and prone to constipation. Prevention is better than cure, so make sure your diet is high in fibre and drink lots of water, herb teas and fruit juices to keep hydrated (coffee and tea have some diuretic properties, depending on their strength).

If you are given iron supplements while pregnant, this may make you constipated; other mothers complain of diarrhoea. Still others suffer neither throughout their pregnancy.

Another reason to keep your bowels in good working order is to avoid straining and the possibility of haemorrhoids.

See also **Constipation, Diarrhoea, Haemorrhoids**

Braxton Hicks Contractions

Even as early as 8 weeks into the pregnancy the uterus begins to generate small contractions, although these are not usually felt until the pregnancy is much further advanced. They become increasingly obvious later on and can be felt as quite strong, although they are not usually painful. In addition they are irregular, even if happening frequently, and last for around a minute. True contractions when they start, are regular and, initially, shorter. There may also be some back pain, and a feeling which is more like a menstrual cramp.

Compare **Labour**

Breastfeeding

For some women breastfeeding is as easy as falling off a log; for many others it is a learned skill that takes time and patience to get to grips with. However, although the breastfeeding rates in the UK are poor, with only around 63 per cent of women attempting to breastfeed (and this figure drops considerably after six weeks), it is possible for almost every woman to breastfeed her baby if she wants to *and* if she gets the help necessary, should problems arise. In Norway, 99 per cent of all women start off breastfeeding and around 90 per cent continue to do so for the first three to four months.

One of the things that makes breastfeeding difficult in the UK is society's attitude – many people disapprove of seeing women breastfeeding and, if out and about, the only place where you may be able to do this with any privacy is in a lavatory! With so few women familiar with the sight of babies being breastfed, it is hardly surprising that the idea of it seems somehow alien. Yet it is perfectly possible to breastfeed a baby discreetly.

Babies are born with an instinct to suck, and it is this apparently endless desire to suck that will stimulate your milk production. In order for this to be effective, your baby will need to suck on the whole nipple and surrounding areola, pulling this in towards the back of his or her mouth. Getting your baby properly 'latched on' is your first key to survival in the early days. Initially your baby will only receive colostrum from your breasts, but when the sucking and feeding begin in earnest you could find the pressure uncomfortable and your nipples could get very sore if your baby is not taking the areola and nipple properly. If this happens, try altering the position of your baby on the nipple: lie alongside each other to feed; lie your baby across your tummy or tuck a small cushion underneath to raise him or her up a little; tuck your baby's body under your arm to feed. Different positions work better for different babies and mothers: take your time to see what suits you, always making sure you are comfortable yourself and not hunching over, otherwise you may end up with backache.

So what can you do to try and get off to a good breastfeeding start? After the delivery:

1   *rest as much as possible in between everything else you find yourself having to do;*
2   *let your baby suckle for as long and as often as he or she likes. Ten minutes isn't long enough, and timing early feeds is inappropriate. Get comfortable, get settled and use this initial lengthy sucking time to rest. You won't be 'spoiling' your baby, or setting up a bad habit; everything needs more effort and practice initially, breastfeeding is just the same;*
3   *drink extra fluids – but not tea or coffee – water, herb teas and diluted fruit juices are better (I avoided coffee altogether for a bit, as the caffeine seemed to make my babies jumpy). You need approximately an additional 2 pints (1 litre) a day while breastfeeding.*

It takes a while for breastmilk to 'come in'. Between two to four days after the birth, and with the stimulus of the baby's sucking, the milk ducts start producing milk. Initially the supply-and-demand nature of breastmilk production isn't particularly efficient – that is, you will produce much more milk than your baby can drink! This can result in your breasts becoming overfull, uncomfortable – even painful – and is referred to as *engorgement*. This happens to just about every mother to a greater or lesser extent. The key things to remember are:

1   *it will pass, and*

2   *continuing to breastfeed is the quickest way for*
       engorgement to be resolved.

The problem during the few days when you are engorged can be getting the baby to latch on effectively. When your breasts are very full, swollen and tight, the nipple isn't so accessible. You may need to express some milk gently by hand to reduce the swelling so your baby's mouth can take enough of the nipple and areola in to feed well. This is another occasion when alternating your baby's position at the breast may help.

Your baby's need to suck/feed every couple of hours will continue through the night, and having your baby in bed with you initially may mean you get more rest and sleep. This period won't last forever, and it won't 'spoil' your child. It will actually establish breastfeeding to the point where you can start lengthening the time between feeds without affecting your milk supply.

Unrestricted feeding in the first few weeks is probably the single most important thing you can do to get breastfeeding going. Your breast produces two sorts of milk: the *foremilk*, stored in the breast ducts immediately behind the nipple and readily available as you begin to feed, and the *hindmilk* which needs the 'let-down' reflex to be stimulated in order to be released. The stimulation for the let-down reflex is your baby's sucking, and it doesn't happen unless your baby has been sucking for long enough. Three minutes isn't long enough and, in the early days, 10 minutes probably isn't long enough either. Your baby needs to receive the more calorific hindmilk as well as the foremilk in order to grow adequately. After a while the let-down reflex becomes more efficient – that is, it comes into operation sooner.

If you find breastfeeding difficult, don't despair. You are not alone. Seek help and advice, preferably from someone whose opinion you trust and respect, and from someone who knows you and your baby. For the first 10 days after your baby's birth you should be visited by your midwife or one from the same team of community midwives. After this you should have access to a health visitor, who may visit you at home or whom you will see at the baby clinic. Both midwives and health visitors are trained to help you; if you need help and advice about breastfeeding, ask them.

In addition, there will probably be a local contact for either the National Childbirth Trust, La Leche League, or the Association of Breastfeeding Mothers (see *Useful Addresses*) in your area. Bear in mind that whomever you consult for advice will have some ideas of their own – so take from their advice what is right for you and your baby.

COMMON PROBLEMS

ENGORGEMENT
See above.

CRACKED NIPPLES
Although this may be quite painful, changing the position of the baby on your breast will probably be enough to alleviate the pain and allow the nipple to heal. Check that your baby is properly 'latched on'. There is no reason to stop breastfeeding or use a breast shield. Try to prevent cracked nipples by keeping them dry and not overwashing with soap. You probably won't need nipple creams to keep your nipples supple as long as you are not overwashing – research has shown that babies prefer an unwashed breast! At the end of a feed, gently insert the tip of your little finger into your baby's mouth to release the suction before removing your nipple. Don't try to pull it out of your sucking baby's mouth.

Homoeopathy is very useful for many breastfeeding problems, and if you have been consulting a homoeopath for other reasons, see him or her again now.

See also **Colostrum, Engorgement, Homoeopathy, Latching On, Let-down Reflex, Mastitis**

Breasts

Contrary to what women may grow up believing, breasts are designed to feed small babies. They are also the focus of a great deal of media attention, so it is hardly surprising that most women are dissatisfied with their own pair, thinking them either too small, too big, lop-sided, etc. They are also the source of both sexual pleasure and sexual attention. While they may be on show in newspapers, on advertising hoardings, top-shelf magazine covers, on television, on film and on the beach, we seldom see them feeding babies. And if we do, there is probably someone tutting.

All this makes breastfeeding more of an emotive issue than it need be, and influences some of the reasons why women aren't happy breastfeeding.

That said, any woman with breasts is capable of breastfeeding the baby she has given birth to. Even women who have adopted their babies have been able to breastfeed partially, with special help and advice.

Throughout pregnancy your breasts will have been responding to pregnancy hormones, in preparation for producing milk after the birth. The main symptom of this will be an increase in the size of your breasts. They may also be quite tender at first and uncomfortable later on. A well-fitting bra will help, but it does need to be properly fitted. Research has shown that many women wear bras that are actually the wrong size, so this is a good opportunity to get properly fitted. The bra you wear during pregnancy will not be the same as a specially designed bra for breastfeeding, which should not be fitted until just before the birth. There is quite a range of feeding bras, with a variety of quick-release devices. Although they may look a bit cumbersome at first, they will prove essential when you are feeding. Although you will increase in size once your milk comes in, once breastfeeding is established your breast size will decrease again as you begin to produce only the amount of milk your baby needs.

Breathing Exercises

Breathing 'normally' when we feel anxious and tense becomes more difficult as we tend to hold our breath, especially at moments of pain. During labour and birth prolonged holding of the breath, or breathing spasmodically, contributes to feeling tired and out of control. By the same standard, if you are able deliberately to breathe 'normally' it increases the feeling that, in spite of everything, you are in control. More than this, it ensures a good oxygen supply to you and your baby which, as for anything energetic, you will need.

There's not much point in waiting until you are in the throes of labour, dealing with contractions, to think about this. It requires some thought and practice beforehand, hence breathing exercises, which are usually combined with relaxation exercises. In these exercises you will concentrate on the out-breath, emptying your lungs while keeping your shoulders relaxed and your mouth open and 'soft'. There is one school of thought that encourages you to think of a link between your soft, open mouth and your soft, opening cervix. Because the uterus, which is muscular, relies on huge tension to contract, you don't want to create your own counter-tension. You also need to relax in between contractions to conserve your strength for the pushing!

Throughout your pregnancy practise relaxing and breathing out in a focused, controlled way. First, you need to be able to identify your muscles in both their tense and relaxed state. Try the following:

- *sit comfortably with your back supported, your legs uncrossed. Rest your hands, palm upwards, loosely on your thighs;*
- *either close your eyes or focus blankly on one spot;*
- *concentrate on breathing gently and deeply in and out, until you find a rhythm that is right for you. You may want to concentrate on some key words, such as 'energy in, peace and quiet out';*
- *screw your facial muscles up into a frown as you breathe in, then deliberately feel the relaxation as you let go on the outward breath. Check that your jaw is relaxed and you aren't clenching your teeth;*
- *work your way down your body, tensing your shoulders as you breath in and relaxing them on the outward breath. The idea is to feel the difference between a tense and relaxed state, so that you know what you are trying to achieve and how to achieve it;*
- *move down through your chest, abdomen, buttocks, pelvic floor, thighs, calves, feet and toes;*
- *all the time, take long, deep breaths – in with the tensing of muscles, out with the relaxing. If you focus on the relaxing out-breath, the in-breath will take care of itself.*

This exercise, which may take some time, should leave you feeling calm but refreshed, partly because by concentrating on getting your body to do what you want it to, you empty your mind momentarily. You can, if you like and it helps, find some beautiful image, object or place to visualize while you are doing this exercise.

During labour, following these steps will help in dealing with the strength, and pain, of contractions. Aim to concentrate on your breathing, focusing your attention inwards as each contraction begins. Breathe in deeply and slowing, pulling the breath all the way down into your abdomen. Concentrate on letting your breath out slowly as the strength of the contraction peaks and fades. Take each contraction at a time, avoiding the urge to hold your breath as it peaks.

If you have a birth partner who has practised your breathing exercises with you, you may want to work together now. Don't make any rigid rules for yourself before the event, and bear in mind that, however much you practised beforehand, it will take you a while to get into the rhythm of breathing through your contractions during your labour. It is worth staying with it, because it *will* help. Try not to give up even if the first really strong contractions quite literally 'take your breath away'.

If you find breathing exercises quite difficult to start with, you might find it easier to learn if taught by someone who can guide you. This could be an antenatal teacher or yoga teacher, or even your husband, partner or friend. Relaxation audio-tapes to listen to might be useful, although you may have to try several before you find one you can actually bear to listen to over and over again. A favourite piece of music might be more conducive.

Once you have practised regularly you will find that breathing in this way becomes second nature. You will have learned a skill of great value, not just for labour and delivery, but for life. It is also a skill that can usefully be taught to your children later.

See also **Exercise, Meditation, Pelvic Floor Exercises, Relaxation**

Breathlessness

As your uterus enlarges with your growing baby, pressure is felt under the ribs; this can contribute to a feeling of breathlessness. This feeling may grow in the last couple of months, and might reach a peak at around 36 weeks. After this, because the baby drops further into the pelvis, pressure under the diaphragm is reduced slightly.

The increasing bulk of your pregnancy makes its own demands on your heart and lungs, but your body's ability to adapt to this demand is extraordinary. In order to ensure not only that you and your baby get enough oxygen during pregnancy, but also that carbon dioxide is efficiently removed, the pregnancy hormone progesterone influences how you breathe during pregnancy. Without noticing it, your breathing is deeper and there is a far greater capacity for oxygen and carbon dioxide exchange. While the number of breaths you take doesn't increase, the quantity of air you breathe in and out increases by up to 40 per cent. So, feeling breathless may just be a recognition of the change in the way you are breathing. This is different from feeling breathless when carrying your extra bulk upstairs!

Either way, you can feel reassured that your body has taken compensatory measures to ensure that your baby is getting enough oxygen. However, if you feel continually breathless even when at rest or when lying down, talk to your doctor or midwife. Sometimes it can be a symptom of, for example, anaemia, which would be best treated before you give birth.

If you are finding breathlessness particularly troubling and it isn't linked to anything that needs treating, you could try shiatsu to alleviate your symptoms. A qualified practitioner, used to working with pregnant women, can be extremely helpful. Also, pressing on the Pericardium 6 point (*see Figure 3*) on the wrist is helpful.

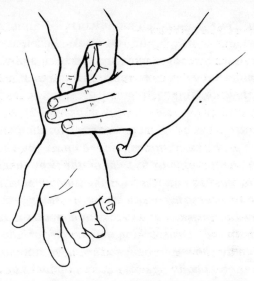

Pericardium 6 – pressing this point helps relieve breathlessness

See also **Anaemia, Shiatsu**

Breech Presentation

About 3 per cent of babies are breech presentation – that is, lying bottom-down (rather than head-down) at term (*see Figure 11, page 232*). It used to mean an automatic caesarean section, but now, as long as other considerations are taken into account, many mothers can opt for a trial of labour and do deliver vaginally successfully. This has to be discussed carefully with your midwife and obstetrician, because there are some quite serious considerations about delivering in this way. Also, you probably want to avoid an emergency caesarean section after having laboured away and become completely exhausted.

If, towards the end of your pregnancy your baby seems to be favouring a bottom-first approach, there are some steps you can take to help the baby turn to a head-down position. There isn't much point worrying about which way up your baby is until around 34 weeks, because prior to this there is enough room to move up and back again. If, by 36 weeks, your baby seems to remain in a breech position, you can try the following:

- *postural tilting – lie on a firm surface, your bed or the floor, with two or three cushions under your bottom, your knees bent and your feet flat on the floor. Remain like this for at least 10 minutes – use the time to relax and practise your breathing exercises, gently massaging your abdomen – several times a day. This position creates a little more room in the uterus, taking the pressure off the pelvic area, and may allow your baby to turn head down.*
- *external cephalic version – this can only be attempted by a skilled midwife or doctor, and isn't always successful. Even if the baby is turned, it often turns itself promptly back to its original position.*
- *acupuncture – midwives trained in acupuncture at the Freedom Fields Hospital in Plymouth, UK, claim a 60 to 65 per cent success rate at turning breech babies with acupuncture. You will need to find a qualified acupuncturist (see Useful Addresses).*
- *moxibustion – this is an adjunct of acupuncture, and involves the burning of the herb Moxa (Chinese for Mugwort, which is St John's Wort) over the appropriate acupuncture point on both feet. While this may be recommended by your acupuncturist, it may also be recommended and applied by other alternative practitioners who have training and experience in moxibustion, for example herbalists, homoeopaths or osteopaths. Moxibustion will need to be applied for 15 minutes, up to 10 times daily.*
- *homoeopathy – the recommended homoeopathic remedy is Pulsatilla 30, one dose every 2 hours for up to six doses.*

This dosage needs to be taken within the course of one day, and then stopped.

Compare **Anterior Position, Brow Presentation, Face Presentation, Occipito-Anterior Position, Transverse Lie, Unstable Lie**

See also **Acupuncture, Caesarean Section, External Cephalic Version, Homoeopathy, Moxibustion**

Brow Presentation

Brow presentation means that although the baby is head-down for delivery, instead of having his or her head tucked in and the top of the head presenting first, the neck is extended and the brow or face presents first.

The midwife will monitor this quite closely, primarily because the face is less robust than the top of the head. If your baby is delivered like this, your midwife may also warn you that there may be some facial bruising – which will quickly subside – and the baby's head may be slightly elongated at first.

Compare **Anterior Position, Breech Presentation, Face Presentation, Occipito-Anterior Position, Transverse Lie, Unstable Lie**

Cc

Caesarean Section

If your baby is born by caesarean section, it will either be a planned – elective – or emergency procedure, and the reasons are varied.

You will need an elective caesarean if:

- *your placenta is covering the cervix (this is known as* placenta praevia*);*
- *your pelvis is too small for the delivery of the baby.*

Other indications that might suggest an elective caesarean include:

- *high blood-pressure;*
- *diabetes (if there are obstetric complications);*
- *breech presentation;*
- *genital herpes, if in an active phase;*
- *you are pregnant with three or more babies.*

Reasons for an emergency caesarean include:

- *cord prolapse;*
- *distress in the baby (including eclampsia), if delivery isn't imminent;*
- *failure to progress in either first or second stage of labour.*

If you are having an elective caesarean, you will be able to deliver with an epidural anaesthetic, awake but with no feeling of pain from the waist down. This means you are fully aware of what's going on, can have your husband or partner with you, and can hold your baby immediately after birth. There is no anaesthetic effect on your baby, and you will be able to breastfeed straight away.

While there should be no feeling of pain during the delivery, you will feel sensations of pressure and pulling, and the sensation of the amniotic fluid escaping. If you have practised relaxation techniques and breathing exercises, this is a good time for them and for focusing on the positive thought of the arrival of your baby.

Giving birth to your baby in this way is no less of a delivery, no less of a birth, than any other way, and you should be able to feel that your experience was a positive one: you have successfully brought your baby into the world.

An emergency caesarean can, however, leave you feeling less positive, partly because there is seldom time for much emotional preparation. You will probably need a general anaesthetic, too, for speed and safety, and there isn't so much time for explanation and information. If you were unconscious when your baby was delivered, you may want to talk at length to your midwife about the individual process of your delivery after the event. It is still unusual for a husband or partner to be there for a delivery under a general anaesthetic, but he or she can provide a good link for a mother, 'filling in the gaps' in the mother's experience of the birth. This could include some photographs of the baby immediately after birth, and some first photos of mother and baby. The effects of the anaesthetic are such that a mother's first memory of her baby may be very hazy, so photos can be reassuring.

There may not be much emphasis on caesarean section in antenatal care and classes. And if you attend classes that promote only 'natural' birth, the omission of any discussion of caesarean may later make you feel a failure. This is not true. Any mother who successfully delivers her baby is not a failure. She is a success.

Recovery after a caesarean section is like that after any other major abdominal operation: it takes time. You will have some pain afterwards, you will probably have a drip for a short while, you will have had a urinary catheter. On top of which you will be encouraged to get going as soon as possible ... And look after your new baby. A caesarean birth is not an easy option, so give yourself time to recover and ask for lots of help. Your priorities are yourself and your baby. You may be able to have a single room in hospital, so exploit it and get lots of rest. Take the time to cherish and admire your baby, this miracle you've produced.

Practical suggestions to aid your recovery include:

- *Rescue Remedy – although you will be unable to take anything by mouth during your caesarean procedure, if you have an epidural, occasional drops of Bach Rescue Remedy on your tongue might be helpful;*
- *homoeopathic remedies – useful ones to have available are* Arnica, Bellis perennis, Chamomilla, Hypericum, Phosphorus *and* Staphysagria. *You will need a proper 'diagnosis' to select the remedy most appropriate for you, so consult a qualified homoeopath;*
- *gentle exercise – while in hospital a physiotherapist will visit and advise on specific exercises to help get you going. If you have had a general anaesthetic, this will probably include deep breathing exercises, too. If you practised*

breathing and relaxation exercises before the birth, use them now. And don't forget your pelvic floor exercises – even if you haven't delivered vaginally your pelvic floor could benefit from continued toning;

- *your abdominal scar – this should heal within 7 to 10 days, and the stitches will probably be soluble and not need removing. Caesarean scars are along the bikini line, and will hardly show in time. Your midwife will advise you on the immediate care of your scar, but once it's healed you can apply Calendula or vitamin E cream to keep it supple and help it fade.*
- *cranial osteopathy – now you are no longer carrying your baby inside, you may want some help in re-balancing your body and rectifying any lingering discomfort.*

See also **Bach Flower Remedies, Blood-pressure, Breech Presentation, Diabetes, Eclampsia, Epidural, Failure to Progress, Genital Herpes, Homoeopathy, Multiple Pregnancy, Osteopathy, Pelvic Floor Exercises, Placenta Praevia, Prolapse**

Calendula Cream

Calendula cream is extremely effective in promoting healing and helping the top layer of skin knit together after minor injury (it is important to make sure the wound being treated has been well cleaned before application).

Calendula cream can be used on an episiotomy wound, or prior to delivery to soften the perineum. It can also be used to help heal cracked nipples if you have this problem during breastfeeding.

See also **Breastfeeding**

Carpal Tunnel Syndrome

Some women find that they experience tingling and numbness in the fingers or hands as their pregnancy progresses. This is caused by a degree of swelling in the wrist that puts pressure on the median nerve as it passes through what is called the Carpal tunnel in the wrist. The condition improves spontaneously after the birth of your baby.

Osteopathy can be helpful in reducing oedema (fluid retention) and alleviating symptoms, as can shiatsu. Consulting an experienced practitioner is recommended in both instances. There is a particular shiatsu point in the wrist, Pericardium 6, situated three fingers' width below the hand (*see Figure 3, page 55*). It needs to be pressed firmly for seven to 10 seconds, three times. Sometimes wearing a loose bandage over the wrists is enough to ease the numbness and/or tingling in the fingers that Carpal tunnel syndrome brings on. The same treatment recommended for breast engorgement – the application of cabbage leaves – can also be effective in reducing oedema.

Homoeopathic remedies can be of use to some women. Consulting a qualified practitioner always produces a better diagnosis and treatment, but those remedies recommended include *Arsenicum*, *Lycopodium* and *Sepia*.

Compare **Common Complaints of Pregnancy**
See also **Homoeopathy**, **Osteopathy**, **Shiatsu**

Cephalopelvic Disproportion

This is a medical term which refers to the baby's head being unable to pass safely through the mother's pelvis during delivery and birth. This may be because the maternal pelvis is very small, or more unusually because the baby's head isn't aligned and its wider diameters present at the pelvic brim. Unless, for example, a woman knows she has a narrow pelvic outlet and the baby is large, cephalopelvic disproportion won't become apparent until the head fails to engage some time after 36 weeks of pregnancy.

Cerebral Palsy

This neurological syndrome is characterized by problems with muscle tone and power, which have an effect on posture and movement. The range of difficulty is wide and there may or may not be some intellectual disorder. In the past, people with cerebral palsy were often referred to as 'spastics', in reference to the spasticity of their muscle movement. If this was very marked, it made assessment of their intellectual capacity difficult.

It is estimated that only about 6 per cent of cases of cerebral palsy are caused by birth trauma. Luckily, nowadays if a baby is born with a degree of cerebral palsy there is a lot that can be done to help the baby's physical development and to assess the full range of his or her intellectual development. In the UK the charity SCOPE (previously known as the Spastics Society) is extremely helpful (*see Useful Addresses*).

People with cerebral palsy do live very full and active lives, and some do go on to give birth and raise families of their own successfully. There isn't thought to be a genetic connection, and there isn't a specific antenatal test available.

Cervical Incompetence

This is the medical term given to a cervix that is weak. As a pregnancy progresses, the pressure of the baby and amniotic fluid on such a weak cervix can cause it to dilate and bring on a miscarriage. It is thought that up to 20 per cent of women who have recurrent miscarriages have, for a variety of reasons, a weak cervix. Once diagnosed, it is possible to insert a purse-string stitch into the cervix to keep it closed. This is referred to, medically, as a Shirodkar suture.

Women who have this stitch need close monitoring immediately afterwards as the stimulation to the cervix can itself sometimes cause a miscarriage. But if everything is OK after about five days, the stitch stays in place until around the 38th or 39th week of pregnancy – or is removed straight away if labour starts before this time.

See also **Shirodkar Stitch**

Cervical Mucus

The lining at the opening of the cervix produces mucus in response to the hormones oestrogen and progesterone during a woman's menstrual cycle.

The hormonal effect on the production of mucus is easy to see during the menstrual cycle, and it is a sign used in natural family planning to indicate when ovulation is close.

Immediately after the end of a period there is no mucus secretion to speak of. Over the next couple of weeks it becomes more apparent, initially sparse and opaque and then much more copious, watery and 'stringy', up to ovulation. After ovulation there is a dramatic change back to thicker, lumpier mucus that decreases in amount over the next couple of weeks to a period.

As one of the sympto-thermic methods of natural family planning it can be enormously useful for some women, once they have 'learned' their individual symptoms to pinpoint ovulation and either achieve or avoid pregnancy.

Cervical mucus is usually odourless and white or clear, unless you have some sort of vaginal infection. This may be accompanied by itching around the vulva, too. You may find you are more prone to vaginal infections during pregnancy.

You may also find that, during pregnancy, because of the increase in the level of the hormone progesterone you produce much more cervical mucus which is quite watery and may be a nuisance. Try using panty liners if this is a problem.

Your first sign of labour may be a 'show', which is the mucus plug that comes away from the cervix as it begins to dilate. This is usually quite a thick, large-ish amount of mucus, quite recognizable if it happens to you, often pinkish in colour or slightly blood-stained. If your labour begins with your waters breaking, however, you probably won't notice a 'show'.

Compare **Natural Family Planning**
See also **Show, Thrush**

Cervix

This is the neck of the womb, through which the sperm passes to fertilize the egg and through which your baby will be born (*see Figure 4*). You are probably familiar with it only because of your regular smear tests.

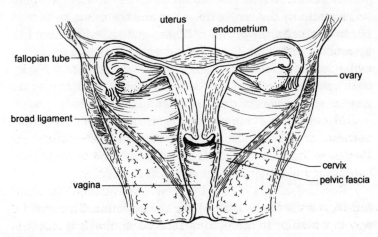

Cervix

You will hear a lot about your cervix when you are pregnant, and particularly when you are in labour. It has to dilate up to 10 cm, and it is this dilatation that is occurring during the contractions in the first stage of labour. As your cervix begins to dilate in labour, you may have a 'show', a plug of mucus that covered the opening to the cervix during pregnancy that comes away as labour begins (or even a few days before this).

The cervix doesn't dilate evenly. You may be 2-cm dilated before you have any sign of a contraction, you may then progress quickly to 8 cm and then spend two hours getting to 10 cm: every labour is unique. With each contraction the baby's head descends, little by little, further into the pelvis. The pressure of the baby's head helps the cervix dilate and also stimulates the production of oxytocin, which in turn stimulates the contractions.

If your waters have broken, the very direct contact between your baby's head and the cervix will increase the stimulation of oxytocin, and the contractions. This is why your membranes are sometimes ruptured artificially, to promote contractions and labour.

Eventually the cervix thins out and opens up, so that at 10 cm dilatation the cervix will have virtually disappeared up around your baby's ears. One description often used, which is useful for visualizing what is happening, is of a polo-neck jumper being pulled on over your head: that is the way in which the cervix opens up and over your baby's head.

After birth the cervix closes again, although the cervical opening, or 'os', is never as fully closed as it was before.

Chiropractic

A chiropractor treats pain by joint manipulation. In this way it is similar to osteopathy, but the emphasis is much more on the vertebral joints, and chiropractors tend to use diagnostic X-rays and high-velocity thrusts as part of their practice.

While chiropractic may not be suitable for use during pregnancy, many postnatal backaches, headaches and other pains can be successfully treated. There is something to be said for visiting a chiropractor or osteopath postnatally for a check-up and to see if there is any need for remedial care following the physical demands of pregnancy and labour (and motherhood!).

Consult your doctor, who may, like many others, increasingly recommend chiropractors, or contact the Chiropractic Association (*see Useful Addresses*).

Compare **Osteopathy**

Chlamydia

Chlamydia is a vaginal infection caused by a parasite. Women with this infection may have no symptoms at all, but it can cause a variety of problems: tubal inflammation, pelvic inflammatory disease (PID), possible ectopic pregnancy, repeated miscarriage and infertility. If a woman has an infection at the time of giving birth, it can cause conjunctivitis in her baby.

It is possible to screen for chlamydia (though this isn't done routinely). It can be successfully treated in pregnancy with the antibiotic erythromycin. It is always worth telling your doctor or midwife if you have any vaginal discharge you are worried about.

Chorionic Villus Sampling (CVS)

This is an antenatal diagnostic test for chromosomal and/or genetic disorders that can be undertaken early in pregnancy – between 8 and 12 weeks. It is usually recommended if the pregnant woman is over 35.

The procedure involves taking a sample of placental tissue by inserting an endoscope into the uterus via the vagina, using ultrasound scanning to guide the endoscope. Because this can be done early in pregnancy, one of the advantages is it provides an early diagnosis should there be any congenital problem. And where there is a family history of a genetic disorder, it can be very reassuring when nothing is found.

If the diagnosis is positive, this allows a couple time to make an informed decision about whether or not they want to have a termination. This is a difficult decision under any circumstances, but one that is always better made with time to reflect. The organization Support Around Termination For Abnormality (SAFTA) provides counselling following a positive diagnosis – without pressure one way or another (*see Useful Addresses*).

Like all antenatal testing, CVS isn't something to be undertaken lightly and it does have some risk factors. For example, there is a 2 per cent chance of spontaneous miscarriage; there is some suggestion that the test results aren't always accurate; and some research suggests a link between CVS and birth defects. You need to discuss your individual circumstances with your obstetrician.

Compare **Amniocentesis, Antenatal Testing**

Colic

Colic is characterized by sharp, intermittent abdominal pains, causing the baby to draw his or her legs up or flail around. It is usually accompanied by a lot of distressed and pitiful crying. All of this will make *you* feel awful. First of all, hang on to the fact that it is not your fault and it *will* pass. Some babies just do take a while – up to three months – to settle, and although this seems a lifetime at the time, in the scheme of things it isn't very long.

That said, there is quite a lot you can do to help your baby and yourself to survive this period. It is quite natural to try and find a specific reason for your baby's distress, and to try and solve the problem: this may not be possible, partly because the 'problem' may be unspecific, or change, *and* your baby can't tell you what it is either. But there are various things you can try:

- *If you are breastfeeding, check what you are eating and drinking. Cutting out coffee, tea, cola and some acidic fruit juices, plus cow's milk, is worth considering, if only in the short term. Some vegetables in the cabbage family (broccoli, etc.) might also cause problems. Garlic apparently doesn't cause any problem, and porridge is good, too, especially as it is thought to encourage a good milk supply. Chewing fennel seeds, or making a fresh infusion of fennel seed tea might help, as might camomile tea, because these soothing herbs pass into the breastmilk.*
- *Freshly brewed fennel seed tea, in small quantities, can be safely given to your baby. Don't use commercially prepared fennel drinks as they contain unnecessary sugar. You can give this to your baby on a sterilized, non-metal teaspoon.*
- *Occasionally offer your baby cooled, boiled water, again from a teaspoon if you are breastfeeding. If you are breastfeeding unrestrictedly your baby is unlikely to be thirsty, but it may be worth a try, especially if it is very hot.*
- *Offer your baby a dummy or fingertip to suck: sucking may help him or her settle, while continuing to feed may just overload his or her tummy. For some babies, comfort sucking is very important.*
- *An abdominal massage may help, especially if you think your baby may also be a bit constipated. Make sure the room is warm and draught-free, and that your baby is*

lying on a soft surface – a well-worn, clean towel is fine – bearing in mind that your massage may produce either urine or a bowel movement. Use a sweet almond oil, perhaps adding a few drops of Roman camomile, and massage gently but firmly in a clockwise direction around your baby's lower abdomen using the tips of your middle three fingers. This will only go down well if your baby doesn't mind lying naked. If it causes extreme panic, don't continue: you can try again another time.

- Shiatsu and reflexology both have a role to play in the treatment of colic. You will need to find someone qualified and with an interest in or experience of working with babies (see Useful Addresses).

- Breastfeed unrestrictedly at first, as the build-up of an adequate supply of milk is important in the first few weeks. You can reduce the number of feed times later. Once you can see your baby is gaining weight satisfactorily, and having lots of wet nappies, you will know that it isn't hunger that is making him or her cry. The close body contact may also be reassuring.

- Have a warm bath together. Some babies love this and respond very well, although most mothers or fathers find that the correct temperature for their baby is a bit cool for them!

- Wrap your baby securely in order that he or she will feel 'contained' emotionally and physically while getting used to being away from you. Some babies really don't like being held and moved around all the time, it makes them jittery, but they do like to feel secure when alone in their pram or cot.

- If you have had a particularly demanding delivery, or needed some sort of intervention, consider taking your baby to a cranial osteopath. The jittery, nervous irritation experienced by many babies during their first few months of life can be very easily helped by a cranial osteopath: it *is well worth a visit (see Useful Addresses). In fact, whatever type of delivery you've had, this is one alternative practitioner who is worth seeing for both yourself and your baby, after the birth, just for a check-up.*

- *If you are really getting to the end of your tether and beginning to feel really tense, seek help. This includes practical help: allow a trusted friend or family member to babysit while you take some time out to recharge your batteries, otherwise you may find yourself spiralling into a circle of tension and frustration. Go off for a sleep, a walk, a massage or bath – anything, even if only for an hour. You may find that sometimes it breaks a cycle, and a fussy baby may find it easier to relax and 'let go' away from you.*

- *Finally, if you have any reason to suspect there is a bigger problem than you can deal with, because the crying is incessant, the baby won't feed, or there is persistent diarrhoea or vomiting, or no wet nappies – seek help from your midwife, health visitor or doctor. And ask for help and advice whenever you need it: better to ask during the day than at 3 a.m. when everyone's at their wit's end.*

See also **Crying Baby**

Colostrum

While your baby is born with a certain amount of passive immunity gained from your own blood-borne antibodies, the colostrum produced by your breasts prior to your milk coming in is another valuable source. Colostrum is rich in protein, and in particular those proteins so essential for early growth and brain development. It is also high in immunity-enhancing substances and anti-infective agents, protecting against a wide range of bacteria and viruses.

Even if you are not planning to breastfeed your baby for any length of time, it is well worth giving your baby the benefit of colostrum.

See also **Breastfeeding**

Common Complaints of Pregnancy

See **Carpal Tunnel Syndrome, Constipation, Cramp, Cystitis, Fainting, Gingivitis, Gums, Bleeding, Haemorrhoids, Hair (changes to) Headaches, Heartburn, Incontinence, Insomnia, Itching, Morning Sickness Nausea, Nosebleeds, Oedema, Ptyalism, Skin (changes to), Stretch Marks, Taste (changes to sense of), Thrush, Tiredness, Varicose Veins**

Community Midwives

Community midwives work within the community rather than in a hospital setting, although they may be employed by a hospital trust and answer to the head of midwifery or women's services, who is hospital-based.

Community midwives will see women for their antenatal care at a health centre or GP practice, or visit them at home. After the birth, and discharge from hospital, you will be visited at home by the community midwife, who will oversee your care and your baby's care for a minimum of 10 days after birth. So, if you spent two days in hospital, she will visit you for eight days, etc. If necessary for any reason, however, your community midwife can visit for up to 28 days.

If you have opted for a Domino delivery, your community midwife will accompany you to hospital. If you have opted for a home birth, your community midwife will deliver you at home.

See also **Domino Scheme, Home Birth**

Complementary Therapies

See **Acupressure, Acupuncture, Alexander Technique, Aromatherapy, Autogenics, Bach Flower Remedies, Biochemic Tissue Salts, Herbal Remedies, Homoeopathy, Hypnotherapy, Kinesiology, Naturopathy, Osteopathy, Reflexology, Shiatsu**

Conception

Conception heralds the beginning of a pregnancy, when the woman's ovum has been fertilized by the man's sperm and this embryonic life has implanted in the wall of the uterus.

Conception requires a number of favourable circumstances: that the sperm should be around at the time of a recently-released ovum; that there should be nothing to avoid their meeting; and that implantation occurs without problem.

For those trying to get pregnant, meeting these three criteria may present difficulties. Because ovulation occurs only once a month, and the ovum only lasts for around 12 hours, timing of intercourse is important. Luckily sperm last for around five days, so there is some lee-way. But sperm, because they are being continually produced, are more susceptible to fluctuations in quality and quantity. They need to be sufficiently robust in order to navigate their way to the ovum and, although only one is required, several million are produced each time in order to increase the chance of one making it 'all the way'.

There is no doubt that a woman's fertility starts to decline after about the age of 35. A couple having regular, unprotected intercourse could reasonably expect to get pregnant within a year. However, if you want to increase your chances it is worth spending a bit of time learning about the fertility cycle, and in particular your own. Natural family planning, because it teaches you about the explicit indicators of fertility, and especially those individual to you, is particularly useful.

Planning a pregnancy is also a time to think about your general health, diet and lifestyle. Without getting obsessional, there are probably areas of your personal health you should consider improving.

See also **Natural Family Planning**, **Pre-conceptual Care**

Confinement

A rather old-fashioned medical term still in use today for the period during which a woman gives birth (in hospital or at home).

Constipation

For many women this is the bane of their pregnancy. Primarily it is caused by the effect of the pregnancy hormone progesterone, which relaxes smooth muscle (including the muscles in the intestine). Intestinal movement is then reduced and sluggish, and this can result in constipation.

Avoid it by increasing the amount of roughage in your diet: fruit, vegetables and whole grains. Avoid over-refined and junk food on a regular basis. You can try a bran-based breakfast cereal (oat bran is gentler than wheat bran). Also increase the amount of fluid you drink – but not tea and coffee, which can have a diuretic effect. Water, fruit juices and herb teas are better. Also make sure you take some exercise every day. This needn't be energetic; regular gentle walks will help.

Although iron supplements aren't routinely given to all pregnant women, if you are prescribed them you may notice that they increase your likelihood of becoming constipated.

Bear this in mind – although some women have found the opposite is true – and take pre-emptive action.

However, if the worst comes to the worst, and you do become constipated, don't despair. There is still quite a lot you can do to help yourself:

- *Start the day with a cup of hot water and lemon, or herb tea. This in itself is sometimes enough to kick-start the bowel into action. Morning is often the best time for a bowel movement, as the digestive inactivity of the night is replaced by activity in the gut after being stimulated by the first food/drink of the day.*
- *Take your time when you go to the lavatory, and make sure you are private, warm and comfortable. Constipation is often a general problem for many women when life is busy.*
- *Try to avoid straining and run the risk of uncomfortable haemorrhoids – you are more at risk of these when pregnant anyway.*
- *Breakfast on lots of fresh fruit and bran-based cereal. Try and have a portion of raw fruit or vegetables with each meal.*
- *Several homoeopathic remedies are useful. Try* Aesculus *(Aesc.);* Lycopodium *(Lyc.)* Kali carbonicum *(Kali-c.);* Nux vomica *(Nux-v.); and* Pulsatilla nigricans *(Puls.). For a more specific prescription, consult a qualified homoeopath.*
- *Vitamin C and magnesium supplements may help, but take advice on this.*
- *Herbalists recommend dandelion root tea: try your local health food shop.*
- *Massage your abdomen in a clockwise direction. Add a few drops of essential oil of* Mandarin *or* Orange *to a base oil or cream and massage your abdomen with this.*

- *Try shiatsu massage – two-finger pressure – halfway between the pubic bone and the navel, for 10 seconds at a time.*
- *Shiatsu massage to the stomach meridian, which runs along the outside of the thigh from the hip to just below the knee, can also be helpful.*
- *Gentle massage of the foot arches, in a clockwise direction, as according to reflexology this area of the foot corresponds to the intestines.*
- *If you are doing any yoga-based exercise, some yoga postures are particularly beneficial. Check with a yoga teacher.*
- *Both osteopathy and acupuncture can be helpful in treating constipation, but you will need to find a qualified practitioner.*
- *Try to avoid purgatives and laxatives, as some may be positively harmful. If you absolutely do need something to help, a glycerine suppository may be better. Take advice from your midwife, doctor or pharmacist.*

See also **Acupuncture, Diet, Herbal Remedies, Homoeopathy, Massage, Nutrition, Osteopathy, Shiatsu, Vitamins**

Contraception

You will probably be asked about what form of contraception you intend to use at your first check-up after your baby is born.

If you are not breastfeeding at all, you can get pregnant again very soon after giving birth. Once your hormones have settled down, you will begin ovulating again quite soon. If you are breastfeeding *unrestrictedly*, and that means throughout the night too, your levels of prolactin will probably be high enough to prevent ovulation, but as soon as you reduce this high level of breastfeeding you run a risk of pregnancy. The problem is that you won't know until you either have a period (or get pregnant!) whether or not you've started ovulating again.

If you are breastfeeding you won't be able to take an oestrogen-based contraception pill as this will interfere with your milk production. The pill isn't prescribed within the first few weeks following delivery anyway, because of the slight increase in the risk of blood clots. A progestogen-only pill could be prescribed even while breastfeeding, as it doesn't prohibit milk production, and it is thought that what little crosses into breastmilk does no harm.

You will have to wait until after your check-up if you wish to have an IUD (Intra-uterine device) inserted, as there is a small risk of damaging the uterus if it is still 'soft' following the birth.

If you were using a diaphragm, or Dutch cap, prior to your pregnancy, you will need to wait until after your first check-up to be fitted with a new one. Your size following pregnancy will have changed, especially if you are still 7 lb or more heavier than you were pre-pregnancy, as is likely.

You may find that, initially, using a sheath or condom is best, especially given everything else you will be dealing with. This is something your husband or partner can take full responsibility for. Condoms are already lubricated, but if you need extra lubrication use only water-based lubricants such as *KY Jelly*. Anything petroleum-based, such as Vaseline, will make the rubber of the condom deteriorate.

Contractions

The uterine contractions felt periodically towards the end of pregnancy are called Braxton Hicks and are different from the contractions of labour.

Labour contractions may begin quite gently and be imperceptible to the mother, occurring about every 15 to 20 minutes and lasting about 30 seconds. The interval between contractions gradually lessens and, by the end of the first stage, they are occurring at 2- to 3-minute intervals and lasting around 50 to 60 seconds. It is at this later stage that, because they are so powerful, contractions may be felt as painful.

Uterine contractions, unlike ordinary muscle contractions, have the ability to 'hold' a little of the contraction within the muscle. The muscle contraction starts from the top of the uterus and radiates across and downwards. This acts strongly on the upper part of the uterus, progressively holding the contraction in order to reduce the amount of space inside for the baby and to assist in its expulsion. At the same time the lower end of the uterus is contracting less strongly and dilating to allow the passage of the baby through the cervix. So the work of labour contractions is quite specialized and, if these two aspects are working harmoniously together, the progression of your labour should be straightforward.

Because of the way in which labour contractions work, your mobility and position during early labour can either work with or against your contractions. This is one of the reasons why an active birth – keeping moving, staying upright – can be so beneficial.

See also **Active Birth**, **Birth**, **Braxton Hicks Contractions**, **Labour**

Co-operation Card

This is the term used to describe the medical notes shared between your GP and the hospital. You have access to these, and keep them yourself during your pregnancy, to take along with you to each antenatal check.

Here is a list of terms and explanations commonly used on antenatal notes:

LMP	*Last menstrual period (date)*
Fetus	*Baby before birth*
Fundal height	*Size of the womb*
Uterine size	*Size of the womb*
B.P.	*Blood-pressure*
Presentation	*Part of the baby coming first*
C./Ceph./Cephalic	*Heading pointing down*
Vx./Vertex	*Head pointing down*
TTr./Transverse	*Baby lying sideways*
B./Br./Breech	*Baby's bottom pointing down*
Relation to brim	*Whether baby's head is in the pelvis*
E./Eng./Engaged	*Whether baby's head is in the pelvis*
FFH	*Fetal heart heard*
FM(N)F	*Fetal movements (not) felt*
Oedema	*Swelling*
Hb./Haemaglobin	*Iron level in the blood*
NAD	*No abnormality discovered*
VE	*Vaginal examination*
Cx./Cervix	*Opening to the womb*
Rubella	*German measles*
AFP	*Blood serum screening test for Spina Bifida*
MSU	*Mid-stream specimen of urine*
U/S	*Ultrasound*

Cordocentesis

Although this antenatal test is done after 20 weeks' gestation, the results are ready in a couple of days and it is the only way to detect some conditions. It is a test usually reserved for women with a known family history of certain disorders, for example cystic fibrosis, some chromosomal problems, and hereditary blood disorders.

Sometimes referred to as fetal blood sampling, the baby's blood sample is taken from the umbilical cord (guided by ultrasound). White blood cells from the sample are cultured and tested. There is a risk of miscarriage with this test (between 1 and 2 per cent) and it is not widely available in the UK, although if necessary it is possible to be referred to a private clinic which performs this test.

Counselling

If you are feeling particularly shaky about your pregnancy, its effect on your life, your ability to mother your child – or even feeling overwhelmed with unknown fears and anxiety, ask your doctor or midwife to refer you to (or help you to find) a suitable counsellor. This needn't be full-blown analysis, but more a helpful sorting out of old feelings that your pregnancy may have dredged up, which can often happen during times of major life change. Although talking to friends can be helpful, the support of a skilled counsellor – even if only for a few sessions – can be invaluable. There is no loss of face, it is a positive step towards coping with change, not an admission of an inability to cope.

Cramp

Muscular cramp in the leg can be extremely painful; why pregnant women are more susceptible isn't really known. It may be linked to a number of factors, including a deficiency of calcium – so you could try increasing your intake of dairy products. Other dietary deficiencies may be Vitamin B, so you could increase your intake with wheatgerm.

If you are suddenly afflicted by cramp in your leg, straighten it and flex the foot towards you. Massage the calf muscle firmly, which will also provide pressure over the shiatsu point known as Bladder 57, effective in reducing cramp. Night cramps might also be reduced by raising the foot of the bed by 25 cm (10 inches).

Regular, gentle exercise throughout pregnancy may help circulation and help avoid cramps. Walking, swimming and yoga are good and can be continued until the end of pregnancy. Yoga also has particular poses that are good for stretching the calf muscles. All exercise aids circulation and, combined with deep breathing and relaxation, will increase your energy levels and help you prepare for the arrival of your baby.

Homoeopathic remedies for cramp include *Calcarea phosphorica* (Calc-p.) and *Magnesia phosphorica* (Mag-p.). *Nux vomica* is sometimes recommended for cramps that occur at night, and *Arnica* might be useful if you feel your cramp occurs because you are generally overtired.

The biochemic tissue salt *Mag. phos.* is thought to be useful as it has an effect on nerves and muscles. Herbalists recommend a decoction of Crampbark, perhaps with the addition of ginger, as this aids circulation.

See also **Biochemic Tissue Salts, Herbal Remedies, Homoeopathy, Shiatsu, Yoga**

Cranial Osteopathy

This is a branch of osteopathy that is focused on the skull, which is made up of eight separate bones, and the cerebro-spinal fluid that surrounds the brain and runs up and down the spinal cord. It is an aspect of osteopathy that is particularly relevant to pregnant women, newborn babies and infants, as it doesn't involve any spinal manipulation.

Qualified osteopaths, and those with additional training in cranial work, are skilled at detecting any distortions or disturbances – which can be very minor – in the flow of cerebro-spinal fluid. Then, through gentle pressure on the bones of the skull and sometimes the sacrum, they can correct the balance and alleviate the symptoms.

The strain of pregnancy, and of the birth itself, can actually cause low-grade symptoms that are accumulatively very wearying: headaches, tiredness, backache, restlessness, depression, etc. – often the very symptoms we associate with early motherhood, which can in fact be reduced or avoided.

Newborn babies may show many symptoms of cranial irritation that respond very positively to this form of osteopathy, or craniosacral therapy as it is sometimes called: excessive crying, colic, sleeplessness, breathing problems, constipation – again, many of the problems routinely associated with the 'normal' pattern of behaviour in newborns.

Osteopaths who have trained at the Osteopathic Centre for Children in London (*see Useful Addresses*) are particularly adept at diagnosing and treating problems in newborns and older children alike. They will also have information on practitioners in your area.

Compare **Chiropractic**, **Osteopathy**

Crying

You may find yourself crying much more easily when you are pregnant, and for a variety of unexplained reasons. You may also find that you cry more easily when angry, frustrated, sad or even when moved by something beautiful. For women who are not 'cryers' by nature, this may be a bit disconcerting. All sorts of suggestions are made about the reasons why this happens, largely relating to your hormones, psychological state, attitude to pregnancy, etc., which may help a little. Unless there is any reason you know of why you may be feeling particularly distressed (in which case you should seek specific help from your midwife, health visitor or doctor), you may just have to live with it. While it may be worse during the first three months of pregnancy, and compounded by perhaps feeling unwell, it will probably ease up later. It is, however, particularly irritating to be reduced to tears by a minor confrontation that previously you would have taken in your stride!

For some women there is a feeling of emotional liberation with this new-found source of expression. Having a baby is, after all, a profound experience and one that should be emotionally considered and integrated. This, however alien it may feel initially, can be positive and is part of the very major changes going on in your life.

See also **Anxiety**, **Depression**

Crying Baby

All newborn babies cry, it is their only vocal form of self-expression. Over time you will begin to decipher your baby's different cries – hunger, tiredness, boredom, crossness, distress – and respond accordingly. Some babies just do cry more than others and, certainly in the first few months, parents can spend a lot of time trying to work out why their baby is crying.

There is nothing more rewarding than being able to console a crying baby, which makes us feel like a 'good' mother, and conversely there is nothing that makes us feel more like a 'bad' mother than a baby who cries incessantly. And it can be very hard not to resent the cause of these negative feelings, on top of everything else about new motherhood.

If, however, your baby's crying is beginning to defeat you, do talk to your health visitor or doctor, who may have some suggestions born of experience with a variety of babies. Sometimes the objectivity of an outsider can put things into perspective, and a couple of key ideas may just help you cope better. In most cases, as long as there is no physical complaint or illness, babies who seem to cry a lot will settle eventually.

See also **Colic**, **Cranial Osteopathy**, **Homoeopathy**

Cystitis

If you were prone to cystitis before you were pregnant, you could find that it is now aggravated. You will already be familiar with some of the things you can do to avoid an attack, including:

- *always empty your bladder as soon as you need to;*
- *wear cotton underwear, avoid 'biological' washing powders, and always rinse clothes thoroughly;*
- *avoid wearing tights;*
- *avoid perfumed toiletries;*
- *always wipe yourself from front to back;*
- *ensure you drink plenty of water: 2 litres a day is recommended;*
- *use a lubricating agent – for example, KY Jelly – during sexual intercourse to avoid any aggravation to the urethra.*

If you begin to suffer the first signs of an attack, immediately check you are following the above suggestions, and also try some of the following tips:

- *make your own lemon barley water by boiling pearl barley in double the usual quantity of water, then draining off the water and flavouring it with a little lemon. In spite of the lemon flavouring, barley water is alkaline and helps reduce the urine's natural acidity;*

- *drink half a pint of fluid – alternating barley water, water, camomile tea, cranberry juice – every half hour for several hours, which may be enough to flush out any potential infection;*
- *cranberry juice is particularly useful as it is thought to prevent any bacteria adhering to the bladder wall;*
- *other herbal teas that are useful are nettle and marigold;*
- *reflexology can be helpful, but you will need to see a qualified reflexologist;*
- *osteopathy can help some cases. If you are already seeing an osteopath he or she should already have checked any susceptibility to cystitis on your part when taking your medical history;*
- *increase your dietary intake of garlic, parsley, whole grains and brown rice. Cut out acidic and refined foods, especially white sugar;*
- *when symptoms are acute, use a solution of warm camomile tea as a vulval washdown after emptying your bladder;*
- *keep warm and try to get lots of rest.*

If symptoms persist, your doctor should take a urine specimen for analysis and prescribe antibiotics. Because of the risk of kidney infection, which can be a secondary problem of cystitis particularly in pregnancy, this must be treated effectively. If at any time you have backache in conjunction with the symptoms of cystitis, which may suggest a kidney infection, see your doctor straight away. Similarly, if you experience a fever, vomiting, headache or blood in your urine, do consult your doctor.

See also **Osteopathy, Reflexology**

Dd

Deep Transverse Arrest

This is the technical term that describes a delay in the second stage of labour because the baby's head, having failed to turn sufficiently to travel down the birth canal, gets 'caught' on the bones of the mother's pelvis. In order to deliver vaginally, the head needs to be turned using Keilland's forceps. This is sometimes referred to as a high forceps delivery and requires delivery by an obstetrically trained doctor. Anaesthetic is also needed, either a pudendal block or an epidural.

Although the forceps are designed to encase, rather than squeeze the baby's head, there is often some swelling and bruising after birth if delivery has been assisted in this way, which will subside quite quickly.

See also **Epidural, Forceps, Pudendal Block, Vacuum Extraction**

Demand Feeding

This refers to feeding babies as and when they appear to be hungry, rather than to any fixed schedule. It is also called feeding 'on demand' or, less assertively, baby-led feeding. It refers to breastfeeding rather than bottle-feeding and, if you are breastfeeding unrestrictedly in order to build up your milk supply, you will be feeding on demand. After a period of time your baby will 'demand' less often, allowing you to introduce a schedule of sorts, albeit by necessity a flexible one.

See also **Breastfeeding**

Depression

Depression after childbirth falls into four categories:

1   *Baby-blues, which usually occur around day three or four, customarily when your milk comes in. After the emotional 'high' of the birth itself, baby-blues are reckoned to be due to an abrupt change in your hormonal levels.*
2   *Mild depression, which may be a quite natural reaction to the emotional intensity of giving birth and becoming a mother, combined with hormonal changes and feeling tired and bruised after the birth and lack of sleep. This may only last a short time and/or be easily resolved with a little more rest and recovery.*
3   *Severe depression: a clinical depression that may come from nowhere or result from a worsening of mild depression. Approximately one in 10 mothers experiences postnatal depression of this type, and for many this goes unrecognized, misdiagnosed as tiredness or anaemia or some other physical problem that we can put a face to and treat.*

4   *Puerperal psychosis: an acute psychiatric illness that occurs within a few days of delivery. It is easily identified and needs prompt treatment. It is also relatively unusual, affecting about one woman in every 1,000.*

Unfortunately it isn't possible to identify the women who will get postnatal depression, only to be alert to the signs and to seek help if necessary. Becoming a mother is such a life-change that it would be surprising if there weren't a strong reaction to the reality of this new life with a small baby and all the upheaval it involves. All other relationships, with your husband or partner, parents, siblings, friends, workmates, etc. change to some degree. If this change is suppressed rather than acknowledged and integrated, feelings of depression can sometimes escalate.

We spend so much of pregnancy dwelling on the physical, rather than the emotional impact of having a baby, when it happens we can be emotionally 'caught short'. If time isn't given to addressing these changes and how we feel about them, it can easily contribute to depression.

Nowadays the average length of a hospital stay after giving birth is two days, whereas in the past it was 10 days, which enforced a period of rest on a new mother. Both have their merits and drawbacks. It's good to get home as soon as possible, but only if you can rest and recuperate there, too. Some suggestions for living with the ups and downs of the early days include:

- *rest, recover and focus on your new baby;*
- *however busy your routine seems, try to eat regularly and well, and keep your fluid levels up if you are establishing breastfeeding;*
- *don't over-do the visitors. Have your husband, partner, mother or friend tell people if you are resting and not to be disturbed;*

- *suggest to friends that they will be very welcome if they make their own tea, or bring a ready-cooked meal around, or want to wash the kitchen floor, or babysit while you take yourself and/or your older children out for an hour;*
- *talk through your delivery with your husband or partner, or midwife or friend, especially if there were aspects of it you feel unhappy about;*
- *however brilliant you are feeling, take it easy and don't be surprised if you inadvertently overdo it one day and feel exhausted the next;*
- *take some gentle exercise, it will keep you going and increase your energy levels;*
- *take some time out just for you: go to the hairdressers, take a walk, visit a friend, have an aromatherapy massage or reflexology session;*
- *see a cranial osteopath for a postnatal check and treatment, and take your baby for a check-up too.*

Avoiding depression isn't always possible, and it may be part of the process of adapting to parenthood. However, even if this is the case support and help are necessary. If things seem overwhelming and you feel you can't cope any longer, it is important to get professional help. This needn't be in the form of any sort of medication, but some sort of short-term counselling might be appropriate. In France women are entitled to much more postnatal support, and this includes a year's free counselling, than we receive in the UK. Try your health visitor and doctor first; there may be a postnatal support group and counsellor attached to your GP practice or health centre.

It isn't a sign of failure to seek help, but more a case of recognizing what an important job parenting your child is, for which we all need help sometimes.

Compare **Anxiety**, **Crying**
See also **Counselling**

Diabetes

If you have diabetes you will, with expert help, be able to enjoy a happy and healthy pregnancy. When well-controlled, the effect of diabetes on pregnancy (and vice versa) is minimal. Pre-conceptual advice and care are particularly important if you have diabetes, as is antenatal care, the aim being to pre-empt and so avoid problems. You might want to contact the British Diabetic Association for further information (*see Useful Addresses*).

Some women develop diabetes only for the duration of their pregnancy; this is referred to as *gestational diabetes*. And occasionally the increased demand for insulin that pregnancy creates can, for some women, make latent diabetes appear.

If you have been well-monitored by obstetrician and endocrinologist alike, and all has progressed smoothly, there is no reason why a woman with diabetes can't enjoy a normal labour and delivery. It used to be thought necessary to deliver the baby between 35 and 37 weeks of pregnancy, but this is no longer the case. Neither is diabetes on its own a reason for a caesarean delivery, only if there are other obstetric reasons in conjunction with this.

It is also perfectly possible to breastfeed your baby if you have diabetes. It may be necessary to increase your intake of carbohydrates and adjust the insulin dose required, but any insulin the baby receives via breastmilk is destroyed in the baby's stomach. The only thing that could interfere with milk production is poor diabetic control, so specialist help may be necessary to ensure that this does not occur.

Keeping diabetes well controlled may be problematic if you suffer greatly from morning sickness and vomiting. If you have diabetes you may also be more susceptible to minor pregnancy problems such as cystitis and thrush.

Other standard health considerations such as smoking, drinking alcohol and taking exercise should also be reviewed.

See also **Cystitis, Morning Sickness, Thrush**

Diarrhoea

You may be slightly more sensitive to foods that are not quite fresh when you are pregnant, and may react by producing stools that are more loose than usual. If you have diarrhoea accompanied by stomach cramps, and feel unlike eating very much, then just make sure you drink more to compensate. Your baby won't suffer if you don't eat much for a couple of days, but you must make sure you don't get dehydrated. Above all, increase your intake of water. And if you have abdominal cramps that are very severe, or getting steadily worse, do see your doctor.

There are a number of homoeopathic remedies that are extremely effective for diarrhoea, but prescribing the correct one depends on your range of symptoms, so it's best to consult a qualified homoeopath.

Sometimes diarrhoea at the end of pregnancy can be an indication that labour is about to start. In these circumstances you may find you experience repeated, small amounts of diarrhoea over a period of time. This may be nature's way of ensuring you have an empty bowel prior to delivery.

Diarrhoea in small babies is another matter. It is unusual for breastfed babies to get gastro-intestinal complaints (one of breastfeeding's many advantages), and a breastfed baby's stool is naturally soft to runny, and quite yellow in appearance. It can resemble lightly scrambled egg, and smell quite sweet. It is also quite normal for breastfed babies to have several dirty nappies a day. Your baby's first bowel movement after birth will produce a sticky, greenish-black stool which is called meconium. This is just an emptying of the gut, and indicates that there is a clear passage through. Over the next few days this colour changes to greenish-brown, to brown, to the yellow of breastfed babies' stools, or the more formed brown stool of bottle-fed babies. There are, quite naturally, some variations of stool depending on your baby's general health, whether he or she is teething, has a slight cold, etc.

However, if there is persistent diarrhoea, especially accompanied by any vomiting, your baby runs the risk of becoming dehydrated – and this can be serious. If this happens you will also notice that there are no, or fewer, wet nappies and the urine smells much more strongly. If you are concerned, especially if your baby is 6 months old or younger, seek help from either your health visitor or doctor. Dehydration is always better avoided. You will also need to seek advice if diarrhoea and vomiting are additional symptoms to, say, a rise in temperature and generalized discomfort perhaps caused by pain.

See also **Homoeopathy**

Dick-Read, Dr Grantley

Dr Grantley Dick-Read was a doctor practising in the 1930s who recognized that women's fear of childbirth lead to muscle tension and, therefore, more painful labour. He recommended that women were given more information about labour and birth, while also being taught specific relaxation and breathing techniques to use during childbirth. His pioneering work is very much embodied in the continued work of the National Childbirth Trust (*see Useful Addresses*).

See also **Fear, Psychoprophylaxis**

Diet

It is particularly important to make sure your diet is balanced and nutritious while you are pregnant, and it is also worth thinking about your diet even before you become pregnant. Your baby will take all it needs from you and your reserves, so to keep fit and healthy you will need to be sure your diet is adequate. This is also a good opportunity to review your eating habits and try to increase your intake of more health-giving foods.

Following a vegetarian diet throughout pregnancy shouldn't present a problem as long as you follow the advice on protein below, using vegetarian sources. You may just have to watch your iron intake, and should let your midwife know that you are vegetarian. With a vegan diet you will need specialist advice; your midwife can refer you to a nutritionist.

Current nutritional advice suggests the following:

Protein (meat, poultry, fish, eggs, nuts, beans, lentils, etc.)	*three servings a day*
Carbohydrates (bread, potatoes, rice, pasta, cereals, etc.)	*four servings a day*
Fresh fruit and vegetables (this would also include salads)	*four servings a day*
Dairy products (milk, cheese, yoghurt, etc.)	*one serving a day*

Also, you should eat as little additional fat as possible in terms of spreads and dressings (there is enough already within the food groups outlined above).

The aim of a good diet is to be low in saturated fats, salt, sugar and refined foods, and to be high in complex carbohydrates, unprocessed foods and fibre. Eating lots of raw fruit and vegetables immediately increases your intake of vitamins and fibre. When you do cook, steam rather than boil, grill rather than fry, and use sunflower or olive oil rather than animal fats to cook. Use yoghurt rather than cream, or look for 'half-fat' varieties, or semi-skimmed milk products.

Obviously a little of what you fancy does you good, occasionally. There's no point being fussy about the foods you eat to the point of obsession, as long as the general principles outlined above apply to the foods you eat. There is also no doubt that the eating habits we develop in childhood last a lifetime, so changing yours to more healthy ones now could be beneficial for your children.

While you are pregnant you do not need to eat for two, neither do you need to restrict your intake in order to keep your weight gain to a minimum. You don't need to eat for two because your body, while you are pregnant, makes better use of the foods you do eat. If you continue to eat sensibly, you won't increase your weight so dramatically that you can't lose it again, and if you breastfeed you will probably lose it again very quickly.

Following the guidelines above will give you the good daily intake of the balance of protein, carbohydrate, fats, minerals, vitamins and fibre that you need. Breastfeeding mothers need to increase their intake of dairy products by an additional serving.

See also **Fibre**, **Iron**, **Minerals**, **Pre-conceptual Care**, **Vitamins**

Domino Scheme

This stands, literally, for 'Domiciliary in and out' where the community midwife cares for the mother antenatally, in conjunction with her GP practice, but delivers the baby at the local maternity unit. It means that you can call the community midwife to your home at the onset of labour, where you remain until the baby is due to be born, then you transfer to the hospital for the actual delivery. Your baby will be delivered by your community midwife, although there is full obstetric back-up on hand if needed. If the birth is uncomplicated, you can return home between 2 and 6 hours later, or the next morning if you deliver at night.

See also **Birth Plan**, **Labour**

Down's Syndrome

This is a chromosomal abnormality with which some babies are born. Babies with Down's Syndrome have a variety of symptoms that include a degree of mental disability and slow physical development. There may also be a degree of congenital heart disease and other physical ailments. Each baby born with Down's Syndrome will be individual in his or her range of symptoms, some of which are immediately apparent and others which need more careful diagnosis.

For many babies born with Down's Syndrome, their life expectancy is good and they have happy and fulfilled lives. This will partly depend on their individual symptoms and what specialized care their families or support services can give them. While there is understandable grief at the birth of a baby with Down's Syndrome because there are many of life's opportunities that won't be available to them and there are often difficult decisions about their care to be made, many parents come to see the disabilities of their baby with Down's Syndrome as just as much a part of them as the colour of their eyes.

However, because there are known risk factors for Down's Syndrome, and antenatal tests for these, it is possible for parents to make a decision about whether or not to continue a pregnancy that will result in the birth of a baby with Down's Syndrome.

Your Age	Your Risk of Having a Baby with Down's Syndrome
25	1 in 1,500
30	1 in 800
35	1 in 300
38	1 in 180
40	1 in 100
45	1 in 30

Also, *see Useful Addresses* for information on the Down's Syndrome Association.

Compare **Amniocentesis, Antenatal Testing, Bart's Test, Triple Test**

Due Date

When your pregnancy is confirmed, you will be given your Due Date, or Estimated Date of Delivery (EDD). This is calculated as being 40 weeks or 280 days from the first day of your last menstrual period (although you will have conceived your baby on or around day 14, if you have a 28-day cycle), which is the average length of a pregnancy. If your menstrual cycle is normally any shorter or longer than 28 days, of if you think you know precisely when your baby was conceived, you can adjust your dates accordingly.

Your due date is only really useful if you deliver early or late, as it provides a guide for the medical care you and your baby may require. Any delivery between 38 and 42 weeks is considered full-term, so the due date is really only a guide and very few babies – between 4 and 5 per cent – are born on their specific due date. But you will endlessly be asked, 'When are you due?', so you may as well have a date to give everyone.

When is your baby due?

Use this chart to work out your expected date of delivery. Pick out the date of the first day of your last period from the figures in light type. The date your baby is due is immediately underneath in bold.

In each row the top figures (light type) are the first day of your last period; the bold figures immediately underneath are the date your baby is due.

Period month	Due month(s)	1	2	3	4	5	6	7	8	9	10	11	12	13	14	15	16	17	18	19	20	21	22	23	24	25	26	27	28	29	30	31
JAN	OCT / NOV	8	9	10	11	12	13	14	15	16	17	18	19	20	21	22	23	24	25	26	27	28	29	30	31	1	2	3	4	5	6	7
FEB	NOV / DEC	8	9	10	11	12	13	14	15	16	17	18	19	20	21	22	23	24	25	26	27	28	29	30	1	2	3	4	5			
MAR	DEC / JAN	6	7	8	9	10	11	12	13	14	15	16	17	18	19	20	21	22	23	24	25	26	27	28	29	30	31	1	2	3	4	5
APR	JAN / FEB	6	7	8	9	10	11	12	13	14	15	16	17	18	19	20	21	22	23	24	25	26	27	28	29	30	31	1	2	3	4	
MAY	FEB / MAR	5	6	7	8	9	10	11	12	13	14	15	16	17	18	19	20	21	22	23	24	25	26	27	28	1	2	3	4	5	6	7
JUNE	MAR / APR	8	9	10	11	12	13	14	15	16	17	18	19	20	21	22	23	24	25	26	27	28	29	30	31	1	2	3	4	5	6	
JULY	APR / MAY	7	8	9	10	11	12	13	14	15	16	17	18	19	20	21	22	23	24	25	26	27	28	29	30	1	2	3	4	5	6	7
AUG	MAY / JUNE	8	9	10	11	12	13	14	15	16	17	18	19	20	21	22	23	24	25	26	27	28	29	30	31	1	2	3	4	5	6	7
SEPT	JUNE / JULY	8	9	10	11	12	13	14	15	16	17	18	19	20	21	22	23	24	25	26	27	28	29	30	1	2	3	4	5	6	7	
OCT	JULY / AUG	8	9	10	11	12	13	14	15	16	17	18	19	20	21	22	23	24	25	26	27	28	29	30	31	1	2	3	4	5	6	7
NOV	AUG / SEPT	8	9	10	11	12	13	14	15	16	17	18	19	20	21	22	23	24	25	26	27	28	29	30	31	1	2	3	4	5	6	
DEC	SEPT / OCT	7	8	9	10	11	12	13	14	15	16	17	18	19	20	21	22	23	24	25	26	27	28	29	30	1	2	3	4	5	6	7

When are you due?

E e

Eclampsia

With good antenatal care, eclampsia is generally avoided. If high blood-pressure and other symptoms are diagnosed, treatment is given to prevent it. Very occasionally pre-eclampsia is so rapid in onset that eclampsia develops and can result in convulsions and coma. If eclampsia does develop, immediate medical treatment is required and the baby is usually delivered as soon as possible by caesarean section. Once the baby is born, the mother usually makes a good recovery.

Compare **Pre-eclampsia**

Ectopic Pregnancy

This is a pregnancy that occurs either in the Fallopian tube or, more rarely, in the abdominal cavity. Sometimes called a tubal pregnancy, it occurs in about 1 in 150 pregnancies. If the pregnancy continues within the Fallopian tube, the tube can rupture, causing an internal haemorrhage, which may be life-threatening to the mother.

First symptoms of an ectopic pregnancy are a missed period, mild pain low down in the abdomen coupled with occasional sharp, stabbing pains and possibly feelings of sickness or dizziness. There is a slightly increased incidence of ectopic pregnancy if you use a coil for contraception, in which case you might not even immediately suspect a pregnancy. The pain of an ectopic pregnancy can also be confused with that of appendicitis, urinary infection, or an ovarian cyst. Diagnosis may not occur until the pain is extreme, and should include a pregnancy test and probably an ultrasound scan.

Treatment involves surgery to remove the pregnancy, and to try and save the Fallopian tube. This may mean an emergency operation if diagnosis has been late.

See also **Ultrasound**

EDD

This stands for Estimated Date of Delivery: *see* **Due Date**

Effleurage

This describes a light, stroking massage technique. It may usefully be applied to the lower abdomen during labour. It is designed to be done in rhythm with the mother's breathing, to aid relaxation and help focus her attention during a contraction. While some women find it immensely helpful, others find any sort of touch distracting, especially when they are nearing transition. Effleurage should be used only if the mother wishes it. Even if it seemed like a good feature of natural childbirth prior to labour, it may not actually be applicable at the time.

See also **Massage**, **Transition**

Embryo

This is the term given for the developing baby for the first 8 weeks after conception (10 weeks of pregnancy), after which the developing baby is usually referred to medically as a fetus.

See also **Conception**, **Fetal Development**

Emotions

Not much attention is usually given to the emotions of pregnancy, birth, and thereafter, except as an adjunct to some of the practical aspects or as an area of concern or distress. Sometimes referred to as 'emotional lability' or 'mood changes', or dismissed as being part of 'hormonal changes', our emotions are usually side-lined as a negative, sometimes problematic, part of the whole procedure. Focus is more readily applied to the effort required to keep our emotions in check and under control.

Attempting to ignore this part of the becoming-a-parent process, however, denies women the opportunity to participate fully in all the changes going on. Throughout pregnancy this transformation needs to be absorbed and integrated into a continuing life with another, as yet unborn, person. Difficult feelings, often explained away as 'loss of body image', or 'overwhelming responsibility', or 'resentment of loss of freedom', not to mention the ubiquitous effect of hormones, etc., need to be expressed if they are to be managed. It might even be argued that it would be inappropriate *not* to be affected emotionally, to the same extent as physically, when having a baby.

For many women, where there is no recognition of how they are feeling internally these emotions and 'mood changes' can be threatening and frightening. Each woman responds individually to her pregnancy, and her experience is rooted in her personal circumstances, her view of herself as a woman and mother, her perceived role in society, her relationship with her baby's father, her relationship with her own mother and maternal role models, etc. A major readjustment to her self-view is required. Is it any wonder, then, that the process is almost just as emotionally demanding as it is physically?

Unfortunately this process can be seen as negative by spouses, partners, family, friends and employers – hence the history of women's emotional unreliability – which is a misinterpretation of what is going on. Rather than relaxing into the emotional changes, efforts are made to suppress them or redirect their energy into practical issues and physical concerns. Women are somehow made to feel that it is unacceptable to say, 'I'm pregnant and I feel different...' when in reality they *are* different, even while remaining the same person they always were.

For many women pregnancy is empowering. These women instinctively seek out kindred spirits, resources and information. There has been quite a move in more recent years to promote this, through the natural childbirth movement and also through the use of alternative and complementary therapies. The message that emerges is that pregnancy is an emotional time – and women should be helped to accept and enjoy this aspect of becoming a mother.

Compare **Anxiety, Crying, Depression, Thick Skin**

Endometrium

This is the inner lining of the womb which, during pregnancy, thickens and increases in its blood supply to nourish the implanted embryo. It is influenced by the hormone progesterone, produced initially in the ovary after the release of the egg. If an egg is fertilized and successfully implants, progesterone continues to be produced by the ovary to sustain the endometrium until the placenta is developed enough to take over this supply, at around 12 weeks.

If no pregnancy occurs after ovulation, or doesn't successfully implant, the endometrium breaks down and is shed as part of the menstrual bleed, or period. If pregnancy does occur and continue, the endometrium becomes known, medically, as the decidua.

Enemas

Enemas are a small amount of warmed gel inserted via the rectum, designed to produce a bowel movement. They used to be given routinely at the start of labour, in order to ensure an empty rectum. Nowadays they are not thought necessary. Very often the bowel empties naturally at the onset of labour, although the length of labour and pushing in the second stage may mean that some faecal matter is passed.

Although the idea of an enema is distasteful to a lot of women, in labour or otherwise, there are occasions when it might be useful. Sometimes a full rectum can actually impede the progress of dilatation of the cervix, so an enema – and emptying the bowel – might help. If you are advised, during pregnancy or labour, that an enema might be helpful, ask why. If the reasons seem justified to you, then you can decide whether or not to have it.

Engagement

Your midwife will be particularly interested in whether or not your baby's head has 'engaged' towards the end of pregnancy. This is because it is an important sign that the pelvis is going to be large enough to accommodate a vaginal delivery. In a first-time mother the baby's head usually engages sometime between the 36th and 38th week of pregnancy. In subsequent pregnancies, the head may not engage until actual delivery. And with a breech presentation it is difficult to tell whether or not the pelvis will be adequate to deliver the head, which is why a caesarean section is sometimes advised for a breech baby.

If this is your first baby, and the head hasn't engaged at around 38 weeks, you may be referred to an obstetrician who will check that there is no cephalopelvic disproportion – that your baby's head can safely pass through your pelvis – as it is better to know this before you go into labour.

Engagement is defined by how far the baby's head has passed through the 'brim' of the pelvis, the brim being at the level of the pubic bone. You may see the level of your baby's head engagement expressed on your antenatal chart as, for example, '4/5 brim'. You may even see, on consecutive visits, the progress of engagement from '2/5 brim' to '5/5 brim' or 'fully engaged'.

See also **Breech Presentation, Cephalopelvic Disproportion, Labour**

Engorgement

A very common but short-term problem at the beginning of breastfeeding is engorgement of the breasts. This occurs as milk production is stimulated by the baby suckling on the colostrum, at around day three or four. One of the immediate problems for a breastfeeding mother is that the breasts are enormous, hot and uncomfortable, and breastfeeding itself becomes a painful, rather unrewarding experience.

The first thing to remember is that this stage will pass within a few days *if you continue to breastfeed unrestrictedly*. Your midwife, who should be trained, competent and experienced at helping mothers begin breastfeeding, should be able to help you. Otherwise find a breastfeeding counsellor via your local National Childbirth Trust group or La Leche League (*see Useful Addresses*). Don't be tempted to bottle-feed just because of engorgement, or to give supplementary bottles to ease your symptoms, as the best way to ease engorgement is to let your baby feed as often and for as long as possible.

One of the immediate problems with a swollen breast is that it becomes difficult for the baby to latch on (*see Figure 7, page 175*), and instead of breastfeeding attempts to nipple-feed, which can make the nipple sore. If you are very engorged and it is difficult for the baby to latch on, try expressing a little milk before the feed to soften the surrounding breast tissue. This can be helped by applying soft cloths, wrung out in hot water, beforehand. In between feeds, apply the same soft cloths wrung out in very cold water to ease the congestion and discomfort. Make sure your nursing bra is well-fitting and provides the right support without digging in anywhere.

Continuing to feed your baby unrestrictedly will help any engorgement to subside in a day or two. It will also help to avoid any problems that could possibly result from the initial engorgement. Try alternating the position in which your baby feeds, always checking that the whole of the nipple and enough of the surrounding areola is taken into your baby's mouth.

Alternative remedies for breast engorgement include placing a cabbage leaf inside your bra. The suggestion is to use very dark green cabbage leaves, as it is thought that it is the chlorophyll that is the active ingredient. Wipe the leaves clean and store them in the fridge until needed. Place one inside each bra cup and replace when wet.

Reflexology has a good effect on breast engorgement, but you will need to see a trained reflexologist. He or she may, however, be able to suggest a reflexology area which you can massage yourself prior to breastfeeding in order to alleviate symptoms.

Two homoeopathic remedies that are recommended for engorgement are *Belladonna* and *Bryonia*, which you can self-prescribe. If you are taking *Arnica* following your baby's delivery you will have to stop taking it while taking one of these other remedies.

The engorgement that occurs when your milk comes in is referred to as 'primary' engorgement. It is possible to become engorged again, although not as dramatically as the first time, perhaps if you have missed or delayed a feed for some reason. For example, your baby may have started sleeping for longer periods at night. Just follow the suggestions above and it will soon subside.

Compare **Breastfeeding, Breasts, Expressing Milk, Latching On, Mastitis**

See also **Homoeopathy, Reflexology**

Entonox

More commonly known as 'gas and air', this is a form of pain relief available during labour and birth. It is a mixture of oxygen and nitrous oxide inhaled via a rubber mask held by the woman herself. The pain-relieving effect begins after about 20 seconds of inhalation, and reaches its peak effect after about 45–60 seconds of use. So if inhalation starts at the beginning of a contraction, it can help reduce the sensation of pain. As the body doesn't store entonox it can be used for relatively long periods; the baby receives very little via the placenta as it is excreted via the mother's lungs.

Some women find entonox enormously effective and all the pain relief that is needed, while others require something stronger. Some women find using the face mask very claustrophobic, and they dislike the smell of the rubber of the mask, although a mouthpiece might be available. Some actively dislike the analgesic effect as it makes them feel somehow out of control. So it is very much a matter of individual choice and just one of the pain relief options available.

See also **Pain, Pain Relief**

Epidural

This is a very effective form of pain relief, where a local anaesthetic is inserted into the epidural space between two lumbar (spinal) vertebrae. The effect is to reduce the sensation of pain by anaesthetizing the spinal nerves radiating from that area, while the mother remains fully conscious.

This procedure can only be performed by a qualified anaesthetist, and one who is fully trained in epidural procedure. This sometimes explains why there is occasionally a delay in providing an epidural for pain relief, because it is dependent on the availability of an anaesthetist.

The initial needle of entry is replaced by a thin plastic tube, through which the anaesthetic is inserted. This remains in place to allow for 'topping up', when further anaesthetic is given as and when it is needed.

An epidural can very often be requested for pain relief by the mother as part of her birth plan. Otherwise there are specific occasions when it is recommended. These include:

- *long labour, especially where there is back presentation;*
- *breech delivery, because it reduces the urge to push when the cervix has not yet dilated fully;*
- *high forceps delivery where the baby needs to be turned;*
- *pre-eclampsia;*
- *caesarean section, as an alternative to a general anaesthetic if it is an elective caesarean;*

- *throughout labour if the mother's blood-pressure is raised significantly.*

If you have an epidural you will have an intravenous drip, and possibly a urinary catheter, and you and your baby will be attached to a monitor to check your progress. In the second stage, when you need to know when a contraction is coming in order to push, monitoring is essential. In addition, your blood-pressure will be closely monitored as epidural anaesthesia does have a lowering effect on this.

In some hospitals the opportunity for a 'mobile epidural' or 'ambulant epidural' exists. This is, as it sounds, pain relief without the loss of mobility. However, it isn't always possible to get exactly the right level of anaesthetic effect – pain relief combined with the ability to walk around – although it is worth a try, if it is available to you.

Recovery from the epidural is rapid: the effect on your ability to walk should have worn off in around six hours. The anaesthetist's aim is to provide exactly the right level of local anaesthetic for only as long as you need it. Because of the close supervision required when an epidural anaesthetic is given, the level and dosage is designed to tail off towards the end of the second stage.

See also **Breech Presentation, Forceps, Monitoring, Occipito-Anterior Position, Pain, Pain Relief, Pethidine**

Episiotomy

Sometimes, in order to help deliver the baby's head or to avoid an awkward tear, the midwife makes a cut in the mother's stretched perineum (the area of skin between the vagina and anus). After delivery an episiotomy needs to be stitched, as would a tear; a small injection of local anaesthetic is given prior to this.

Episiotomies aren't routine in most places, and this may be something you want to discuss with your midwife. She may recommend one, or may feel that you can manage without, or that a small tear is better. Of course, your perineum may stretch so adequately that none of this is necessary!

See also **Perineum**

Equipment for a Hospital Stay

A basic kit for going into hospital, for you and your baby, is worth thinking about several weeks before your due date. Having a small bag packed ready is also a good idea.

The following checklist may be helpful:

For you:

- *2–3 nightdresses. While you may want to include a new or specially pretty one for those first precious photo sessions, you may find that comfortable old ones fare better. Front-opening ones make it easier to breastfeed.*
- *dressing gown and slippers. Although hospital wards are notoriously warm, you will still need something as a cover-up for moving around.*
- *super-absorbent sanitary pads. Stick-on ones are probably easiest, so remember some extra pairs of pants. You may want to include some paper pants, too.*
- *your usual toiletries and make-up.*
- *lip salve. Your lips can become very dry from breathing and panting in labour.*
- *water spray, either an aerosol or a plant spray filled with fresh water*
- *Bach Rescue Remedy to take during labour when the going gets tough*
- Arnica *tablets (strength x30), to take after delivery*

- Lavender *essential oil: add a few drops to your bath, as this is calming and mildly antiseptic*
- *bath and face towels: many hospitals no longer supply these, so check first.*
- *nursing bra and breast pads*
- *coins and/or phone card*
- *reading and writing materials*

For your baby:
- *vest, stretchsuit (babygro), hat, oversuit or cardigan (for going home in). It's a good idea to wash new baby clothes through, in a non-biological washing powder, before use.*
- *first-size nappies: don't buy a huge amount of these, though, because if your baby is large they won't fit him or her for long.*

Essential Oils

See **Aromatherapy**.

Exercise

Regular exercise is important for all of us, and if you have kept fit in some way prior to becoming pregnant you can probably continue quite safely and happily to do so. You may need to make some sensible concessions, for example swopping a high-impact, aerobic exercise class for a gentle stretch and relaxation one or one designed specifically for pregnant mothers. But walking, swimming and other forms of gentle exercise are positively beneficial to both you and your baby. If you participate in any more active sports or activities, it will depend on your individual pregnancy whether or not you can continue. Check with your midwife or obstetrician.

In a sense, pregnancy is a time of physical preparation for an event as demanding as running a marathon, which you certainly wouldn't attempt without some quite serious training. Lots of health authorities run antenatal groups that include appropriate exercise classes; your midwife should be able to advise you about these. And don't forget those very important pelvic floor exercises: start getting into the habit while you are pregnant.

Postnatally you should be given a list of progressive tummy and other exercises devised by an obstetric physiotherapist. You will need to exercise carefully at first because your ligaments will still be 'soft' from the effects of the pregnancy hormones, an effect that lasts between three and four months. Exercise will strengthen your muscles, thus protecting your joints and ligaments from strain. Take care when lifting and check your posture, especially when breastfeeding or carrying your new baby, to avoid additional strain. Your midwife will be able to advise you, so do ask her.

If you have had a caesarean delivery, you should be given quite specific postnatal exercises by an obstetric physiotherapist. Ask to see him or her while you are in hospital recovering, and work out the exercise programme that suits you best.

See also **Breathing Exercises**, **Pelvic Floor Exercises**, **Posture**

Expressing Milk

It may be helpful to express a little milk at the beginning of a feed if you are engorged; there may also be times, as your baby gets older, when you may want to express a full feed to leave for him if you want to go out for a time. Once your supply of milk is established this is perfectly possible, though it does take practice.

Whether you use a breast pump or express milk by hand, you will need to make sure your hands are washed, then dried with a clean towel, and that any utensils you use to collect and store the milk are sterilized. Choose a time when you are relaxed and in no hurry. Various tips that women have found useful are:

- *try first thing in the morning, when your supply might have built up a bit overnight;*
- *breastfeed your baby first, as the sucking will stimulate the let-down reflex and make it easier to express;*
- *feed one side only, then express from the other, again benefiting from your baby stimulating your let-down reflex;*
- *apply warm cloths to your breast and gently stroke with the flat of your hand towards the nipple, not forgetting the underside of the breast;*
- *if you want to express milk, say during the middle of the day when you are away from your baby (perhaps at work), choose a time that corresponds to a feed-time. You will probably feel the tingling sensation of your let-down reflex and experience some leaking, and expressing the milk will be easier.*

Don't be surprised if you find expressing milk a little difficult and awkward to begin with. Like everything else about motherhood, it takes practice! Ask your midwife or health visitor for advice. You may have a National Childbirth Trust or La Leche League breastfeeding counsellor living locally, too (*see Useful Addresses*).

Breastmilk can safely be stored in the fridge for 24 hours or up to three months in the deep freeze. Don't use a microwave to defrost breastmilk, and it isn't advisable to re-heat milk in this way either.

See also **Breastfeeding, Engorgement**

External Cephalic Version

This is a procedure that should only be attempted by an obstetrically trained doctor, as it is an attempt to turn a baby head-down for delivery. If your baby is still in a breech position after 32 weeks, external cephalic version may be suggested; although trying to turn a baby before 37 weeks is usually a waste of time, as the baby is likely to turn back again.

See also **Breech Presentation**

F f

Face Presentation

Rather than the top of the baby's head presenting first at delivery, the neck is extended and the baby's face, chin forward, presents first. This makes delivery more awkward, and may account for some delay in the second stage. It is also much more demanding on the baby, who may be born with a degree of bruising and swelling to the face and head. This will quickly subside and leaves no lasting damage.

As this is a more difficult birth for a baby, especially as the neck has been flexed backwards, it might be beneficial to take your baby to see a cranial osteopath.

Compare **Breech Presentation**, **Brow Presentation**, **Occipito-Anterior Position**

See also **Cranial Osteopathy**

Fainting

During the first three months of pregnancy the hormone progesterone makes the blood vessels dilate; this has the effect of lowering blood-pressure. This may make you feel faint, especially if you have to stand for any length of time. After the first three months a pregnant woman's volume of blood increases and faintness becomes less of a problem. Although this can be an irritating problem, it is seldom anything to worry about, and your baby isn't at any risk.

You can take various steps to try to avoid feeling faint. These include:

- *keep your fluid intake up. Drinking a full glass of water will have an almost immediate effect on blood volume;*
- *always get up gently, as standing up suddenly may make your blood-pressure drop dramatically;*
- *sit down if you feel faint, and put your head between your knees – try to avoid actually passing out;*
- *eat small amounts regularly, especially if you have any morning sickness. Low blood sugar will aggravate the feelings of faintness;*
- *mention this to your midwife. She may want to check that you aren't anaemic.*

Towards the end of pregnancy the weight of the abdomen pressing on the main blood vessels may also make you feel faint, especially if you lie on your back. You may be one of around 10 per cent of women who are particularly affected by this during pregnancy. Lying on your side brings about a rapid recovery.

Fallopian Tubes

Within the woman's reproductive system are two tubes which extend from the top of the womb to the ovaries. They are not actually attached to the ovaries but are designed to 'catch' the egg when it is released and transport it down to the womb. If the egg is fertilized on its way, it will continue on its journey and implant in the lining of the womb.

Occasionally a fertilized egg will implant before it reaches the womb, actually within the Fallopian tube. This results in a tubal, or ectopic, pregnancy.

Sometimes, following an infection within a woman's reproductive organs or within the pelvic cavity, the Fallopian tubes may become blocked. This is one cause of infertility in women.

Sterilization, a form of permanent birth control, involves the tying of the Fallopian tubes, so that no egg can pass through and run the risk of fertilization.

See also **Conception, Ectopic Pregnancy**

False Labour

You may find it difficult towards the end of your pregnancy actually to tell whether or not your labour has started (especially if it's your first time). Braxton Hicks contractions feel stronger towards the end of pregnancy because your abdomen is so much larger, but their pattern may change to such an extent that you may feel labour has actually started. However, instead of becoming stronger and more frequent, they fade again. This may happen on and off for some weeks before true labour actually begins, and it may be that your womb is contracting in order to manoeuvre your baby's head down into the pelvis.

False labour seems to be more common with first babies, perhaps because we feel more apprehensive and less sure of what is about to happen. Talk to your midwife and check with her whether your symptoms are indicative of true or false labour. She will be able to reassure and advise you.

See also **Braxton Hicks Contractions, Contractions, Labour**

Family

Families come in all shapes and sizes, and are organic in nature. Your family might consist of yourself and your child, in which case you may be referred to as a 'one-parent family'. But in a year's time you may have created a different family by living with someone and his or her children, and perhaps having a child together. Whenever someone refers to 'my family' they will mean something specific to them, and quite unlike anyone else's family although there may be elements in common.

A lot of focus is given to the nuclear family as being the only possible ideal: a man and woman, married to each other, have children together and continue to stay married to each other. Three out of four families start out like this, and out of those, two out of three will continue to stay married. But this is just one type of family, no more nor less legitimate than any other type.

The term 'single mother' has been largely replaced by the term 'single parent', which is just as well as no one I know has ever had more than one mother at a time! Single parent also applies equally to those families with only a father. And children born to unmarried parents are more accurately defined as 'non-marital'; they are legitimate by their very presence and legitimate in law.

An extended family – grandparents, aunts, cousins, etc. – is only as good as the relationships that exist within it. At its best, an extended family is wonderful at supporting and appreciating you, at its worst it isn't even your last port of call.

Finally there are those family members who are chosen, because of their involvement and commitment to your family unit. Whether this takes the formal form of godparents, or is just because someone is a loved and trusted friend, they become part of your family. For your children this may well include any permanent care-giver, a nanny, childminder or *au pair*.

See also **Fathers**

Fatigue

See **Tiredness**

Fathers

Fathers are extremely important to children, for two main reasons: for conception, and to love them unconditionally. This may not necessarily be the role played by the same man if, for example, a baby is adopted or born to a couple through the use of artificial insemination by donor, or if the biological father quits the scene for some reason. Not all children have positive experiences of their fathers; an absent father can dramatically affect a child's self-esteem, for example.

Just as becoming a mother is emotionally demanding, so is becoming a father. The progress of pregnancy and the necessary primary maternal preoccupation with the growing fetus offers women the opportunity to prepare emotionally for this major life-change, while the father can feel left out. Many couples find that the birth of their first child creates changes to their own relationship for which they were unprepared.

While there are few real guarantees in this life, it should be possible for two adults who have once been close enough to conceive a baby, to find some way to support that baby throughout its childhood. It shouldn't be a question of choice for either parent, the existence of their child demands it. A child has the right to the love and commitment of both parents, whether or not they continue to live together, and government and the society at large must change its expectations of 'family' accordingly. If fathers and mothers work together, the changes necessary to make parenting a happier and more constructive process for everyone concerned will be easier to cope with.

See also **Bonding, Family, Paternity Leave**

Fear

Fear is an emotion that can immobilize the strongest among us. Fear of the unknown is particularly potent, and for many women fear of childbirth is very much fear of the unknown. Dr Grantley Dick-Read recognized this in the 1930s, and so pioneered the change in maternity care that recommends that women are fully informed about the process of pregnancy, labour and childbirth, in order to alleviate their fear. He found that a mother's fear during labour actually served to delay the process, so he recommended breathing and relaxation exercises that could be learned beforehand, for use during labour.

Acute symptoms of fear include shallow breathing, palpitations, feeling sick in the stomach and feeling faint. Sometimes just dealing with the symptoms by using deep breathing and relaxation exercises alleviates these feelings. Various complementary treatments from Bach flower remedies to aromatherapy to reflexology can help nurture a feeling of strength that makes dealing with fear more possible. Some homoeopathic remedies are particularly useful for fear. But to prevent recurrences, dealing with the root cause of the fear is essential; this may mean finding a counsellor, or someone to help you structure and deal with your fearful thoughts. Talk to your midwife, or contact the British Association for Counselling (*see Useful Addresses*).

Compare **Anxiety, Crying, Depression, Emotions**
See also **Aromatherapy, Bach Flower Remedies, Counselling, Homoeopathy, Reflexology**

Fertility

This describes the ability to produce a baby. Female fertility depends on the monthly production of a healthy egg and the proper functioning of female hormones that assist in the fertilization of this egg by a sperm, the smooth transit of this fertilized egg to the womb, the safe implantation of the embryo in the lining of the womb and the continuation of the pregnancy to term. Male fertility depends on the production of healthy and mobile sperm.

The reverse of fertility, infertility, is the result of a malfunction of any part of the fertilization or implantation process, which can occur either in the female or in the male partner, or anything that impedes a continued pregnancy. Infertility is termed as 'primary' if pregnancy has never occurred, or 'secondary' where there has been a previous, successful pregnancy.

Fertility is dependent on a host of different factors individual to either a woman or her partner. Most couples are able to take their fertility for granted, as most couples having regular sexual intercourse without using contraception will conceive within a year of trying. For one couple in eight, however, there is a problem. And for most of these couples it is a problem with a solution, although expert help is often required.

See also **Conception**

Fertilization

This is the first stage of pregnancy, when an egg and sperm successfully unite. This usually occurs within the Fallopian tube and the fertilized egg then travels to the womb where it implants. Sometimes the fertilized egg won't implant and, even before a woman notices that she might be pregnant, she has an apparently normal period.

However, once a fertilized egg has implanted, various signs and symptoms including a missed period, will indicate to a woman that she is pregnant.

See also **Conception**, **Fertility**

Fetal Development

The growing baby is referred to as a fetus from the eighth week after conception (10 weeks after the beginning of the last menstrual period), before which it is referred to medically as an embryo. The development of a fertilized egg into a baby capable of life over a 40-week period is phenomenal – especially during the first three months, when the development of all the organs and systems of the body occurs, albeit in a rudimentary form.

1 to 4 Weeks:
- *rapid cell division and growth*
- *heart develops and begins to beat*
- *formation of limb buds*
- *early development of central nervous system*

4 to 8 Weeks:
- *all major organs appear in primitive form*
- *facial features begin to develop*
- *formation of genitals, but not yet possible to tell the gender of the baby*
- *early movements begin*
- *embryo/fetus visible on ultrasound*

8 to 12 Weeks:
- *fetal circulation is now functioning*
- *fetus moves freely, but not yet felt by mother*
- *eyelids fuse*
- *fetus is able to swallow surrounding fluid*

- *sex of the baby is apparent*
- *kidneys begin to function and, from 10 weeks, urine is passed*

12 to 16 Weeks:
- *fine, downy hair (known as lanugo) appears on the baby's body*
- *meconium – the black substance within the baby's gut – is present*
- *rapid development of the skeleton, which would now be visible on X-ray*
- *the nasal septum and roof of the mouth fuse*

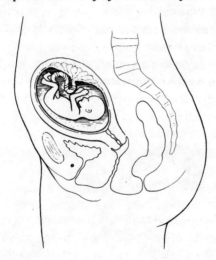

16 to 20 Weeks:
- *fetal heart can be heard by listening to the mother's abdomen*
- *mother feels the movement of her baby – 'quickening'*
- *protective layer of white, creamy covering to the baby's skin – vernix caseosa – appears*
- *skin cells can now renew themselves*
- *fingernails appear*

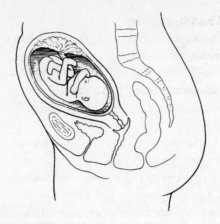

20 to 23 Weeks:
- *the baby experiences periods of activity and rest*
- *responds to sound*
- *most body systems are now fully functional*
- *baby's skin is red and wrinkled*

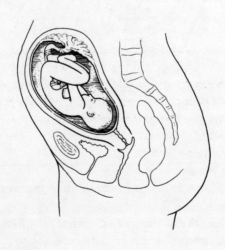

24 to 27 Weeks:

- *the eyelids re-open*
- *breathing movements begin*
- *with specialized care, the baby would probably survive if born now (the fetus is said to be 'viable')*

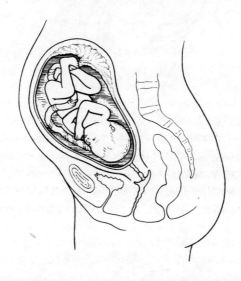

28 to 32 Weeks:

- *the covering of body hair disappears from the face*
- *skin becomes less red and more smooth*
- *stores of body fat and iron are laid down*
- *in a boy, the testes descend*

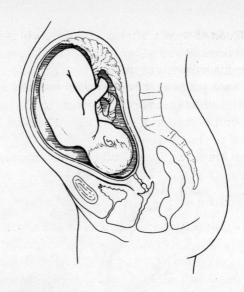

32 to 36 Weeks:

- *body hair disappears*
- *body becomes more rounded as fat stores increase*

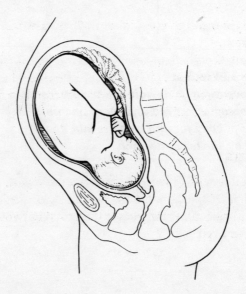

Between 36 and 40 weeks after conception, which is the same as between 38 and 42 weeks after the beginning of the last period, the baby is due. A baby isn't considered to be 'late' unless the pregnancy has gone beyond 42 weeks from the beginning of the last period, and isn't considered premature unless it is born earlier than 37 weeks from the beginning of the last period.

See also **Amniotic Fluid, Embryo, Meconium, Vernix**

Fetal Sac

The fetal sac is sometimes known as the amniotic sac, or you may hear it referred to as the membranes. It is contained by the womb, where the baby grows and develops over the 40 weeks within the cushioning effect of the amniotic fluid.

Either before or during labour, the waters break; this is the membranes rupturing and is part of the process of labour. Occasionally the membranes are deliberately ruptured, in order to start labour off or to enhance contractions.

During the third stage of labour, when the placenta is delivered, the midwife also checks the expelled membranes to ensure that no part has been left within the womb, where it could cause a problem.

Fetus

Term used for the growing baby from the eighth week after conception (10 weeks after the beginning of the last menstrual period). Prior to this the growing baby is referred to as an embryo.

Fibre

This is the indigestible part of the food we eat, which creates bulk. This in turn makes the bowels function better and makes passing faeces easier. Adequate fibre is always important in a healthy diet, but particularly important when you are pregnant because the effect of the pregnancy hormone progesterone on the bowel makes it more sluggish and less efficient. Adequate, or even extra bulk, in the form of fibre makes the bowels' action more effective. This can be extremely helpful in avoiding or dealing with constipation in pregnancy.

The cellulose part of all vegetables and fruit is indigestible, so providing a high level of dietary fibre. Make sure you have at least four servings of fresh fruit and vegetables every day.

See also **Constipation**, **Diet**

First Stage of Labour

See **Labour**

Fluid Retention

See **Oedema**

Folic Acid

One of the most important recent discoveries relevant to pregnant women is that a diet low in folic acid increases the risk of neural tube defects in babies. Neural tube defects include Spina Bifida, anencephaly and other disorders of the spine. Consequently, all women considering pregnancy are advised to take a 0.4 mg folic acid supplement, available over the counter – ask your pharmacist. If there has been any previous, or family history, of neural tube defects a woman's doctor may advise a higher dose. This supplement should be taken for at least a month before getting pregnant and throughout the first 12 weeks of pregnancy.

Folic acid is one of the B group of vitamins. Good dietary sources include dark green, leafy vegetables, wholemeal bread, fortified breakfast cereals, whole milk, mushrooms, sprouted grains, yeast extract and nuts. In the UK the Department of Health provides a booklet listing folate-rich foods. This booklet should be available from your midwife or doctor; otherwise, contact the Department of Health direct (*see Useful Addresses*).

See also **Diet, Minerals, Vitamins**

Food Safety

Most of the food hygiene precautions that you take routinely are all that's required when you are pregnant, with a few additional recommendations: *see* **Listeria, Salmonella, Toxoplasmosis**.

See also **Diet**

Forceps

Primarily, there are two uses for forceps when assisting a delivery. High forceps, or Keilland's forceps, are used to turn a baby's head if the presenting part is too wide to descend through the birth canal. These are sometimes referred to as rotational forceps as they are needed to rotate the baby's head.

There are a number of different styles of forceps used for non-rotational delivery, where the head is low down in the vagina but the mother needs some assistance with its delivery. Perhaps after a long labour the mother is too tired to push hard enough to finish the delivery without help.

A delivery that is assisted by forceps needs to be fully explained at the time. An appropriate analgesia will be offered, which may mean an epidural if a Keilland's forceps delivery is required.

A forceps delivery may be recommended for a number of reasons, including:

- *fetal distress*
- *exhaustion and distress in the mother*
- *second stage delay*
- *badly positioned baby, who needs turning.*

However, forceps can only be used to assist delivery if the cervix is fully dilated, the membranes have ruptured, the baby's head is engaged and there is no evidence that the pelvic cavity is too small to deliver the head. The doctor making a decision about the use of forceps should fully advise a mother about why he or she is recommending it, because the reasons will vary according to each individual case.

Compare **Deep Transverse Arrest**, **Epidural**, **Vacuum Extraction**

See also **Delivery**

Foremilk

The foremilk is, as it sounds, the breastmilk the baby receives at the beginning of his or her feed. It comes primarily from a reservoir, the lactiferous sinus, immediately behind the nipple so that there is a supply readily available for a hungry baby at the beginning of the feed. It is ample in quantity but less calorific than the hindmilk that follows.

In order for your baby to benefit fully from both types of milk provided by your breasts, he or she needs to feed for a reasonable length of time. In the early days of breastfeeding, unrestricted feeding will ensure that your baby quickly regains his or her birth weight and sets up a good supply-and-demand system that will meet all his or her nutritional needs.

See also **Breastfeeding**

Fundus

The fundus is the top of the uterus, the part furthest away from the cervix. During antenatal care your midwife will measure the fundal height, from the pubic bone to the top of your pregnant abdomen. This, in relation to the number of weeks of pregnancy, gives a very good indication of the healthy growth of the baby.

Gg

Gas and Air

See Entonox

Genital Herpes

This is caused by an infection of the herpes simplex virus type 2. For those mothers who have recurrent bouts of the virus, their babies probably acquire some level of maternal antibodies in the womb. The main risk to a baby is during birth, but only if the infection is active at the time, in which case delivery by caesarean section is advised.

If a woman is familiar with the symptoms that herald a forthcoming attack of genital herpes, and what it is that might reactivate it, there are steps that can be taken to try and avoid it, thus making a vaginal birth possible. The transmission rate of the virus under these conditions is low, and if for any reason infection of the newborn baby is suspected or diagnosed immediately after birth, antiviral therapy for the newborn is possible.

If you do have genital herpes, your midwife and doctor

will need to know and it should be included in your medical history. Do all you can to try and avoid triggering an attack, especially as you near your due date. However difficult, try to avoid stress and fatigue. Make sure you get enough nutritious food, rest and relaxation in order to boost your immune system. Treat any minor ailments to avoid their impact escalating. Nurture yourself with aromatherapy massage, reflexology to boost your system, or acupuncture. If you do have an outbreak during your pregnancy, do all you can to speed its healing. While complementary therapies cannot cure herpes, they can help the healing process and keep you strong, thus averting an attack.

For more information, contact the Herpes Association (*see Useful Addresses*).

See also **Acupuncture**, **Aromatherapy**, **Homoeopathy**, **Reflexology**

German Measles

See **Rubella**

Ginger

This is a particularly useful substance during pregnancy as it has many applications. Fresh ginger root, cut into thin slices and infused in boiling water, makes a very refreshing tea. This is extremely useful during early pregnancy if there is any nausea or vomiting. It is also useful for heartburn, constipation, and exhaustion during labour.

In addition to ginger root, powdered ginger can also be used in cooking, or it can be taken in capsule or crystallized form. Many women find it extremely good for relieving their symptoms, so it is worth a try. If you don't like the taste of ginger, use the capsules.

See also **Morning Sickness**

Gingivitis

You may be more prone to gingivitis (inflammation and infection of the gums) during pregnancy because the increase in the hormone oestrogen makes the gums spongy and more susceptible to these problems. Brush and floss your teeth regularly – at least twice a day – and visit your dentist and oral hygienist at the first sign of trouble.

See also **Gums, Bleeding**

Glucose Tolerance Test

The aim of this test is to assess how someone responds to an increasing glucose (sugar) intake. From this it is possible to assess whether the body is coping normally with this increase, or not – and from this information, whether the person has diabetes or not.

You may be asked to take a GTT if there is a history of diabetes in your family. The first step is to take a blood sample after you have been fasting for a number of hours: this gives a baseline. Then a measured amount of glucose is given in a drink (this will be warm and tastes pretty horrible). Further blood tests are then taken to measure the amount of glucose in your blood, over a period of time. These results can be compared against the normal range. Initially the level of glucose in your blood will rise, but if all is well it should return to normal with a given amount of time; under normal circumstances the secretion of insulin will transport the glucose in the blood to the cells for metabolism.

Gums, Bleeding

The increase in oestrogen during pregnancy has an effect on the gums, making them spongy, more likely to bleed and susceptible to gingivitis. This can give rise to dental problems, and explains the old wives' tale that 'you lose a tooth for every pregnancy'. This is no longer necessary as, in the UK, dental treatment provided by the National Health Service is free to every pregnant woman and for a year after the birth.

It does pay to take extra care of your teeth and particularly of your gums during pregnancy. See an oral hygienist, whose individual and specific advice is well worth it.

See also **Gingivitis**

Guthrie Test

This is a heel-prick blood test for phenylketonuria carried out on a baby between 6 and 14 days after birth. The baby needs to be well-established on milk feeds before it is worth carrying out a Guthrie test.

See also **Phenylketonuria**

Hh

Haemoglobin

Haemoglobin is the pigment in red blood cells that allows them to transport oxygen around the body. Oxygenated haemoglobin is bright red in colour. Anaemia is a reduction in the blood's capacity to transport oxygen.

During pregnancy you will hear reference made to your haemoglobin levels (Hb levels as recorded medically on your notes). The level of haemoglobin appears to decrease during pregnancy because the quantity of blood increases and the concentration of haemoglobin falls. So although under normal circumstances a haemoglobin level of 10.5 g/dl would signify anaemia, many doctors would ignore this level in a pregnant woman, unless it fell further.

Even if anaemia is diagnosed, its cause won't be apparent. It is most likely to be an iron-deficient or folic acid-deficient anaemia, so giving a woman a course of combined iron and folic acid tablets usually resolves the problem. These used to be given routinely, but this is now thought unnecessary and even counterproductive. Make sure that your diet contains adequate foods rich in iron; if you are vegetarian you may need special nutritional advice. Contact the British Dietetic Association (*see Useful Addresses*) or speak to your midwife or doctor.

See also **Anaemia**, **Diet**, **Iron**

Haemorrhage

Haemorrhage describes any loss of blood, but for the pregnant or newly delivered mother it is usually defined as either antepartum (before the birth) or postpartum (after the birth). Haemorrhage associated with childbirth is now no longer the problem it once was, given the good antenatal and postnatal care most mothers in Westernized countries receive.

Any bleeding in pregnancy needs to be reported immediately, especially after 24 weeks, as it may be an indication of placenta praevia, which may need monitoring, or the more serious abruptio placenta. Signs of haemorrhage include not only evidence of bleeding, but also physical symptoms of shock: weak pulse, pale complexion and clammy skin.

Postpartum haemorrhage, which is now extremely rare in Westernized countries, usually occurs because the third stage of labour – the delivery of the placenta – has not been concluded satisfactorily. One of the reasons why this problem is now so rare is that the third stage of labour is assisted by administration of the drug Syntometrine, which reduces the risk of postpartum haemorrhage.

See also **Placenta Praevia**, **Syntometrine**

Haemorrhoids

These are, effectively, varicose veins that occur around the anus and are caused by the effect of the pregnancy hormone progesterone on the smooth muscle tissue of the veins.

Circulation is less efficient and varicosities can occur. They are also known as piles, and you may first notice them because there is some blood present after you've opened your bowels.

Haemorrhoids can range from being extremely painful to mildly itchy. Try to avoid becoming constipated, or straining to pass faeces, by making sure that you have adequate fibre in your diet – or try eating prunes, which work as a natural laxative.

As well as avoiding straining, keep the anus clean, washing carefully after each bowel movement. Try either a hot or cold compress (whichever works best for you) to ease the discomfort. Avoid standing for long periods, and practise pelvic floor exercises, which will help increase circulation and ease congestion.

See also **Fibre**, **Pelvic Floor Exercises**

There are a number of complementary approaches that are extremely effective in the treatment of haemorrhoids. This is particularly important postnatally, as the pain of haemorrhoids may make a mother sit awkwardly and get into a poor position for breastfeeding:

ACUPUNCTURE
There is a specific acupuncture point in the calf which can ease the pain and swelling in a very short time. *See* **Acupuncture**

HOMOEOPATHY
There is a range of remedies, including *Pulsatilla*, *Arsenicum*, *Nux vomica* and *Sepia*, that can help; as with any homoeopathic prescribing, seek the advice of a trained homoeopath. The homoeopathic cream Aesculus/Hamamelis can be bought and applied to the anus to relieve the itching and discomfort. *See* **Homoeopathy**

REFLEXOLOGY

Haemorrhoids can be treated by reflexology. With the help of a trained practitioner you can learn to massage the appropriate part of your foot to alleviate acute symptoms. *See* **Reflexology**

SHIATSU

A number of pressure points are indicated for help in treating haemorrhoids, and if you have seen a practitioner he or she will be able to recommend self-treatment in acute episodes. *See* **Shiatsu**

Hair

Most women find that their hair grows faster and appears more luxurious during pregnancy. However, after the birth you may find your hair falling out in alarming quantities. This is quite common, and takes several months to settle down. Hair loss around the hairline is a feature, but this too will grow back.

Eating and resting properly after the birth, especially if you are breastfeeding, will help your hair loss to diminish. Use a mild shampoo, wash your hair regularly and massage your scalp thoroughly to stimulate your scalp. A haircut can improve the look of your hair, making the ends appear thicker.

If you are seeing an acupuncturist, aromatherapist or reflexologist for any other reason, mention any concern about hair loss, as there may be something he or she can advise to help. One homoeopathic remedy sometimes recommended is *Natrum muriaticum*. Alternatively, a trichologist, someone who specializes in scalp and hair care, might be worth consulting.

Hamamelis

Also known as witch hazel, *Hamamelis* is useful for bruises where the skin is broken. It can also be applied as a cold compress for both piles and varicose veins.

Hamamelis obtained from a homoeopathic pharmacy is much more effective than that sold through an ordinary chemist, although this will help if it is all you can find to use. Some homoeopathic pharmacies provide a mail-order service (*see Useful Addresses*).

HCG/Human Chorionic Gonadotrophin Levels

Once the fertilized egg has embedded in the wall of the womb, a layer of cells, called the chorion, forms around it from which finger-like projections, called the chorionic villi, branch out. It is the chorion that produces the human chorionic gonadotrophin hormone. This tells the ovary to continue producing progesterone to suppress the possibility of a period and prevent the lining of the womb being shed.

It is the HCG hormone that pregnancy tests are sensitive to. And its high levels for the first 12 weeks of pregnancy, until the placenta takes over the ovaries' hormonal function, are thought to be a prime contributor to morning sickness.

See also **Morning Sickness**

Headaches

Headaches occur for a variety of reasons whether or not you are pregnant. If you get recurrent headaches, run through the following checklist to see if it is possible to identify a cause:

- *eyesight, which may deteriorate during pregnancy. Have your eyes checked or your prescription checked if you already wear glasses.*
- *posture, which will change as your pregnancy evolves – are you inadvertently overcompensating, causing musculo-skeletal strain?*
- *eating regular meals: during pregnancy your metabolism changes and you may have to adjust your eating patterns accordingly. If you are suffering from early pregnancy nausea and vomiting, don't let this make you more susceptible to headaches. Also, avoid caffeine (in tea, coffee, chocolate, cola, etc.).*
- *rest and relaxation: are you getting enough gentle exercise and adequate sleep?*

Headaches are actually quite common during early pregnancy, because the hormone progesterone affects the cerebral blood vessels, causing them to dilate. Taking paracetamol (within the limits of its dosage) is thought to be safe, but you may wish to try some alternative approach to ease or prevent your headaches. Make sure your fluid intake is adequate; you may have cut down to keep yourself from having to pee so often. Or you may have cut out tea and coffee without replacing these drinks with others. Try camomile tea, which aids relaxation, and other herbal teas, plus fruit juices and water.

Osteopathy, in particular cranial osteopathy during pregnancy, can be very effective. Reflexology, acupuncture and massage are all extremely useful in treating headaches. Applying pressure to the shiatsu points at the top of the eye sockets is also effective. *Magnesia phosphorica* is considered to be 'homoeopathic aspirin', and should form part of your homoeopathic first aid kit. Firm scalp massage, perhaps using *Lavender* oil, might help relax muscular tension.

Headaches are always worth mentioning to your midwife or doctor, because there are some occasions during pregnancy when, coupled with other physical symptoms, headaches serve as an advance warning of, for example, high blood-pressure, which will need monitoring.

If you have a history of migraine, talk to your doctor about this as you may not be able to take your usual migraine treatment during your pregnancy. Many women find that their migraines diminish or disappear while they are pregnant. One homoeopathic remedy which is helpful for migraine is *Natrum muriaticum*.

See also **Acupuncture, Aromatherapy, Cranial Osteopathy, Diet, Homoeopathy, Massage, Reflexology, Shiatsu**

Healing

Healing after childbirth takes time, and will depend partly on the type of childbirth you experienced: the major abdominal surgery of a caesarean section takes longer to recover from because your muscles and skin tissues have to regenerate.

With a combination of rest, gentle exercise and good nutrition, your recovery should be rapid. How you are feeling emotionally also plays a part. There are also a number of simple steps you can take to aid your healing process. These include:

- *Homoeopathic remedies* – Arnica *in particular, and also* Bellis perennis *for aches and pains caused by the bruising. Homoeopathic remedies are also good for helping emotional healing, especially if the birth was very painful and you have been left with feelings of resentment. A qualified homoeopath will be able to prescribe most accurately for any postnatal condition.*

- *Aromatherapy – massage with oil of* Clary sage *postnatally helps reduce abdominal pain and sacral backache.* Clary sage *can be used alone or combined with the very beautiful smelling oil of* Rose, *which is also recommended for its use postnatally.* Lavender *oil massaged over the sacral area is also helpful.*
- *Osteopathy – especially cranial osteopathy – is particularly helpful postnatally because it rebalances the body after the impact of pregnancy and childbirth, and helps relieve any musculo-skeletal pain caused by pregnancy and the birth. Long-term pressure on the sacral area during the process of childbirth can create frontal headaches which can be effectively treated by cranial osteopathy.*
- *Acupuncture – particularly good for relieving pain and discomfort postnatally and helping to rebalance the body's energy.*
- *Reflexology – again, this is useful for both general and specific recovery postnatally, as is Shiatsu.*

See also **Acupuncture**, **Aromatherapy**, **Cranial Osteopathy**, **Diet**, **Homoeopathy**, **Reflexology**, **Relaxation**, **Shiatsu**

Health Visitors

In the UK, Health Visitors are trained nurses with additional training in social and preventative medicine. They provide care, information and advice for mothers, babies and children under five. For the first 10 days after birth your care is the responsibility of your midwife, either the hospital midwife or, when you return home, the community midwife. You are entitled to a daily visit, and should be able to contact her whenever you need help or advice.

After 10 days this role is usually transferred to the health visitor, who will probably only visit you once in your home, unless you need more support, after which you will probably see her, or one of her team, at your local baby clinic. It will be your health visitor who explains about your baby's feeding needs, when to consider weaning onto solids, the immunization programme you are entitled to, hearing tests and developmental checks. Many mothers, especially first-time mothers, get to know their health visitors really well, perhaps visiting the baby clinic once a week to have their baby weighed and to be reassured that all is well. Health visitors are an invaluable resource, providing information, support, advice and reassurance to mothers.

Heartburn

Because the hormone progesterone relaxes smooth muscle, it affects the muscles at the opening at the top of the stomach. This can allow reflux of some of the stomach contents up into the oesophagus and, because of the acidic nature of the stomach's contents, causes the burning sensation typical of heartburn. This is most problematic towards the end of pregnancy, because the growing baby pushes upwards, compressing the space between the oesophagus and the stomach.

If you suffer from heartburn, try taking smaller meals. Sleeping in a more upright position might help, as might lying in a semi-reclining position on your right side. Persistent heartburn can be helped by taking antacids, but check with your doctor because he or she will be able to prescribe something that is safe for you to take. You should avoid those containing aluminium, as this can cross the placenta and be absorbed by the baby.

Tea, coffee and other drinks containing caffeine should be avoided, as should fatty foods. Although milk and milk products are traditionally recommended for heartburn, they have limited use for this purpose, although they won't aggravate the discomfort. Try camomile or ginger tea, both of which have calming properties. Increasing your intake of garlic (up to a clove a day – preferably raw) – is the recommendation of herbalists. Herbalists also recommend slippery elm, available from wholefood shops as lozenges or in powdered form.

There is a specific reflexology point for heartburn: four fingers' breadth above the navel, on the midline. Press intermittently with two fingers for 10 seconds at a time, over a 5-minute period, to alleviate acute symptoms.

Osteopathy has proved very effective at relieving heartburn, but you will need to find a qualified practitioner. Various homoeopathic remedies that may be recommended include *Arsenicum album*, *Calcarea carbonica*, *Magnesia carbonica*, *Magnesia phosphorica* and *Natrum phosphoricum*. Consult a qualified homoeopath for further advice.

See also **Herbal Remedies, Homoeopathy, Osteopathy**

Herbal Remedies

The premise on which herbal medicine is based is that it seeks to enhance health rather than 'cure' disease. The approach is holistic, in that any herbal prescription focuses on the needs of the individual rather than on his or her specific complaint. Herbalists also use the whole plant, rather than isolating a key chemical, thus providing a lower concentrate and more dilute solution which lessens the possibility of any side-effects. For this reason, properly prescribed herbal medicines are very safe and often better tolerated than their more conventional counterparts.

That said, any potent plant has to be treated with respect. In the UK, properly trained medical herbalists will have completed four years' study, with over 500 hours of clinical attendance. A qualified and accredited member of

the National Institute of Medical Herbalists will have
either the initials MNIH or FNIH after his or her name.

We are already familiar in the use of herbs in our
cooking, to enhance or improve the flavour of foods, and
there are other foodstuffs that we recognize as having
health benefits, such as garlic. Using herbs medicinally
takes this known beneficial effect and applies it
more specifically.

There are numerous ailments in pregnancy (such as
morning sickness, heartburn, engorgement, threatened
miscarriage, urinary infections, moodiness, poor milk
supply and exhaustion) which can be helped by judicious
use of specific herbs, whether as infusions, decoctions,
added to other foods, or added to baths or bidets. If you
intend to use herbal medicines, however, you should seek
the advice of a qualified herbalist (*see Useful Addresses*)

HIV

The Human Immuno-deficiency Virus is the virus that
causes Acquired Immune Deficiency Syndrome, or AIDS.
Mothers who are HIV-positive may pass the virus on to
their unborn child. It is thought that the risk factor of this
happening is around 1 in 6, and a few babies have become
infected through breastfeeding. Mothers who know they are
HIV positive shouldn't donate milk to milk banks, although
all human breastmilk available from milk banks is heat-
treated to ensure no risk of infection.

Since 1985, all donated blood in the UK is heat-treated
to avoid the risk of passing on the virus via contaminated
blood.

Pregnant mothers are not automatically tested for HIV
in the UK, although in some areas it will be offered. A
pregnant woman who finds that she tests positively for HIV
may be offered a termination.

Care of a pregnant woman who is HIV positive is no different than for any other. HIV is only spread via the blood and secretions of an infected person and, as universal precautions apply in the UK, the standard procedures and safety measures are the same for everyone. Only during actual labour, where there is an increased amount of body secretions and blood, are extra precautions observed by medical staff.

All babies born to mothers who are HIV positive are born with HIV antibodies. It can take up to 18 months for the child to lose these antibodies, so it won't be possible to say whether or not he or she is infected until after this time.

Additional information can be obtained from AVERT (the National AIDS Helpline) and Positively Women (*see Useful Addresses*).

Home Birth

Having your baby at home is one of the options available for women in the UK. Every year about 1 per cent choose to give birth at home. The majority of mothers only choose a home delivery if they feel confident that this is the right choice – medically and/or socially – for them. The choice can be made only if full information about the possible complications is available. This is something to discuss with your midwife.

Having your baby at home is your legal right, and you don't need either your doctor's permission or to have him or her present at the delivery. It is perfectly possible to have a midwife-only delivery. It is also enshrined in the Midwife's Code of Practice (UKCC 1989) that a community midwife must 'continue the care of the mother' under just about all circumstances, and this includes a mother insisting on staying at home, perhaps against the advice of the midwife's clinical judgement.

There are two main objections that might be raised should you express a wish to have your baby at home: one is the possibility of postpartum haemorrhage in the mother, the other the risk of breathing difficulties in the baby. Both complications need expert care, and fast. Having said this, both are uncommon, and midwives are trained and equipped to deal with both at home.

Conditions for which a hospital birth is recommended:

- *placenta praevia, because the only safe delivery will be an elective caesarean section, usually at 38 weeks;*
- *known cephalopelvic disproportion, where the pelvic outlet is too small to allow the baby's head to be born;*
- *high blood-pressure caused by the pregnancy; pre-eclampsia;*
- *a pre-existing disease, such as cardiac disease, kidney disease, diabetes mellitus, and sexually transmitted disease.*

There are also a number of other considerations that may need to be taken into account, for example:

- *mother's past obstetric history;*
- *mother's age (under 18 or over 35), although in fact evidence shows that many mothers over 35 deliver safely at home;*
- *mother's height (under 1.5 metres), as this might indicate that her pelvis will not accommodate the baby's head;*
- *first birth – your physical reaction to giving birth is something of an unknown quantity at this stage, although this consideration is slightly spurious because every woman and every birth is different;*
- *multiple pregnancy, as each baby will probably be smaller and more vulnerable than singletons, and sometimes born pre-term;*

- *breech presentation; although vaginal delivery is possible, there is always some concern about the delivery of the head after the body.*

However, if it is possible to have your baby at home, there really is no better place to be. Statistics prove that home birth is in many ways safer than a hospital birth, and that mothers recuperate better and feel happier with the experience after a home birth than after delivering in hospital. On a personal note, my second son was born at home even though I was over 35 and had had a very difficult first birth, with a delay in the second stage that had required a Keilland's forceps delivery with an epidural anaesthetic. I did not select a home birth the second time because I thought there was anything remiss about my hospital delivery; quite the contrary, I just felt more confident and more comfortable with the idea of having my baby at home.

If you want to consider a home birth, ask for information about its possibility at your first 'booking-in' visit. Even if you opt for a home birth, a hospital bed will be booked for you, just in case. There are a number of individual considerations about having a baby at home, for example, where you actually live, availability of a flying squad, etc. A useful resource is the Society to Support Home Confinements (*see Useful Addresses*) and, if you feel you are not getting the support you would like in the area where you live and you have the necessary financial resources, you might like to consider an independent midwife (*see Useful Addresses*).

Compare **Hospitals**
See also **Independent Midwives**

Homoeopathy

Homoeopathy is based on the principle that 'like cures like', that a small dose of whatever causes the symptoms of an illness will activate the body's own corrective and healing potential. Orthodox medicine tends to rely on using opposites to cure disease – the example often quoted is giving laxatives, which cause diarrhoea, to cure constipation. Homoeopathy takes a very holistic approach: if you are going to stimulate the body's ability to cure itself, you also have to take the emotional aspect of the individual into account.

With homoeopathy, the more diluted a remedy, the more effective its action. This is the opposite of how we view most medicine, where more is usually considered better. The potency of a remedy is measured as x6, x12, x24 and x30, which is the number of times it was diluted. So a remedy diluted 30 times will be more potent than a remedy diluted six times.

Another application for homoeopathy is to enhance health, rather than treating illness. Constitutional remedies are used to strengthen an individual's ability to deal with distress or illness, and therefore to reduce his or her susceptibility to disease. Preparing for pregnancy might occasion a first visit to a homoeopath.

Homoeopathy is both an art and a science, and remedies work gently and effectively, without side-effects, for a wide variety of illness and complaints, including emotional ones. This makes them ideal during pregnancy, birth and, afterwards, for babies, too. It is perfectly possible to learn to self-prescribe or to prescribe for your baby, but you need a good resource. One homoeopath who comes highly recommended, especially for mothers and babies, is Miranda Castro (*see Further Reading*). She combines her homoeopathic expertise with her own experience as a woman and mother, and her work is accurate, thoughtful and easy to understand.

Finding your own homoeopath, and establishing a relationship with him or her, is also advantageous when you need help in prescribing. The Society of Homoeopaths in the UK keeps a register of qualified homoeopaths (*see Useful Addresses*).

Many midwives and health visitors do the three- to four-year course to qualify as homoeopaths, thus adding to the range of care they can provide to mothers and children. In the UK names of family doctors who are also trained homoeopaths can be obtained from the Family Health Services Association (*see Useful Addresses*).

Homoeopathic remedies come in a variety of forms: tablets, powders, granules, pills and drops. They need to be stored away from substances that could destroy their beneficial effects: coffee, peppermint, eucalyptus and any other strong, pungent materials, including essential oils. It goes without saying that you should not drink coffee (or suck on peppermints!) while taking a remedy. Remedies should be physically handled as little as possible: tip tablets into the container lid; shake granules onto a clean spoon – try not to touch the remedies at all.

If you would like to obtain a particular remedy, there are a number of excellent mail-order companies (*see Useful Addresses*).

Hormones

Hormones are the body's chemical messengers. They are excreted by an endocrine gland in one part of the body, to have an effect in another area. For example, the hormone progesterone is secreted by the ovary in order to prepare the womb's lining for the possible implantation of a fertilized egg. And oxytocin, secreted by the pituitary gland in the brain, causes the muscles of the womb to contract during labour.

The hormones of a woman's sexual cycle all interplay. For example, following childbirth the level of oestrogen in a woman's body falls, which in turn stimulates the production of prolactin, by the pituitary gland, telling the breasts to start producing milk.

Hormones can also be produced synthetically and used to emulate or enhance normal hormonal activity. The action of the contraceptive pill is hormonal. While the Pill is taken, the body believes it is pregnant, so ovulation doesn't occur. Labour can be induced by giving prostaglandin pessaries, or a Syntocinon drip, both of which are synthetic hormones.

See also **Oxytocin**, **Progesterone**, **Prolactin**

Hospitals

The majority of women in the UK have their babies in hospital, whether they have a 6-hour discharge or leave after two days. The advantage of hospitals is that both medical equipment and expertise are on hand should you or your baby need it. And, if you want to have an epidural for pain relief, you can only do this in hospital.

Because of the excellence of antenatal care in Britain, more women could probably deliver at home, although there is always an unknown quantity about any delivery. However, the majority tend to choose hospitals because they feel happier about it. Certainly most doctors, whose medical business is largely with the difficult and abnormal, view hospitals as the place to deliver because of all the medical equipment to hand. There is, however, no evidence to suggest that this makes a hospital any safer than home. Many midwives, however, would like to see more emphasis on home birth with better 'flying squad' provision. There is a view that hospitals tend to medicalize birth, and endorse greater interventions. Also, the changeover of staff and high numbers of personnel in hospitals tend to make the process less personal.

Facilities vary at different hospitals, and in some areas there isn't much in the way of patient 'choice', but it's certainly worth investigating all the options for maternity care provided in your area.

Compare **Domino Scheme, Home Birth**

Hospital Stay

See **Equipment for a Hospital Stay**

Hydrotherapy

Hydrotherapy is the use of water for therapeutic purposes. It is well known that soaking in a warm bath is relaxing, especially with the addition of appropriate essential oils, and swimming as an exercise is particularly good for easing backache. Using water when pregnant, in both the ways outlined above, is advantageous. In addition, doing antenatal exercises in water is an extremely effective way of supported exercise – the water bears some of the weight.

'Aquanatal' classes exist in some areas of the UK, run by midwives. Exercising in this way will help maintain muscle function and improve circulation. In addition, practising relaxation techniques and controlled breathing while floating is useful antenatally and postnatally. Your midwife will probably know of any exercise classes specially for pregnant women in your area.

Ideally the pool in which aquanatal classes can take place should meet the following criteria:

- *both a midwife and someone with an Amateur Swimming Association lifesaving qualification should be in attendance;*
- *the pool should be exclusively reserved for this use at this time;*
- *the pool should be graduated, with a shallow and a deep end, so that non-swimmers can participate;*
- *the temperature should be between 29°C and 30°C to relax muscles and reduce tension. Any hotter and mothers can feel dizzy; any cooler and mothers could experience muscle cramps.*

Another benefit of using water antenatally, either for aquanatal classes or just for swimming, is that a mother-to-be can see whether or not she likes the sensation of being in water when heavily pregnant. If she doesn't enjoy this, then the option of a water birth can be ruled out.

See also **Water Birth**

Hypnotherapy

Many women have utilized the benefits of hypnosis in relieving pain during labour and childbirth. They are able to create a level of consciousness, somewhere between sleep and wakefulness, that means they are fully conscious but unable to feel pain. They have also found it extremely beneficial in removing anxieties about the impending birth.

Not everyone finds that hypnosis works for them and, if you intend to make use of it during labour and delivery, you will need several sessions with a medically trained hypnotherapist during pregnancy. You will probably also need your hypnotherapist with you during labour and delivery, although some self-hypnosis techniques can be learned.

However well hypnosis works for you under ordinary conditions, you may need to consider the impact of labour and delivery. Under these circumstances it may not be as effective, so it would be wise to consider alternatives should they be necessary, as you would with any form of pain relief.

To find a properly trained medical hypnotherapist in your area, you might need to contact the British Hypnotherapy Association (*see Useful Addresses*). Your relationship with your hypnotherapist needs to be a close and trusting one. You wouldn't expect to find this with everyone you meet, so if you do not feel really comfortable with your hypnotherapist, try another one. Hypnotherapy won't work for you unless you feel relaxed and confident about it.

See also **Pain Relief**

Ii

Immune System

The body's immune system consists of two forms of defence against infection: the *lymphocytes* or white blood cells (found in the lymph system as well as the bloodstream), and *antibodies* circulating in the blood which are produced by certain types of lymphocytes. Antibodies are produced in response to specific infections, giving protection against re-infection by the same virus or bacteria. This is what we understand by immunity.

Immunity can be either passive – conferred to a newborn baby via his or her mother's blood supply or through antibodies present in breastmilk – or acquired. Acquired immunity can occur because of past infection, or through immunization.

Pregnancy suppresses a woman's immune system, otherwise the fetus might be rejected by her body as a 'foreign body'. This can make pregnant women more prone to infections, which has implications for her own health as well as for her developing baby. So it is especially important to try and promote positive health while pregnant through a combination of good, nutritious food, rest, relaxation and gentle exercise. For those who don't exercise regularly, yoga is a good choice when pregnant, particularly in a class specially designed for expectant mums.

Complementary therapies are particularly useful – for reducing morning sickness, for example. Any hands-on therapy has the additional benefit of enhancing a feeling of well-being. Homoeopathy can play a role in correcting any physical and emotional imbalances created by pregnancy; reflexology, shiatsu and acupuncture can stimulate energy levels as well as alleviating specific complaints which could be sapping your energy and causing you mild distress; cranial osteopathy has a similar role to play. Labour and birth are physically demanding, as will be the next 18 years of motherhood!

See also **Acupuncture, Allergies, Cranial Osteopathy, Diet, Homoeopathy, Immunization, Passive Immunity, Reflexology, Relaxation, Shiatsu, Yoga**

Immunization

By giving someone an injection of either dead or weakened virus or bacteria, the body recognizes it as 'foreign' and produces antibodies. Should that person come into contact with the virus or bacteria at some later date, the already present antibodies are activated to prevent an infection. Numerous distressing and debilitating illness are avoided in most Westernized countries now because of a long-standing immunization campaign.

The current immunization programme for children in the UK is offered as follows:

At 2 months: Diphtheria/Tetanus/Whooping Cough (triple vaccination); Polio (drops); Hib (protects against *Haemophilus influenzae* type B [bacterial meningitis], but not against meningococcal, pneumococcal or viral meningitis)

At 3 months: As above.

At 4 months: As above.

At 12 to 18 months: Measles, Mumps, Rubella (MMR)

At 3 to 5 years: Diphtheria/Tetanus booster; Polio booster; MMR (unless previously received)

The immunization programme used to begin when a baby was between 4 and 6 months old but, because of numerous whooping cough outbreaks, this was brought forward. A baby is born without any passive immunity from his or her mother for whooping cough, because the mother's immunity doesn't cross the placenta. So small babies were particularly vulnerable not only to infection, but also to the full impact of this illness and its debilitating and long-term effects. While some controversy remains about the safety of this vaccine, it is still safer than risking the disease.

While the majority of mothers choose to have their child immunized, the few who don't should remain protected. If the level of those immunized drops below a certain level, the risk to the population at large increases.

Babies and children can be immunized even if they have a cold – unless there is a high fever – and while taking most medicines, including antibiotics. However, when you take your baby for immunization the nurse or doctor will always check the baby and ask you about his or her general health at the moment. They will be able to advise you. Should your baby have a mild reaction to any of the vaccinations (such as irritability or a slight fever), give an appropriate dose of infant paracetamol and extra breastfeeds or drinks. It should only be a 24-hour reaction.

Talk through any concerns you may have with your health visitor or doctor, so you feel happy and informed about any choice you make. The organization Informed Parent (*see Useful Addresses*) can provide advice and support.

See also **German Measles, Rubella**

Implantation

If an ovum (egg) is fertilized successfully, then implantation will occur roughly seven days later. For some women, implantation creates bleeding which, depending on the usual length of a woman's menstrual cycle, can be confused with a period. This can sometimes give rise to confusion later about her due date, although this can be verified with an ultrasound scan.

Very early miscarriage, when the fertilized ovum fails to implant, is thought to be caused in part by a deficiency of the mineral zinc in the mother.

See also **Embryo**, **Fertility**, **Fertilization**, **Fetal Development**

Incontinence

This means a temporary or permanent loss of control over the bladder or bowels. Women are sometimes prone to urinary stress incontinence following childbirth, and experience some leakage if they run, sneeze or laugh. The pressure on the pelvic floor of pregnancy and birth can weaken the muscles there. Thankfully, in almost all cases, this can be rectified by doing pelvic floor exercises.

See also **Pelvic Floor Exercises**

Independent Midwives

Independent midwives are fully qualified midwives who have chosen to work outside the National Health Service, although continuing to support its aims and ideals. This is a private facility and the midwife is paid for by the parents. For this you get one midwife who cares for you during pregnancy, birth and afterwards, although they often work in teams to ensure availability.

This service provides excellent continuity of care, with its emphasis very much on working *with* the mother to ensure the best possible experience of birth. A large proportion of independent midwives take bookings for home births, and the rest are for booked hospital births. Independent midwives work with other healthcare practitioners if and when necessary.

In the UK, an Independent Midwives Association was set up in July 1985 (*see Useful Addresses*). They hold a register of midwives, which is updated every six months, and provide a central resource for enquiries from parents, midwives and other interested people.

See also **Midwives**

Indigestion

See **Heartburn**

Induction

This is generally taken to mean the initiation of labour by artificial means, although this entry will include a number of recommendations for alternative approaches.

Artificial induction should only ever be carried out for medical or obstetric reasons, if the health of the mother or her baby would be adversely affected if the pregnancy continued.

Most inductions occur because pregnancy has continued to 42 weeks. After this length of time, the rate at which the placenta begins to deteriorate speeds up. Close monitoring will indicate whether or not the birth should be induced. In mothers over 35, placental insufficiency is more common after 40 weeks, so it might well be recommended that the birth is induced.

Other reasons for induction include:

- *high blood-pressure – where there is concern that this might escalate;*
- *unstable lie – labour might be induced after turning the baby to a head-down (cephalic) position;*
- *spontaneous rupture of membranes – if the waters have broken after 36 weeks of pregnancy, but labour hasn't commenced after a further 24 hours;*
- *genital herpes – some mothers are induced at 38 weeks if the disease is in remission, in order to avoid a caesarean section if spontaneous labour causes a flare-up of active disease;*
- *previous large baby – if a previous baby's birthweight was over 4 kg (8 lb), as subsequent pregnancies tend to produce bigger babies. Birth may be induced at 38 weeks, to try and prevent a difficult labour and delivery.*

Pregnancies are managed differently by different people, and some obstetric consultants have more rigid 'rules' than others. It is always worth discussing fully the basis on which suggestions are proposed and decisions made. In any event, you need to be fully aware of any treatment and how it will affect you.

Artificial induction occurs in one of three ways:

1 *use of prostaglandin – pessaries which may ripen the cervix enough to start labour off. Prostaglandin can also be used within the cervical canal, actually inserted around the outside of the amniotic membranes, or orally.*
2 *artificial rupture of the membranes – sudden loss of the amniotic fluid may bring the baby's head into closer contact with the cervix which can, in itself, help stimulate labour.*
3 *an intravenous infusion of the synthetic hormone Syntocinon – used to stimulate contractions.*

There are a number of things you can do to help initiate labour; one is for you and your husband or partner to make love. The stimulation of your nipples may encourage the secretion of the hormone oxytocin, which stimulates contractions (although only one nipple should be stimulated at a time). Prostaglandins in semen help to 'ripen' the cervix, and the internal contractions of an orgasm may start the contractions of labour off. It is certainly worth a try! Others have been known to swear by a hot curry ...

One homoeopathic remedy that is recommended is *Caulophyllum* 30, every two hours for up to six doses in 24 hours. More specific prescribing requires a homoeopathic consultation. If you have been drinking raspberry leaf tea since 28 weeks, increase the amount from either one cup or tablet a day, to four cups or tablets a day. Acupuncture can be effective, as can reflexology, although both require the help of a skilled practitioner. An aromatherapy massage to the lower back, using a blend of *Lavender* and *Mandarin* essential oils, may enhance and co-ordinate contractions. Exercise, for example a brisk walk, could also help get labour started.

Even if you have a particular medical reason to be artificially induced, there may be a number of complementary therapies you can utilize in conjunction with this. And, because the contractions of an artificially induced labour can be quite strong and demanding, any additional, complementary pain relief should be considered as part of your pain relief options.

See also **Acupuncture, Aromatherapy, Homoeopathy, Pain Relief, Raspberry Leaf Tea, Reflexology**

Insomnia

There are many reasons why you may suffer from an inability to sleep even before you are pregnant, but the additional discomfort of an enlarging and cumbersome abdomen certainly won't help. While some women don't have any problem sleeping during pregnancy, for the majority the last few months of pregnancy produce a fair few disturbed nights. You may like to think of it as part of practising for what is to come after the birth!

Just trying to get comfortable in bed with a kicking baby inside your growing abdomen can seem, on some nights, impossible. Make sure your mattress is firm enough – insert a board under your mattress if it isn't. As you get bigger, sleeping on your back may no longer be comfortable and may make you feel faint, because of the pressure of the baby on your main internal blood vessels. Sleeping on one side or the other may be your only option. And if you regularly slept on your stomach prior to pregnancy, you had better start practising sleeping some other way, although, at least until very late in the pregnancy, some women do manage to adopt a position that allows them to almost sleep face-down (one leg bent at the knee and drawn up, most of their weight actually borne by the other side of their body). Additional pillows might be useful in order to prop yourself up a little more, or to slip between your knees when you are lying on your side.

You may also find that physical symptoms such as heartburn need rectifying before sleep is comfortable, or that the need to get up to pee in the night contributes to broken nights. In any event, try to ensure that you take some form of gentle exercise every day. Then find time to relax and wind down before you go to bed, allowing yourself at least two hours during which you perhaps take a warm bath with essential oil of *Camomile* added to the water, and drink a cup of camomile tea. General massage, with or without essential oils, can be beneficial, as can a shiatsu massage, although you will need to find a qualified practitioner to help you with this. Various homoeopathic remedies may also help, so long as the chosen remedy matches your overall physical and emotional profile.

If you find you are waking early and worrying about seemingly intractable problems related to your pregnancy, you may find some counselling helpful (*see Useful Addresses*). Even if the actual cause of your insomnia is emotional rather than physical, the complementary therapies outlined above will still be useful. In many cases, easing any physical discomfort, increasing your ability to sleep and easing your sense of fatigue can make some of the emotional stuff easier to deal with. If you have been heavily overdoing it on all fronts and your sleep has become affected, you may have to give yourself a week of self-nurturing in order to regain the balance you need to ensure restful nights. It will be well worth it, as lack of sleep makes everything else seem worse. This philosophy of self-care will also help you through the early weeks and months of parenthood, with all the emotional and physical demands they will entail.

See also **Aromatherapy, Homoeopathy, Shiatsu, Sleep**

Intercourse

Intercourse is only one aspect of your sexual relationship with your husband or partner. Making love involves a lot of intimate activity which may or may not include intercourse. For most couples, though, making love involves intercourse and, during pregnancy, this may raise questions about safety. Generally speaking there should be no problem about intercourse unless:

- *you have a history of early miscarriage, in which case*
  you may want to avoid penetrative sex until after the
  14th week;
- *if you are bleeding, or spotting, at all;*
- *if you experience any pain, whatever position*
  you attempt;
- *your waters have broken, as there is some risk*
  of infection.

Making love, and intercourse, can be even more pleasurable than usual during pregnancy. During the middle three months, many women find their sexual interest is greatly heightened, so this can be a time of increased sexual activity in a marriage or partnership. Good sex is energizing, and very good exercise for your pelvic floor muscles!

Some women, however, find that pregnancy means a temporary loss of libido. This is quite normal, too, especially in the first few months if you have all-day 'morning sickness' and feel generally grotty. If a loss of libido also indicates some kind of emotional withdrawal from your husband or partner, you may need some psycho-sexual counselling to uncover the root of it. Some men, too, find that they can't cope with their wife or partner's changing shape, or her physical and emotional needs, or with the idea of the responsibility of a baby. This aspect of your relationship needs looking at now, either formally or informally, otherwise problems may escalate after the baby is born.

After the birth, you will probably find that you are asked whether you have ' ... resumed sexual intercourse ... ' at your first postnatal check-up. This is to establish whether or not everything is functioning more or less OK after your delivery. (You will also be asked about contraception.) You can resume your sexual relationship with your husband or partner as soon as you feel like it. If you are concerned about your vaginal discharge post-delivery, this should have cleared completely after between two to three weeks. You may, however, find that it takes quite a long time for your libido to return postnatally, especially if you are breastfeeding. This is perfectly normal, too – and though it may sound a cliché, keeping the lines of communication open with your partner is the best way to ensure that your relationship doesn't suffer permanently.

See also **Lochia**, **Orgasm**

Involution

This describes the process by which the womb returns to its normal size after pregnancy, labour and delivery. The process can take up to two months, but can be helped in a number of ways – most readily by breastfeeding. As your baby suckles, oxytocin is secreted and this helps the womb continue to contract down in size. You will probably be aware of this from the afterpains at the beginning of each breastfeed during the first few weeks. You will probably also experience an increased blood loss in the first few days, as feeding stimulates the womb to contract and expel its contents. Obviously if you are bottle-feeding your baby, involution takes a little longer.

See also **Afterpains**

Iron

Iron supplements used to be given routinely to pregnant women to avoid the problems associated with iron-deficient anaemia. Nowadays iron supplements are usually only given as necessary, as the inappropriate prescribing of iron supplements can inhibit zinc absorption, causing its own problems. Iron is required in order to produce haemoglobin, which is the oxygen-carrying part of the red blood cells. We get most of what we need from our diet, as long as it is complete with the nutrients we need. Iron is found primarily in red meats, and requires an adequate intake of vitamin C in order to be utilized properly by the body.

See also **Anaemia**, **Diet**, **Haemoglobin**, **Minerals**, **Zinc**

Itching

Many women find that, as the skin of their abdomen stretches during pregnancy, it becomes very itchy. The skin may also become dry and flaky. Other women are unfortunate enough to itch all over, especially at the end of pregnancy. Your doctor may suggest a course of anti-histamine tablets if it becomes so bad you can't sleep.

Other things you can do to ease the itchiness include:

- *keep cool – this may be difficult if the weather is very hot, but try;*
- *bathe in tepid (not hot) water;*
- *wash with aqueous cream, or add essential oil of* Camomile *mixed up in some milk (which will create an emulsion and diffuse the oil) to your bath water;*
- *keep your skin, and especially that of your growing abdomen, supple with plenty of non-scented cream or lotion.*

Be reassured that the itching will cease almost as soon as your baby is born, though if it is very severe and persistent, do mention it to your midwife or doctor.

See also **Skin**

J j

Jaundice

Many babies have slight jaundice after birth, and this is considered within the normal range if it occurs after the second or third day. When a baby is in the womb it needs a much higher than normal level of haemoglobin to attract sufficient oxygen across the placenta. After birth this high level is no longer necessary, so the excess is broken down, resulting in a temporary excess of a substance called bilirubin. This is what gives the customary yellow tinge of jaundice, because the baby's liver is not yet mature enough to deal with it.

Usually all sign of jaundice is gone within seven days or so. Breastfeeding unrestrictedly is the single most helpful thing you can do, although because of the jaundice you may have to work harder to persuade your baby, who may be rather sleepy, to feed. Keep at it, and by the time the jaundice has passed, you will have the extra benefit of a well-established milk supply.

Homoeopathy can be helpful, and exposure to daylight, but make sure this is only to gentle, indirect sunlight.

Joints

Because of the effects of the pregnancy hormones progesterone and relaxin on ligaments and smooth muscle in the body, the stability of your joints can be affected. This is beneficial where the joints of the pelvis are concerned because, during delivery, the pelvis is able to increase in size to allow the descent of the baby.

However, these hormones have an effect on all the joints in the body and can make them vulnerable to strain, causing aches and pains. The joints of the back are particularly vulnerable, because of the increased weight of the growing baby, so it is important for women to be aware of their posture during pregnancy in order not to cause additional strain.

Other joints can also be affected, and you will be more susceptible if you were unfit to start with. You don't, however, want to start exercising vigorously at the beginning of pregnancy; regular gentle exercise is best and will be helpful in protecting your joints.

If you do strain any joint, it will eventually recover with rest. Use an ice pack, or packet of frozen peas, to ease any pain or swelling. Back pain or backache might be more difficult to shift, so resort to alternative therapies. Osteopathy would probably be your first port of call, but also try a *Lavender* oil massage to the lower back (only use *Lavender* after the first three months); the homoeopathic remedy *Arnica* may help, as would a course of Alexander technique lessons to help alleviate postural deficiencies.

See also **Alexander Technique**, **Backache**, **Posture**

Kk

Kegel Exercises

See Pelvic Floor Exercises

Ketones

Ketones occasionally show up in the urine of a pregnant woman, but probably mean nothing more serious than that she has missed her lunch. Ketones are the result of the body metabolizing protein, rather than carbohydrate, so as to provide energy – and your body's energy demand during pregnancy will increase. Ketones in large quantities are toxic to the body, but if your urine test throws up ketones, you probably need to go and have something to eat; if ketones are present regularly (which is very rare), you are probably not eating enough.

Kick Chart

Kick charts are sometimes given to a mother for her to record the number of times she feels her baby kick inside her. This is usually part of an exercise in reassurance if a mother is concerned that the baby is moving less, as well it might towards the end of pregnancy when space becomes more confined.

A kick chart has space on which to record kicks felt, against a period of observation, which is usually 12 hours. That period of observation will be decided by the known time of fetal activity, which may be, for example, late evening. Evidence of at least 10 movements a day is considered a reliable sign of the baby's well-being.

Kinesiology

Applied kinesiology can be useful in rebalancing your body's energies to restore and promote health. It is based on the principle that energy displacement can give rise to or aggravate disorders. Rebalancing is achieved by fingertip pressure at key points.

Kinesiology can be especially useful in treating allergies. You may find that your susceptibility to allergic responses is increased while you are pregnant, because of the effect of your pregnancy on your immune system. Kinesiology may help identify certain foods that would be advisable to avoid, and help treat ailments such as catarrh, headaches, muscular tension, depression and tiredness. You will need to find a qualified and experienced kinesiology practitioner who has experience of working with pregnant women, so in the first instance contact The Association of Systematic Kinesiology (*see Useful Addresses*).

Compare **Acupressure**

Kitzinger, Sheila

Originally trained as a social anthropologist and then as a childbirth educator, Sheila Kitzinger, MBE has researched, written and lectured extensively on pregnancy, sexuality, motherhood, childbirth, breastfeeding and parenting. Her contribution to women's understanding about these issues has been immeasurable and has changed many attitudes over the past 20 years. Her books include *The Experience of Childbirth*, *Pregnancy and Childbirth*, *Women as Mothers*, *Breastfeeding* and *Woman's Experience of Sex*. For many years she was on the panel of advisors of the National Childbirth Trust. She is now President of the Oxfordshire branch of the Royal College of Midwives, a member of the Royal Society of Medicine, and Honorary Professor at Thames Valley University. She is also the mother of five daughters, including twins.

L l

Labour

Labour is the process by which the womb contracts and the cervix dilates in order for the baby and placenta to be delivered. It is divided into three distinct stages.

STAGE ONE
Stage one is the time from first contractions until the cervix is fully dilated. The waters will usually break sometime during this stage, if not at the onset of labour. In a first-time mother this stage may take between 18 and 24 hours; in a subsequent birth it may take as few as 3 to 8 hours. All labours and all women are, however, different, so this is only a guide.

STAGE TWO
Stage two begins when the cervix is fully dilated, and lasts until the baby is born. This can be very quick in a woman who has previously had a baby, but may last up to 2 hours in a first-time mother. Transition is the period between stages one and stage two.

STAGE THREE

Stage three lasts from the time of the birth of the baby until the placenta and membranes have separated from the womb and been delivered.

See also **Birth**, **Stage Three**, **Transition**

Labour Companions

In addition to your midwife, who is there to guide, support and care for you, you will probably also want your husband or partner or another companion with you while you deliver.

As long as their labour companion doesn't inhibit them in any way, or give them cause for concern when they should be concentrating on themselves, most women find their labour companion invaluable primarily just because they are *there*. A labour companion is also a point of contact with the life into which the baby is going to be born, a connection with the mother's own life, which can be very reassuring in the clinical environment of a labour ward.

If you want to have more than one labour or birth companion, you may have to ask about this beforehand: some hospitals have a policy to limit labour companions to just one. While most women want the father of their child to be there, in some circumstances this isn't possible, so a close friend, mother or sister may be a good alternative.

Ideally your labour companion should attend some antenatal classes with you and be familiar with how you hope your birth to be.

While some men are quite happy to accompany their wife or partner while she gives birth, others are extremely ambivalent and are very resistant to seeing the birth of their child, or to see their partner in pain. If this is the case it's probably better to give the privilege of attending your baby's birth to someone else! It's not that long since men started attending the birth of their children, prior to this it was thought to be a restrictedly female activity. Those men who do attend the births of their children, however, usually feel it's an experience they wouldn't have missed for the world, however uneasy the thought of it made them feel beforehand, or how difficult it was to see their partner in pain.

A research study done in the US showed that the presence of lay birth companions is extremely beneficial to the successful outcome of labour and delivery. It needs to be someone empathetic, perhaps someone who has had a baby herself. You may also want to consider asking your acupuncturist, osteopath or homoeopath – especially if he or she has been involved in your pregnancy.

Lactation

This is the medical term for the secretion of milk by the breasts. It is stimulated by the hormone prolactin, which increases after delivery when the level of oestrogen falls. It takes between 2 and 3 days for this sequence of events to occur, and during this time your baby can suckle on the colostrum produced by your breasts. The sucking itself stimulates not only the secretion of prolactin, but also the secretion of oxytocin, which stimulates the let-down reflex.

See also **Breastfeeding, Colostrum, Let-down Reflex, Oxytocin**

La Leche League

This is a breastfeeding support group (*see Useful Addresses*) founded in 1957, providing information and help in the form of trained La Leche League teachers.

See also **Breastfeeding**

Lamaze Method

Devised by French obstetrician Fernand Lamaze, this method of preparation for childbirth is based on Russian psychoprophylactic techniques. The training exercises are designed to prepare the body and mind for the rigours of labour and childbirth and, through using relaxation and breathing techniques, avoid the unnecessary use of pain-relieving drugs.

See also **Active Birth, Leboyer Method, Natural Childbirth, Psychoprophylaxis**

Latching On

Latching on is the way in which a baby takes the whole nipple and enough of the surrounding areola into his or her mouth in order to breastfeed. Unless your baby is securely and adequately latched on in this way, breastfeeding will seem an unrewarding and difficult process because your baby's ability to milk the breast properly will be impaired, your nipples will become sore and you will both end up extremely frustrated.

You can breastfeed your baby sitting up or lying down, as it is possible in both circumstances to ensure your baby is properly latched on. The following checklist may help remind you of what your midwife should have explained to you:

- *Your baby's body, as well as his or her head, should be turned towards your breast and body. The aim is to keep your baby's head and body more or less in a straight line.*
- *Your baby's mouth should be opposite your nipple and, if you support his or her head either in the crook of your arm or with your other hand, his or her neck will be slightly extended, which is helpful.*

- *If you gently stroke your baby's mouth with your nipple this will stimulate the rooting reflex, making your baby open his or her mouth wide. It is at this point that you should introduce the whole nipple and surrounding breast tissue.*
- *If you try to ensure that your baby's bottom lip is about half an inch from the bottom of your nipple, this will help you to be sure you have got the position right.*

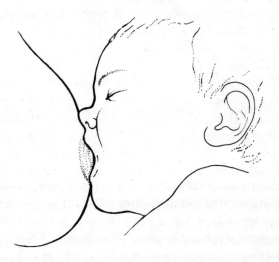

- *You need to ensure that enough of your nipple and breast fills your baby's mouth in order to reach his or her soft palate: this is because it is this contact that stimulates the sucking reflex. And it is this sucking that stimulates the secretion of oxytocin and the let-down reflex, so that your milk is actively squirted into your baby's mouth.*
(See Page 176)

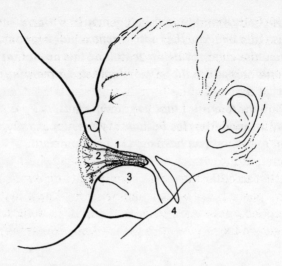

1) nipple; 2) areola and breast tissue, 3) baby's tongue; 4) throat

Latching on

Once you have got this first step sorted out, many of what are termed 'common breastfeeding problems' shouldn't actually occur. If you need your midwife to help you position your baby in order to latch on efficiently, or if you need reassurance about whether or not you've got it quite right, ask her.

See also **Breastfeeding, Let-down Reflex**

Leboyer Method

Frederic Leboyer was a French doctor who advocated that babies should be born gently and quietly, without harsh lights or loud noise. He recommended that the baby should be placed on his or her mother's abdomen until the placental cord stopped pulsating, being allowed to take a first breath in his or her own time before the cord was cut.

Then the baby should be placed gently in a warm bath to welcome him or her to the world. The whole emphasis was to reduce the shock of being born, and the argument was that these babies would be more contented because of it. Indeed, photos of babies born in this way were dramatic in their depiction of alert, smiling newborns.

While few deliveries follow this pattern exactly, Leboyer's method has influenced ideas about the environment into which a child is born, and there is no doubt that to enter the world calmly and surrounded by love and peace is far better than being held upside down and slapped on the bottom, once thought (though thankfully no longer) to be necessary to get the baby breathing.

Let-down Reflex

When you are breastfeeding your baby you will probably notice that, after he or she has been sucking for a few minutes, there is a strong tingling sensation in your breasts. This is the sensation of the let-down reflex which makes the milk ducts in the breast contract, squirting the milk out through the nipple.

It is your baby's sucking that stimulates the secretion of the hormone oxytocin, responsible also for the contractions of your womb during labour. While there is enough milk in the reservoirs immediately behind the nipple to meet your baby's immediate needs, the let-down reflex is essential to release the milk further back in the breast tissue (the hindmilk).

You may find that you notice this tingling sensation on other occasions, perhaps if you hear your baby cry, or as his or her normal feeding time approaches. You may also find that this is accompanied by some degree of leakage from the breasts. This may happen quite dramatically on one side when you are feeding your baby from the other, especially at first, but it should soon settle down as your milk production and feeding pattern become more closely synchronized.

See also **Breastfeeding**, **Oxytocin**

Ligaments

Ligaments are tough, fibrous strands of tissue in the body designed to support the internal organs or to connect bones together. They occur wherever there are joints, including the vertebral joints, and are worth a mention in a book on pregnancy because they are affected by the pregnancy hormones progesterone and relaxin. These make the ligaments more 'soft', thus able to expand greatly, which is of particular value in the joints of the pelvis. It also makes ligaments more susceptible to injury, whether this is back strain or a sprained ankle.

Exercise helps to keep the muscles fit and therefore take some of the strain off the ligaments. Take extra care with your posture, bending and lifting in order to avoid injury.

The other ligaments to consider are those supporting your growing womb. Because these don't stretch much, as your womb enlarges you can experience quite sharp pains in the groin. Mention it to your midwife should it occur, just to be sure. And report any pain accompanied by bleeding immediately.

If the pain is a continuous problem or very bad, your midwife may suggest you wear a 'maternity belt', specially designed to help support your abdomen. You will also find it helpful to support your abdomen with your hands when you turn over in bed or get up from a seated position. You also want to avoid straining your back, if you find yourself standing or moving awkwardly to avoid the pain in your abdomen.

A number of homoeopathic remedies are helpful for ligament pain, including *Bellis perennis*. As for any

homoeopathic prescribing, consulting a qualified
practitioner is your best bet, although you can self-
prescribe adequately for a wide range of minor problems.

See also **Homoeopathy**, **Posture**

Listeriosis

Listeria is an illness caused by a bacteria called *Listeria
monocytogenes*, and if contracted causes a mild, flu-like
illness. The problem during pregnancy is that, although not
a serious illness in itself, it can cause miscarriage or
stillbirth, or severe illness in the baby.

While it is serious, *it is also very rare* (1 case in 30,000
live and stillbirths in 1990). And you can take steps to avoid
running the risk of catching it. If suspected during
pregnancy, it can be treated with antibiotics.

Because of the increasing use of convenience foods –
pre-prepared or cook-chill (not frozen) foods – there has
been a growing emphasis on advising pregnant women
about their use. Make sure that if you eat any of these types
of food they have been re-heated thoroughly – until they are
steaming hot – before you eat them.

High levels of listeria may exist in certain soft cheeses –
Camembert, Brie and blue-veined cheeses – and also some
meat patés. To be on the safe side, don't eat either the
cheeses described above or any form of paté while you
are pregnant.

For the few women who work with sheep, they should
be aware that sheep are susceptible to listeria and may
provide a source of the infection to pregnant women,
especially during the lambing season.

None of these precautions is necessary either before
you are pregnant or after you have given birth or are
breastfeeding. It is only *during* pregnancy that your baby
would be at risk, and then only if you contracted listeriosis.

Lithotomy Position

In this position for labour a woman lies on her back with her knees bent and her feet supported and held in place by lithotomy poles. This allows unrestricted access in order to carry out a forceps delivery, or perhaps to suture a tear. Certainly if you have had an epidural, either for a forceps delivery or a caesarean, your legs will need to be well-supported. Otherwise, even for suturing it is sometimes unnecessary, and very few women will actually deliver like this.

Lochia

This is the medical term for the vaginal discharge following childbirth. It consists mainly of blood from the placental site. This should only last for between two and three weeks after the birth; you will need to wear some form of sanitary protection – towels and then pads as it becomes lighter. Tampons shouldn't be used.

Your midwife will check on the amount and type of discharge with you, when she visits for the first 10 days postnatally. The lochia will only be of concern if it suddenly increases in quantity or contains lots of fresh blood or clots, or if its smell becomes offensive, suggesting an infection.

Low Birthweight

Sometimes referred to as 'small-for-dates or 'light-for-dates', this is any baby born weighing 2.5 kg (5½ lb) or less. This may be because the baby was born before 37 weeks, or pre-term (premature), or because of a number of factors during pregnancy which may include poor nutrition, cigarette smoking, maternal age or multiple pregnancy, for example. Good antenatal care helps to prevent some of these problems, but should your baby be 'small-for-dates', he or she may need the advantage of a special care baby unit for a while.

See **Special Care Baby Unit**

Mm

Massage

Massage, whether or not in conjunction with aromatherapy oils, has a therapeutic value all of its own. The actual process of massage relaxes muscle tension, improves circulation and relieves many minor aches and pains. Massage can also incorporate shiatsu and reflexology techniques.

Massage is particularly good as an aid to relaxation, and at stimulating the body's self-healing properties. For these reasons it is often used in conjunction with other alternative therapies. Apart from relieving tension, massage is also proven to be useful for reducing high blood-pressure, helping with insomnia, headaches, back and neck ache, and relieving anxiety and depression.

It is important to find a trained and qualified practitioner (although your husband, partner or a friend can give you a light general massage) if you want to try and alleviate any minor discomfort of pregnancy. Personal recommendation, as well as checking a practitioner's qualifications, is a good place to start – your midwife, doctor or health centre may be able to suggest someone. Alternatively, try The Massage Training Institute (*see Useful Addresses*), which keeps a national register of high-quality, trained holistic masseurs.

See also **Aromatherapy**

Mastitis

Mastitis means, literally, inflammation of the breast. Many women suffer from some degree of mastitis without being pregnant: they have tender, lumpy breasts particularly just before a period. This is uncomfortable but harmless, and caused by the fluctuating hormones of the menstrual cycle.

When mastitis occurs during breastfeeding, it is usually non-infective and probably caused by a poor feeding technique or an ill-fitting bra. It is usually characterized by a wedge-shaped area of inflammation which feels tender and warm and looks red. Whatever the cause, continuing to feed – having removed your bra and checked the position of the baby on the breast – will help the problem resolve itself quite quickly. If you become engorged, take steps to deal with it so that it doesn't give rise to mastitis.

If you don't continue to breastfeed with mastitis, the blockage that gave rise to the inflammation in the first place provides an ideal breeding ground for infection – and that could, in the worst case, give rise to a breast abscess. Infection can sometimes arise because the nipple has become sore and allowed access to infection. Sore nipples will usually only happen if your baby isn't latched on properly, or positioned badly. Ask your midwife for advice, or contact your local breastfeeding counsellor through either the National Childbirth Trust or La Leche League (*see Useful Addresses*).

Depending on the severity of any infection, you may need a course of antibiotics to treat it. This would not mean you have to stop breastfeeding.

See also **Breastfeeding, Engorgement, Latching On**

Maternity Rights

Maternity rights in the UK for mothers-to-be at work are both wide-ranging and complex, and subject to change! In addition, some employers offer an enhanced arrangement for their staff which exceeds the legal minimum set down by law, so you will need to check with your boss, union representative or personnel department.

The four main statutory rights for pregnant women at work are:

1   *time off for antenatal care;*
2   *protection against unfair dismissal on maternity-related grounds;*
3   *maternity leave and maternity absence;*
4   *maternity benefit.*

The extent and range of maternity rights for which you are eligible will be influenced by a number of factors, including length of time in that particular job, whether or not you are full-time or part-time, whether or not you are self-employed, etc.

Key information about maternity rights is available from a number of sources including your local Social Security office, the Benefits Agency, and The Maternity Alliance (*see Useful Addresses*).

See also **Benefits**

Meconium

During fetal life, the gut of your baby begins functioning after around 12 weeks. Amniotic fluid, containing various skin cells and other debris, is constantly being sucked in, swallowed and passed through. Digestive juices, present before birth, act on this material to produce a black-coloured, sticky substance called meconium. This forms the first bowel movement after birth, and you will probably be asked whether or not your baby has passed any black-coloured faeces. This indicates that all is working well and, after your baby begins feeding in earnest, the colour of his or her stools will change.

Occasionally, if there is a difficult labour and delivery and a baby becomes distressed, meconium is passed before birth and may be seen in the amniotic fluid. This is a useful signal to midwives and doctors that they need to take special care to deliver the baby as soon as possible.

Meditation

Meditation is an extremely useful tool that allows you to relax and focus your concentration, reducing stress and enhancing peace of mind. A meditative state of mind has a direct effect on physical well-being: it reduces the rate of breathing, heart-beat, and the activity of the sweat glands – all of which can be extremely beneficial during pregnancy, labour, birth and parenthood! However, to be effective it has to be practised, because it is an acquired skill.

You can teach yourself to meditate, although many people enjoy learning with a teacher and in a class. There are three main ways in which you can begin to practise meditation, and you should practise for at least 10 to 15 minutes twice a day to become efficient. The aim is to concentrate clearly on one thing – your breathing, a sound, or an object – to the exclusion of all else, in an attempt to empty your mind of all other thoughts.

BREATHING

Find a comfortable and relaxed position in an upright posture, and concentrate at first solely on the process of your breathing, the breath filling your lungs and being exhaled. Focus on the sensation of your breathing and, if other thoughts begin to intrude, gently return your attention to your breathing.

MANTRA

By choosing a word or sound to be repeated over and over in your mind, you should find it possible to clear your head of all other thoughts. Buddhists use the word 'om', meaning 'everything that ever was, is and will be'.

OBJECT FOCUS

Concentrating on a particular object or image also serves to empty the mind of all other thoughts. Not everyone finds it possible to hold on to an image in their heads, so may need an actual object on which to focus. Try using a lighted candle, or a flower, or a favourite picture.

The choice of approach to meditation is entirely personal; the aim is to find an individual route to a calm, inner place where it is possible both to relax and recharge your batteries.

There are a number of pregnancy-related ailments for which meditation may have a positive and therapeutic effect: insomnia, high blood-pressure, tension headaches, the pain of labour, and anxiety and stress.

See also **Breathing Exercises, Relaxation**

Membranes

If you hear mention made of the 'membranes' while you're pregnant, or after delivery, this is a reference to the fetal membranes or the amniotic sac. After delivery the midwife checks to see that the membranes are intact and fully expelled from the uterus.

See also **Fetal Sac**, **Third Stage**

Menstrual Cycle

The series of events that occurs between each of a woman's periods, when she is not pregnant, is referred to as the menstrual cycle. The build-up of the lining of the womb, in preparation for implantation should fertilization occur, the release of a ripe egg from the ovary, the break-down of the lining of the womb if no egg implants, and the subsequent period are the chief features of the cycle, and are under the influence of the female sex hormones oestrogen and progesterone.

The average length of the menstrual cycle is 28 days, although this varies quite considerably not just from woman to woman but also from cycle to cycle. Very few women have completely standard menstrual cycles throughout their fertile years. The relevance of the length of your normal cycle to pregnancy is that this will have a bearing on the length of your pregnancy. If you normally have a very short cycle of, say, 22 days, then you will probably have ovulated and conceived at around day 8 of your cycle – 14 days before your next period was due; if you normally have a long cycle of, say, 35 days, then you would have ovulated and conceived at around day 21 – again, 14 days before your next period was due. It's quite important to remember this when you are trying to conceive, because it will influence your timing for sexual intercourse. By the same token, if you want to avoid conception, you need to have as clear an idea as possible of when you ovulate.

The average length of pregnancy is 266 days from conception, but it's seldom possible to say exactly when conception occurred, so the calculation is done from the date of the first day of the last period. So, by adding the 14 days of an average 28-day cycle to 266 days gives you 280 days, or 40 weeks. This gives you your Estimated Date of Delivery (EDD).

Knowing the normal length of your cycle can be quite useful when looking more closely at your EDD: if your cycle is usually long you may deliver later than estimated, if it's short, then earlier. However, most babies seem to arrive when they're ready, only very few (between 4 and 5 per cent) turning up on the day designated for them.

See also **Conception**, **Due Date**, **Fertility**, **Hormones**, **Natural Family Planning**

Midwives

Your midwife will be your first port of call for support, information and advice during your pregnancy, labour and delivery. With a bit of luck you will develop a close and trusting relationship with your midwife, which will enhance your experience of having your baby.

Midwives are either fully-qualified nurses who have done an additional training in midwifery, or practitioners who have done a three- or four-year course devoted to all aspects of midwifery. While midwifery training is hospital-based with some work in the community, after qualification midwives may choose to work either in hospital maternity units or in the community. Some midwives also choose to work independently.

See also **Community Midwives**, **Independent Midwives**

Minerals

An adequate dietary intake of minerals is necessary for the body to function healthily. The body contains about 25 essential minerals – chemical elements needed in small proportions by all living things. Pregnant women need a slightly higher daily intake, but if they fail to get it their baby doesn't suffer, unless the deficiency is great, as the mother's own stores will be depleted to meet the baby's needs.

Minerals that are necessary include iron, calcium, magnesium, potassium, sodium, iodine, phosphorus, chromium, fluorine, manganese, selenium, sulphur, copper, molybdenum, cobalt, and zinc. The majority of these are present in a well-balanced diet and supplements aren't needed while pregnant or breastfeeding.

The only two dietary minerals you may want to make sure you are getting in adequate amounts are calcium (recommended daily amount 500 mg before pregnancy, 1,200 mg during pregnancy) and iron (12 mg RDA before pregnancy, 13 mg during pregnancy and 15 mg while breastfeeding). If your iron stores were low to start with and you find that what you are eating isn't particularly rich in iron, then it's worth redressing any imbalance.

Sources of calcium include: dairy products, fortified cereals, white flour products, sardines, pilchards and other fish whose bones are eaten, and watercress.

Sources of iron include: red meat, pulses, dried apricots and figs, fortified breakfast cereals, nuts (especially almonds), cocoa, and fortified white flour products. To ensure that the iron content of what you eat is properly absorbed and utilized, drink a glass of fresh orange juice. You need vitamin C to utilize the iron in your diet, and as this vitamin is water-soluble and can't be stored, it needs to be taken in regularly.

See also **Diet, Vitamins**

Miscarriage

This is the loss of a baby anytime between conception and 24 weeks of pregnancy. Medically it is termed 'spontaneous abortion', sometimes occurring so early on that a woman hadn't even realized she was pregnant.

The majority of miscarriages occur between the 8th and 12th week of pregnancy. It can occur because the level of the hormone progesterone produced in the ovaries drops before the level produced by the placenta reaches an adequate level to sustain the pregnancy. In around 60 per cent of miscarriages within the first three months of pregnancy there is some sort of chromosomal abnormality, too.

The earliest sign of a threatened miscarriage is bleeding, either a blood-stained discharge or fresh blood. There will also be some pain felt in the lower, central abdomen much like a period cramp, indicative of the womb contraction. Backache may also be felt. If the cervix dilates, the miscarriage becomes inevitable. Approximately 20 per cent of mothers who have recurrent miscarriages have a weak cervix.

Any bleeding in pregnancy should be reported, though it may not herald the worst. If a miscarriage threatens close to the 24-week point it may be possible to sustain the pregnancy for long enough to save the baby's life with specialized care.

Whatever the reason for miscarriage, and whatever its timing, the loss of a baby is profoundly sad. For many women the loss of a much-longed for pregnancy means real grief for their lost *baby*, not for some unformed person. Anyone who fails to recognize this can only heighten this sense of loss through misguided and inappropriate comments.

There can be no pain like the death of a child, whether from miscarriage or stillbirth, or even termination for abnormality. This pain is entirely individual, although it will bear similarities to the pain others have gone through if they have suffered a similar experience. There is a whole process of grief that needs to be worked through which may, for some, take a long time. You may want to contact a support group such as the Miscarriage Association or SANDS, the Stillbirth and Neonatal Death Society (*see Useful Addresses*).

Any emotional shock can have physical consequences, so taking care of yourself after a miscarriage is essential, especially as it is self-nurturing and that will help you feel better emotionally. Treat any specific symptoms – insomnia, headaches, nausea, etc. – with homoeopathy, aromatherapy massage, shiatsu or acupuncture. Although you may feel OK and immediately prefer just to continue getting on with life, allow yourself time to convalesce and you will recover more fully.

See also **Cervical Incompetence**

Monitoring

Monitoring refers to the checking of your baby's heartbeat during labour and birth. Midwives do this in one of three ways:

1   *with a Pinard (a hand-held 'ear trumpet')*
2   *using a hand-held ultrasound machine called a Doppler*
3   *with an electronic fetal monitor (EFM), for which two receivers are strapped to the mother's abdomen. (Sometimes EFM is used by attaching an electrode to the baby's head, via the mother's vagina.)*

The reason midwives check your baby's heartbeat is that during contractions the blood supply between the placenta and your baby is reduced. While most babies cope with this during labour and the birth, if their oxygen supply is reduced to a level that may endanger them, then their heart rate changes. Checking the heartbeat regularly ensures that, should a problem arise, appropriate action can be taken.

For the majority of women, the Pinard or Doppler is more than adequate. EFM may be used routinely in some hospitals, or may be used only on and off during your labour to check all is well. If EFM reveals a possible problem, a blood sample may be taken from the baby to assess the level of oxygen in his or her blood. Although this sounds unpleasant, it is the most accurate way of judging the situation and may help preclude an unnecessary caesarean section.

See also **Labour**

Morning Sickness

Morning sickness affects about 50 per cent of all pregnant mothers to some extent. Some just feel mildly nauseated at some point in the day and then it passes; others feel sick from the moment they get up until they go to sleep again but are never actually sick; some vomit constantly for three months and are then fine; some feel nauseated and are occasionally sick for the whole nine months. Every woman's morning sickness is unique to her, as will be the steps she takes to alleviate it. If you are suffering, then bear in mind that in most cases it does stop at around 14 weeks.

Morning sickness is thought to be caused by an excess of the hormones oestrogen and human chorionic gonadotrophin, which are highest early in the pregnancy (this is why the symptoms tend to pass after 14 weeks). There is also some indication that morning sickness is made much worse by low blood sugar, hence the traditional advice about eating a dry biscuit and having a cup of tea before getting up in the morning.

In fact there is quite a lot you can try to alleviate your symptoms, although of course you may find that some things work well, and others not at all, or that some things work some of the time ... However you are feeling it is sure to be exacerbated if you are overtired, and in the early stages of pregnancy you will probably feel tired, if not exhausted, a lot of the time. Try to make time for extra rest and sleep. You will probably find that this tiredness will pass, too.

Over-the-counter homoeopathic remedies recommended for morning sickness include *Nux vomica*, *Ipecacuanha* and *Sepia*; remember that it is always worth consulting a trained and qualified homoeopath for a more individualized prescription. You may find that your midwife knows of someone to recommend, or has homoeopathic training herself.

Acupuncture has been proved successful with many cases of nausea and vomiting and, received at the hands of a skilled practitioner, is completely safe for use in early pregnancy. Acupressure points in the wrists can be utilized; wrist bands, used also to alleviate travel sickness, are available from many chemists now.

Ginger (crystallized, in capsule form, as ginger root tea or even non-alcoholic ginger ale) is often helpful. Cutting out tea and coffee and substituting herbal teas (in particular camomile) is recommended. Eating small, regular and nutritious meals while avoiding fatty and spicy foods can help. Taking zinc and vitamin B_6 supplements (50 mg of each a day) is sometimes suggested by nutritional therapists, particularly if pregnancy follows use of the contraceptive pill. Reflexology performed by a trained practitioner is beneficial and, in extreme cases, might even help put an end to continual vomiting.

However bad you are feeling during this early part of your pregnancy, hold fast to the fact that in the majority of cases it will disappear – seemingly overnight – at around 14 weeks. If you can just manage to eat reasonably, keep rested and not become overwrought, then you will avoid taking an exhausted self into the next phase of pregnancy. It is worth trying to do what you can to keep going by using alternative therapies, but if you need to go to bed at 8 p.m. six nights a week just to be able to get up in the morning, then submit gracefully. Women who don't suffer won't understand your problem, neither will men, but if they have ever suffered from travel sickness, point out to them that morning sickness is similar but lasts day-in, day-out for three months. You get used to it, and you get on with the rest of what you have to do, but it's wonderful when it goes away!

See also **Acupressure, Acupuncture, Ginger, HCG, Homoeopathy, Reflexology**

Moxibustion

By applying the gentle heat of burning mugwort (Chinese wormwood) over a specific acupuncture point, the therapist aims to regulate, stimulate or tone the flow of energy within the body, known as Qi. Usually applied as part of acupuncture treatment, smouldering cones of moxa wool may be attached to the top of an acupuncture needle inserted at an appropriate point.

See also **Acupuncture**

Multiple Pregnancy

This describes the development of more than one baby in the womb. Twin pregnancy occurs in around 1 per cent of naturally occurring pregnancies in the UK, triplets occur once every 8–9,000, and quadruplets around once in every 700,000. The increased use of fertility drugs and fertility procedures such as IVF has meant an increase in the number of multiple births. Whatever the reason for a multiple pregnancy, it is associated with an increased risk to mother and babies.

Twins can either be identical (also known as monozygotic or uniovular) – that is, produced from the splitting of one egg fertilized by one sperm and sharing the same placenta; or non-identical (or dizygotic or biovular), having been the result of two eggs fertilized by two sperm. Non-identical twins are more common. There is an inherited, genetic tendency to conceive non-identical twins that is passed from mother to daughter – so if your mother had non-identical twins, there is an increased chance that you will, too.

Diagnosis of multiple pregnancy can be confirmed as early as 8 weeks by ultrasound scan. Symptoms of pregnancy may be exaggerated in a mother with multiple pregnancy, and she will appear larger than her dates suggest. Early diagnosis is important because there are some complications associated with multiple pregnancy that good antenatal care can help avoid, for example anaemia and high blood-pressure.

Nearer the estimated date of birth, the position of the babies will need to be checked and assessed to ensure a safe delivery. Many multiple-birth babies arrive before their due date, and some have to be delivered by caesarean section, so good antenatal care and monitoring are essential. Some multiple-birth babies will also need special care; again, good antenatal monitoring should mean that any baby at risk has been identified.

N n

Natural Childbirth

Rather than imposing unnecessary pain-relieving drugs and interventions on women during childbirth, the emphasis of natural childbirth is to inform and support women and encourage them to work with their bodies – without fear – in order to participate fully in the birth of their child. By regaining control in childbirth and being an active participant in the process, many women have found they can actually do without pain-relieving drugs, which also proves better for them and their babies after birth.

For a time, however, there seemed to be a bit of a tussle, with women labouring through painful labours yet refusing to take any analgesic lest they prove 'failures'. Very high standards were set, and many women, feeling that they had flunked some unwritten test if they had to use pain relief/an enema/an episiotomy/Syntometrine/a caesarean section, seemed to have completely missed the point that they were safely delivered of a healthy baby. Turning up with a birth plan writ in stone cuts no ice with babies, who have their own ideas about birth, too. And while pain may be a natural part of the process, it hurts, too!

Thankfully, one good aspect of all this was that there was a new look at what was appropriate for women during their pregnancies, labour and deliveries, and who was going to supply it. Everything became much more female-orientated, with the very good effect of emphasizing the key role a woman's midwife plays. Antenatal care improved, community midwifery services opened up, home births became easier to get, and greater choice both in and out of hospital became available. You can give birth in hospital in a birthing room, using a birthing stool or a birthing pool while having an anaesthetist on standby should you need an epidural, an operating theatre at hand should you need a caesarean section, and a special care baby unit if your baby is unwell. You may never need it, but it's there if you do.

Fundamentally, the most natural birth is the one that feels most natural to you. So think about what you would like, talk it through with your husband or partner and your midwife, see what is available and keep an open mind as your pregnancy progresses. You may also like to contact the National Childbirth Trust (*see Useful Addresses*). What you think you might like during week 3 of your pregnancy may be different by week 33, and different again after 16 hours of labour. Trust yourself to do what is best for you and your baby.

See also **Active Birth**, **Lamaze Method**

Natural Family Planning

A woman with a thorough understanding of her own, individual fertility cycle can become extremely proficient at discerning her most fertile time of the month. If a woman wants to conceive, this is obviously the best time to have intercourse. If she doesn't want to get pregnant, then she needs to abstain from penetrative intercourse or use a barrier method of contraception (condom or cap) at this time.

The best way to work out your most fertile time is through a combination of signs and symptoms, which provides a double check, rather than relying on just one of the methods described below.

CERVICAL MUCUS

The cervical mucus in the vagina changes during a woman's cycle as it is influenced by the same female sex hormones that control ovulation. Immediately after a period there is little or no cervical mucus present. Over the next few days there is a gradual increase in the quantity of (initially thick, sticky white) mucus. Towards the middle of the fertile cycle the effect of oestrogen, which will cause ovulation, makes the cervix produce much thinner, more watery and stretchy or stringy mucus until, at the most fertile phase, the mucus is similar in texture to the clear stretchiness of egg white. After ovulation there is a quite dramatic shift back to non-fertile mucus as the cervix responds to the effect of the hormone progesterone, until the next period.

TEMPERATURE

Immediately following ovulation the secretion of the hormone progesterone makes body temperature rise by 0.4°F (0.2°C). This small rise is quite recognizable when recorded on a specially-designed chart (*see Figure 8, page 200*). You have to take your temperature at around the same time every morning, before you get out of bed. It will probably take a while before you feel confident of your ability to read and record your temperature to reveal the pattern of your fertility cycle, but as with anything else, practice makes perfect.

CERVIX

The cervix itself changes in response to the changing influence of the female sex hormones. Oestrogen secretion around the time of ovulation makes the cervix soften and dilate slightly. You will probably have to become familiar with the feel of your cervix throughout a succession of cycles before this change becomes recognizable to you.

CALENDAR METHOD

If you keep a record of six menstrual cycles, an average length can be assumed. If your shortest cycle length is 27 days, and your longest is 30 days, and ovulation is assumed to occur on day 14 *before* your next period, then you would expect, on the basis of the information from your six cycles, to be fertile any time between day 13 and day 16 of your cycle. If sperm can live for around five days within the female reproductive tract, and an egg can survive for around 12 hours, then on this basis you should either abstain from penetrative intercourse or take precautions from day 7 to day 20 of your cycle if you do not wish to become pregnant.

If you use a combination of the four methods outlined above, and record them together on a specially designed chart (*see Figure 8*), you will be able to get a pretty clear picture of your fertile cycle over a period of time. You will also become aware of any particular indicators of fertility that are specific to you, for example pain at ovulation, breast tenderness, an outbreak of small spots on your nose, etc.

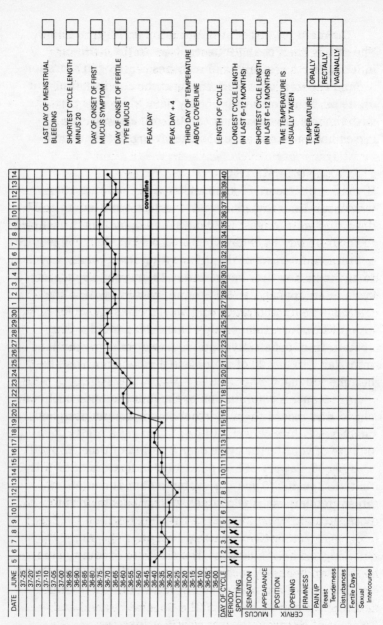

Natural family planning chart

The main resource for information on Natural Family Planning is from the NFP Centre (*see Useful Addresses*), which is also a research and resource centre. In the UK, there are specially trained teachers who can be helpful when you first start using natural family planning. They can also help when you need additional advice during particular times, for example if you work shifts (which may disrupt your cycle) or take any medication that affects mucus production.

You will also need some advice if you want to continue with natural family planning as a contraceptive measure after pregnancy. Breastfeeding will inhibit ovulation while you are feeding unrestrictedly and throughout the night. The problems arise as you regulate, or cut down on breastfeeding, or introduce solids after your baby reaches 4 or 5 months of age. It will only be possible to tell when you've first ovulated retrospectively, that is, once you've had your first period after giving birth, unless you are very clued up to the changing signs and symptoms of your returning fertility. Given the routine disturbances of early motherhood, this is bound to be difficult to assess, so take advice if you are having a full sexual relationship with your husband or partner again and don't want to get pregnant.

See also **Contraception**

Naturopathy

Naturopathy is a holistic approach to healthcare aiming to treat the underlying imbalance that has resulted in illness or disease, rather than treating the symptoms alone. By restoring the body's balance, the aim is to encourage the body's own healing processes using an individually tailored combination of alternative therapies. Details of qualified naturopaths can be had from the General Council and Register of Naturopaths (*see Useful Addresses*).

Nausea

Nausea can result from a number of reasons completely unrelated to your pregnancy. If you have had no morning sickness but feel nauseated later in pregnancy this could be caused by a tummy bug or something you have eaten. Because your immune system is operating slightly under par you may be more susceptible to tummy bugs while pregnant.

Without worrying unduly, you do need to mention this to your midwife or doctor because there are some bacteria, for example Listeria, that need to be treated if contracted during pregnancy.

See also **Immune System**, **Listeria**, **Morning Sickness**.

Nipples

Your nipples and surrounding areola will become darker during pregnancy, and remain so afterwards, although they will lighten somewhat eventually. Whatever your nipples are like, you should have no problem breastfeeding because your baby will breastfeed, not nipple-feed. If you have especially large, long or inverted nipples, some adaptation to positioning may be necessary, though often not. Your midwife should be able to advise you.

There isn't much you can do to prepare your nipples for breastfeeding and there is nothing you can do to avoid soreness should it occur initially *except* ensure that your baby is well-positioned and properly latched on (*see Figure 7, page 175*). Even with a sore or cracked nipple it is possible to feed comfortably if you change the position in which your baby feeds.

Washing nipples between feeds is unnecessary, as are nipple sprays and creams. You may like to tuck a disposable breast pad inside your feeding bra, though, and keep your nipples dry. If your nipples do become sore, then not keeping them dry between feeds will aggravate this.

From your baby's point of view, the smell of your body and the milk you produce for him or her are perfect, and research has shown that babies actually prefer unwashed nipples! Your baby won't be susceptible to infection from you as you will already have provided him or her with a bountiful supply of antibodies, both before birth and in your breastmilk itself. Washing your nipples unnecessarily will only dry out your skin.

See also **Areola, Breastfeeding, Latching On**

Nosebleeds

Some women find that they are troubled by nosebleeds during pregnancy. Again, the pregnancy hormones are partly to blame, as is the increased volume of blood in your body. Routine first aid measures are required:

- *sit leaning forward;*
- *pinch just below the bridge of your nose;*
- *apply an ice-pack or cloth wrung out in icy water to your nose;*
- *don't blow your nose violently.*

Mention this problem to your midwife or doctor, especially if the nosebleeds are very frequent or troublesome. It is unlikely that you would ever lose so much blood that, over a period of time, it could contribute to anaemia, but you should mention it at any antenatal visit.

Nuchal Translucency Scan

This is a high-definition ultrasound scan that can identify the risk factor for Down's Syndrome and other chromosomal abnormalities. It has an accuracy rate of around 85 per cent at 11 weeks' gestation. It makes it possible to measure the fluid behind the neck of the fetus, where the neural tube will form, and thereby given an indication of the level of risk. Developed at the Harris Birthright Centre in London, it is still only offered at a few hospitals in the UK, but should become more widely available in time.

As this test only indicates the risk factor for abnormality, further diagnostic testing may be necessary if more information is to be gained.

See also **Antenatal Testing, Down's Syndrome, Ultrasound**

Nutrition

See **Diet**

O o

Obstetrician

Obstetrics is the branch of medicine concerned with pregnancy, labour, childbirth and postnatal care; an obstetrician is a doctor with additional training and a qualification in obstetrics.

Obstetricians tend to be experts in 'abnormal' births, while the majority of births are straightforward and can be delivered by midwives. There is no legal requirement for a doctor to be present at a birth, as midwives are considered (and indeed are) fully competent in normal deliveries. The benefit of good antenatal care is that any pregnancy which appears to pose a degree of risk to mother or baby can be referred to an obstetrically trained doctor ahead of time.

See also **Midwives**

Occipito-Anterior Position

The occiput is the back of the head; the occipito-anterior position means that the back of your baby's head is facing the front of your pelvis as it comes down the birth canal.

Occipito-posterior means that the back of your baby's head is lying against the sacral (back) area of your pelvis.

During delivery your baby's head normally rotates gently from whatever position it was in to an occipito-anterior one as he or she descends down the birth canal. Occasionally the baby's head remains in an occipito-posterior position (sometimes referred to as a 'back' labour), in which case progress is slower and you may experience more discomfort. Sometimes, by getting onto all fours and lowering your shoulders, you can assist your baby's head in turning, but you would need to take your midwife's advice on the timing of this.

If your baby is delivered with his or her head in this position (sometimes referred to as a 'face to pubes' position), you may later notice a degree of 'moulding' or swelling on the top of your baby's head. This will soon disappear and causes no harm to your baby. It may, too, be necessary for you to have an episiotomy with delivery of the head like this: because the emerging part of your baby's head is wider in diameter in this position, there is more risk of tearing from the centre of the perineum, which is better avoided.

Because delivery in an occipito-posterior position is more demanding on both you and your baby, you may want to consider seeing a cranial osteopath who can help with any residual backache you may have, and who can check and re-balance your baby's head if necessary. Cranial-osteopathic checks are a benefit for any baby after delivery, but especially if it was a long or difficult labour, and should certainly be considered if your baby is very unsettled, a difficult feeder, or colicky.

See also **Anterior Position, Breech Presentation, Brow Presentation, Cranial Osteopathy, Face Presentation, Occipito-Anterior Position, Transverse Lie, Unstable Lie**

Odent, Dr Michel

Michel Odent is a French obstetrician famous for his work
on natural childbirth and water births. Originally based at
Pithiviers in France, he now continues to work privately as
an obstetrician in the UK, while lecturing and writing. He
has published numerous books, most notably *Birth Reborn*,
documenting his work and ideas (*see Further Reading*).
  See also **Natural Childbirth**

Oedema

Some degree of swelling in your ankles and feet is
considered 'normal' towards the end of pregnancy.
Generally it builds up over the course of any given day, and
is worse in hot weather, if you are overweight, or if you are
carrying more than one baby. You can sensibly avoid the
worst of this if you take gentle exercise to keep your
circulation efficient (flexing your calf muscles regularly also
helps). Wear flat shoes and sit with your feet raised when
you can, gently rotating your ankles.

  Mention any water retention or swelling to your
midwife; she will check that it is not indicative of anything
serious by gently pressing around your ankles. If the
indentation of her finger pressure remains, and you have
other related symptoms such as a rise in blood-pressure
and protein in the urine, she may want you to see the
obstetrician to check that there is no risk of pre-eclampsia.
Otherwise there is no need.

  Provided the oedema you have is not serious, there are a
number of alternative therapies you can try to ease any
discomfort. An osteopath might be able to improve your
lymphatic drainage by gently manipulating your ankle, knee
and hip joints. A homoeopathic remedy that is often
recommended is *Natrum muriaticum. Apis mellifica* or

Phosphorus may also be suggested, although a full consultation and prescription based on a holistic diagnosis is always best. Increasing your intake of parsley, garlic and onions is also thought to be effective.

Gentle but firm massage, working up the leg in the direction of blood flow to the heart, can help relieve the discomfort, and essential oil of geranium is recommended by aromatherapists for ankle oedema. Care is needed if there are any varicose veins, however, in which case massaging the leg should be avoided. Foot massage alone is better in this case. A reflexologist can increase the benefit of foot massage by working on the reflex zones for the lymphatic system, to help fluid drainage.

Shiatsu techniques can also help with oedema, particularly with Carpal tunnel syndrome. There is a shiatsu point, Pericardium 6, situated in the wrist three fingers' width below the hand (*see Figure 3, page 55*). This point needs to be pressed firmly for between 7 and 10 seconds, three times in succession. Sometimes wearing a loose bandage over the wrists is enough to ease the numbness and/or tingling in the fingers that Carpal tunnel syndrome brings on. The same treatment recommended for breast engorgement – the application of cabbage leaves – can also be effective in reducing oedema.

See also **Carpal Tunnel Syndrome, Homoeopathy, Massage, Osteopathy, Pre-eclampsia, Reflexology, Shiatsu**

Oestrogen

See **Hormones, Progesterone, Prolactin**

Operculum

This is the medical term for the plug of mucus that seals the cervix, the entrance to the womb, during pregnancy. It comes away at some stage just prior to or at the beginning of labour, and is commonly referred to as the 'show'.

See also **Show**

Orgasm

Orgasm during pregnancy can cause no harm to your baby, although you may find that the contractions of orgasm in your womb are particularly noticeable towards the end of pregnancy. In fact the process of orgasm can be positively beneficial to you in releasing tension and any feeling of pelvic congestion, promoting relaxation and sleep.

While you may not feel particularly sexy during the first few months of pregnancy, especially if you are tired and nauseated, during the middle three months many women find themselves with a strong sexual drive, and this can be a particularly enjoyable time in a couple's life. Towards the end of pregnancy, especially if you feel very large and cumbersome, feeling sexy may wane, but the benefits of orgasm remain.

Sheila Kitzinger, natural childbirth advocate and prolific writer, has described the build-up, climax and fading of labour contractions as being similar to the process of orgasm. Physiologically they may be comparable, but there the similarity ends for most women. However, she has also stressed that babies should be born into the same environment in which you would be happy to make love: peaceful, intimate, private and surrounded by love. For those women who are able to deliver their babies in this sort of atmosphere, they may feel their contractions to be orgasmic in nature rather than painful or overwhelming.

Orgasm is also thought to provide an element of pain relief, but unless the conditions for labour and delivery are very private indeed, there isn't much chance of testing this out! Orgasm as part of intercourse, complete with penetration and male ejaculation (because of the prostaglandins in semen, and those released by the cervix in response to the thrusting of the penis) can be effective in starting labour off, but *only* if everything else is ready. Only very rarely are couples advised not to make love for fear of starting off a premature labour.

See also **Intercourse**

Osteopathy

Our bodies are made up of a framework of inter-connecting bones, joints, muscles and ligaments, all of which absorb the physical stresses and strains of walking upright, carrying shopping, driving, typing, sitting, etc. – not to mention the emotional tension of anxiety, stress or depression. Very few of us do the range of gentle exercises required to compensate for the rather negative way in which we treat our bodies.

Osteopathy uses both massage and manipulation techniques to restore the balance in the body's framework, in order to alleviate minor discomforts and specific pain. Osteopathy is an extremely well-respected alternative therapy, one that is constantly being recommended by doctors, because of its safety and effective results, and the thorough training which practitioners undergo.

During pregnancy, all the stresses and strains on the body outlined above are exaggerated by the growing size and weight of the abdomen. Women tend to compensate for this additional weight at the front by leaning slightly backwards. This additional and increasing weight, poor posture, and softening of the ligaments places the lower back at risk, and in fact many pregnant women are quite badly troubled by lower back pain. After delivery the demands of labour followed by the release from the weight of your pregnancy, plus the continued effect of progesterone and relaxin on your ligaments, mean that your body's framework remains out of alignment for a while.

It is perfectly possible through continuing exercise and being mindful of your posture to avoid any back trouble during pregnancy. However, if you should have any physical problems, the holistic approach of osteopathy makes it a particularly useful therapy for both minor ailments and more serious problems.

Osteopathy is not just beneficial for back pain; it can be useful for a number of problems where manipulation or massage can have a knock-on effect elsewhere, for example oedema or headaches.

Osteopaths with additional training in cranio-sacral work with the very subtle fluctuations in cerebro-spinal fluid and the bones of the head. Their extremely gentle work is beneficial both to a pregnant woman and also to her newborn baby. Many cranial osteopaths specialize in work with children and newborns, and can have a positive effect on many symptoms seen in babies following a difficult birth – such as jumpiness, excessive crying, colic, sleeplessness, feeding problems, etc. It is well worth consulting a cranial osteopath if any of these apply.

The main techniques of the osteopath, following a thorough examination and assessment of movements in an individual's 'normal' range, are dependent on the diagnosis and include the following. Obviously, appropriate adaptation has to be made when treating a woman at different stages of her pregnancy.

MASSAGE
Soft tissue techniques to relax the muscles surrounding an area of pain, injury or sensitivity.

FRICTION
Steady pressure applied to improve the blood circulation in that specific area.

ARTICULATORY TECHNIQUES
Moving a supported limb through a range of repeated movements while applying steady but gentle pressure, to stretch muscles and ligaments.

HIGH-VELOCITY THRUSTS
A classic osteopathic technique that accounts for the associated 'cracking' noise of a particular back joint being put through a specific range of movement, while all the other joints are supported and remain unaffected.

You will need to find a fully trained and qualified practitioner, either through recommendation – ask your midwife or doctor if they know of anyone – or by contacting the General Council and Register of Osteopaths (*see Useful Addresses*) for a list of registered osteopaths in your area.

Compare **Cranial Osteopathy**, **Chiropractic**
See also **Headaches**, **Oedema**

Overdue

If the average pregnancy lasts 40 weeks, you can be said to be overdue if you exceed this. However, because this 40 weeks is based on an average menstrual cycle of 28 days, the length of your particular average cycle will have to be taken into account when calculating whether or not you are actually overdue.

It is usual for a woman to go to 42 weeks before inducing labour, after which time the placenta may begin to work less efficiently, thus potentially putting the baby at risk. With the use of ultrasound estimated delivery dates are now generally much more reliable. Babies should only ever be induced when it is necessary for their safety.

You can try to induce labour naturally in a number of ways:

- *making love: semen contains small amounts of prostaglandins, which help to 'soften' the cervix;*
- *nipple stimulation can release the hormone prolactin, which also softens the cervix (although stimulation has to continue for some time to achieve this effect);*
- *homoeopathy: a qualified homoeopath can recommend which remedy would be best for you;*
- *acupuncture has shown good results, so is worth a try;*
- *reflexology: a skilled practitioner can help;*
- *raspberry leaf tea: you need to start drinking this some time before your due date if it is to be effective in toning the uterus in preparation for labour and the birth.*

Compare **Due Date, Induction, Menstrual Cycle, Ultrasound**

See also **Acupuncture, Homoeopathy, Raspberry Leaf Tea, Reflexology**

Ovulation

This is the point during a woman's menstrual or fertile cycle when the mature egg is released from the ovary. It occurs around 14 days before a period. Depending on the average length of your cycle, this would occur at around day 14 after a period (in a 28-day cycle), at around day 10 (in a 24-day cycle), day 20 (in a 34-day cycle), etc.

See also **Conception, Menstrual Cycle, Natural Family Planning**

Oxytocin

Oxytocin is a hormone secreted by the pituitary gland in the brain. It makes the womb muscles contract strongly during labour, and is sometimes given in its synthetic version (Syntocinon) to induce labour and delivery. Nipple stimulation also stimulates the secretion of oxytocin, which is why it is sometimes recommended as a way to bring on labour or to increase the strength of your contractions during labour.

During the third stage of labour oxytocin is instrumental in the separation of the placenta from the wall of the womb. Putting your newborn baby to your breast and allowing him or her to suck immediately after birth further stimulates the secretion of oxytocin necessary for the placenta to be delivered.

Oxytocin is also secreted in response to nipple stimulation when a baby breastfeeds, and activates the let-down reflex in the breasts, causing the milk to be released from the milk ducts. Allowing your newborn baby to suckle unrestrictedly when you are trying to establish breastfeeding ensures the let-down reflex and your baby receiving adequate milk.

See also **Induction, Let-down Reflex, Third Stage**

Pp

Pain

The experience of pain is entirely individual and can be
influenced by a number of different factors. Under normal
circumstances, pain is an indication that there is something
wrong; the pain of labour, on the other hand, is sometimes
described as 'positive' pain – that is, pain that is
accomplishing something positive: the birth of your baby.
However, for the majority of women labour pain is pain,
pure and simple. And it is worth thinking about how you
are going to deal with this, before the event.

The pain experienced by women in labour occurs
because of the increasing strength of the contractions of the
womb, and the dilatation of the cervix, in the first stage.
During the second stage, the delivery of the baby, pain is
felt because of the stretching of the vagina and the pressure
on the pelvic floor muscles.

Our experience of pain may be increased by fear and
anxiety, which is one reason why it is useful to understand
the process of labour fully and, having discussed it with
your midwife, what pain relief might be useful at what

stage. You may not need any at all, many women don't, but if you do, you will be able to relax in the knowledge that it is available.

Pain is also affected by expectations, which may be influenced by social and cultural factors. If your mother experienced little pain in childbirth it is likely that your expectation will be that it will be a manageable experience for you. Perhaps the most significant factors that will influence how you cope with labour are whether you have enjoyed a happy and healthy pregnancy, and how tired you are by the time you get to this stage. Fatigue exaggerates tension, fear, and consequently pain. Make sure you have adequate rest before your delivery date. Like any physically demanding event, feeling fit and strong beforehand helps a lot.

See also **Pain Relief**

Pain Relief

The majority of women in the UK give birth in hospital where pain relief medications are readily available in a number of different forms. However, there may be other steps you will want to take in order to prepare yourself for whatever pain may arise. If this is your first baby, you may want to keep things very flexible, working with your midwife and taking each stage as it comes. If this is a second or subsequent baby what you may have more of an idea of how you want things to be and what you might need, although you should bear in mind that all labours and deliveries (much like all babies) are different, even for the same mother.

Even if you have been practising your relaxation and breathing exercises and expect to manage any pain through psychoprophylaxis, you should also consider moving around and changing your position during labour. This can help enormously in helping to keep the contractions going, the cervix dilating, and the baby's head descending smoothly. Again, your midwife should help in making recommendations about helpful positions to try during labour and delivery.

Conventional forms of pain relief during labour and delivery include:

- *Entonox, or 'gas and air', which is inhaled as and when needed during contractions;*
- *Pethidine, given as an intra-muscular injection;*
- *Epidural anaesthetic, given via a tiny tube in the spine.*

Alternative approaches to pain relief include:

- *TENS (Transcutaneous electronic nerve stimulation), which works by applying a mild electrical current to the skin of the back, which has the effect of 'damping down' the pain of contractions;*
- *Acupuncture, which stimulates the body's own pain-control resources;*
- *Hypnosis, which can work extremely well for some women but which requires practice and skilled help;*
- *Massage and aromatherapy: can be usefully administered by husband, partner, friend or midwife during labour and delivery;*
- *Homoeopathy: requires having the appropriate remedies to hand, following consultation with a qualified practitioner.*

Also bear in mind that your body's own response to pain is to produce endorphins, chemical that provide pain relief.

Because the alternative approach is holistic, greater emphasis is placed on your emotional reaction to your labour than on your physical reaction. Prior consultation with practitioners of each therapy is essential, and it may prove necessary to have your practitioner with you during your labour, as in the case of acupuncture or hypnosis. Many midwives now use alternative therapies. You may just strike it lucky and find that your midwife is also a qualified acupuncturist, so it's well worth asking around and finding out what local midwifery practices can offer.

Compare **Active Birth**, **Breathing Exercises**, **Entonox**, **Epidural**, **Pethidine**, **TENS**

See also **Aromatherapy**, **Acupuncture**, **Homoeopathy**, **Hypnotherapy**, **Massage**, **Position**, **Psychoprophylaxis**

Passive Immunity

Because of the exchange of blood between mother and baby while the baby is still in the womb, antibodies from the mother are present and effective in her baby's body for the first few months of life. So a baby is born well protected from a wide number of infectious diseases, although only for a while. Some passive immunity is also provided by a mother's milk, and in particular the colostrum produced before her milk 'comes in'. Breastfeeding does an enormous amount to provide your baby with protection against infectious disease, allergies and gastro-intestinal infections.

However, there are some infectious diseases where the mother's antibodies don't cross the placenta for the benefit of her baby, one of which is whooping cough. Babies are born with no passive immunity to this disease, which can be very distressing to both your baby and you.

See also **Antibodies**, **Colostrum**, **Immune System**, **Immunization**

Paternity Leave

Although not yet a legal entitlement, the more fathers who ask for it the more likely that attitudes will – eventually – change. But every father should have the right to spend time with his newborn baby and its mother, without taking holiday time or time off sick. So ask for it.

See also **Families, Fathers**

Pelvic Floor Exercises

The pelvic floor is primarily a number of layers of muscle fibres which create a supportive base for the pelvic organs – the bladder, vagina and rectum and, during pregnancy, the enlarging womb. Because the pelvic floor is muscular it has the ability to expand and contract, and during pregnancy

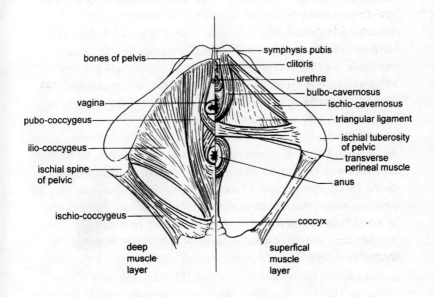

Deep and superficial muscles of the pelvic floor

works hard to contain the pelvic organs. However, the combined impact of pregnancy, labour and delivery needs to be counteracted, and the pelvic floor muscles, like any others, need exercising to get back into shape.

Pelvic floor exercises are important for every woman, and should be done regularly throughout life. After childbirth they are especially important and may prevent the problems of stress incontinence and vaginal prolapse later in life. If you do no other exercise, make sure you do these! Stress incontinence is a very common problem for many women but, *in the majority of cases*, can be effectively treated by pelvic floor exercises. If you have problems with stress incontinence, practise these exercises 10 times in succession, at least six times a day every day for a month – you will be pleasantly surprised at your rapid improvement.

Exercising your pelvic floor muscles should begin in pregnancy, if not before; once you are familiar with pelvic floor exercising it will be easier to get going again after your baby is born. Immediately after delivery you will find it difficult if not impossible to contract your pelvic floor muscles, but keep trying. There is an additional benefit during these early days in that your efforts also stimulate the blood flow to this area, which will help heal up any cut or tear you may have had.

First, find the pelvic floor muscles: one way to recognize them is to try and consciously stop peeing in mid-flow. The muscles you use to do this are your pelvic floor muscles. Once you know what contracting these feels like, you can do it whenever you like. Deliberately contract and hold for as long as you can manage at first, and then to a count of 10. When you get really good at this, you will be able to do it without holding your breath! If you can get into a regular habit of exercising these muscles it will really pay off. Keeping them strong also can improve your sexual pleasure!

See also **Incontinence, Prolapse, Stitches**

Perineum

This is the medical term for the area of the body between the pubic bone and the coccyx, which takes in the urethra, vagina and anus. An episiotomy is the cut made in the perineal body, sometimes referred to as the perineum, in order to increase the vaginal opening and allow easier passage of the baby's head. If you are not given an episiotomy the force of delivering the baby may make the perineum tear, requiring stitches.

Massaging the perineum area daily with wheatgerm or almond oil during the last three months of pregnancy is a good way to increase its suppleness in preparation for labour and the birth.

See also **Episiotomy**, **Stitches**

Pertussis

See **Whooping Cough**

Pessary

Pessaries can take the form of tablets inserted into the vagina, where they dissolve to provide some kind of medicinal effect – for example, antifungal pessaries for thrush. Progesterone pessaries are sometimes used to 'soften' the cervix and bring on labour.

Pethidine

Pethidine is commonly used in labour to relieve the pain of contractions, particularly towards the end of the first stage when the cervix is dilating. It is given as an intra-muscular injection and works well for some women, though less so for others who find it makes them drowsy and detached without providing adequate pain relief. Some women complain of nausea, or may actually vomit following administration of pethidine; the addition of another, anti-nausea drug helps to avert this. The addition of a tranquillizer can also help to relax the woman in labour and to increase the effect of the pain relief.

Pethidine crosses the placenta, and so can affect the baby. The main effect is depression of the respiratory centre, which may mean the baby is slow to breathe spontaneously after delivery. Other neuro-behavioural studies show other, subtle effects: babies are slightly less alert and suck less efficiently. This can last for around 48 hours, but can be reduced considerably if pethidine is not given less than two to four hours before delivery, allowing the maternal system to 'detox'. This is why it may not be given if a woman is too close to delivery, in which case alternative forms of analgesia may be offered. If it is given and delivery follows soon after, an antidote can be given to the baby – naxolone – which reverses any respiratory depression.

As with any pain-relief option, talk this through with your midwife before the birth, and, if at all possible, during labour.

Compare **Entonox**, **Epidural**
See also **Pain Relief**

Phenylketonuria

Every newborn baby is tested for phenylketonuria, or PKU, when he or she has the Guthrie test within the first 10 days of life. If the test result is positive it means that the baby is unable to break down the chemical phenylalanine, which occurs naturally in our diets; the poisonous effect of this chemical can in this case have severe consequences for an otherwise normal baby. The incidence is about 1 in 10,000

and, if diagnosed early enough and a special diet is
followed, there are no ill-effects. Later on it is possible
for a child to graduate to a normal diet.

The only occasion when it is essential to follow a strict
diet again is if a PKU-sensitive woman is pregnant, when
high levels of phenylalanine would have a negative effect on
her developing baby. If possible, this special diet should be
introduced pre-conceptually.

See also **Guthrie Test**

Pica

Pica is the term used to describe the cravings for odd and
unnatural substances, for example coal or chalk, which
pregnant women occasionally experience. No one really
understands why this happens, and it is only a problem if
the substance craved is potentially harmful to the mother
and/or her unborn child. It should be mentioned to your
midwife or doctor, just to ensure that it isn't an indication
of anything serious.

Piles

See **Haemorrhoids**

Placenta

The placenta is fully formed by the 12th week of pregnancy,
and is literally the baby's lifeline. It is about 17.5 to 20 cm
(7–8 inches) in diameter and about 2.5 cm (1 inch) thick, and
weighs approximately one sixth of the baby's birthweight.

Its function is to transmit oxygen and nutrients from
the mother's blood to the baby via the umbiblical cord,
and to remove carbon dioxide and waste matter. It provides
a barrier to many infections, although not to viruses.

Antibodies cross from mother to baby, providing the baby with passive immunity for around the first three months after the birth. The placenta also produces the hormones progesterone and oestrogen throughout the pregnancy.

The placenta is delivered during the third stage of labour, as the contractions of the womb continue. It is important that the placenta is fully and completely delivered; your midwife will check this carefully. In many cases Syntometrine is given at the end of the second stage to help reduce the risk of excessive bleeding.

See also **Afterbirth**, **Passive Immunity**, **Syntometrine**, **Third Stage**, **Umbilical Cord**

Placenta Praevia

Sometimes the position of the placenta is close to the exit of the womb, or obstructing it. If it is too close there is a problem during labour and delivery because the dilation of the cervix damages the placenta and causes excessive bleeding. If the exit of the womb is completely obstructed, it becomes impossible to deliver the baby safely vaginally; in these circumstances a caesarean section will be performed.

Placenta praevia is classified into four types:

Type 1: *vaginal delivery is still possible and safe;*

Type 2: *vaginal delivery* may *be possible, depending on the exact location of the placenta;*

Type 3: *because the placenta precedes the baby, and bleeding is likely to be severe, vaginal delivery isn't possible;*

Type 4: *because the placenta is located over the exit to the womb, vaginal delivery is impossible and a caesarean section is needed in order to protect the lives of both mother and baby.*

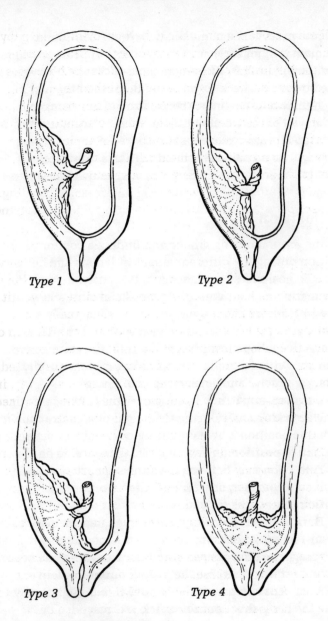

Type 1

Type 2

Type 3

Type 4

The four types of placenta praevia

225 ❈ Placenta Praevia

Placenta praevia is usually diagnosed via ultrasound scanning. If at an early scan the placenta appears to be low down, it will probably be recommended that another scan is done later on to check its position. Because of the way in which the womb expands, the placenta often seems to move up the wall of the womb. Without having a scan, the first sign of placenta praevia may be some degree of vaginal bleeding. There will be no pain associated with this. Any bleeding should be reported immediately to your midwife or doctor.

Position

Moving around during labour and finding a comfortable position during the different stages of labour and delivery are to be positively recommended. Primarily, if you follow your instincts about what feels beneficial, and take your midwife's advice about what position will actively help your progress, you will be working with your body and towards an effective labour resulting in a straightforward delivery. What you will also find yourself doing, quite naturally, is assisting gravity and conserving your energy.

Kneeling, squatting, leaning over the back of a chair or using a rocking chair during the height of a contraction may help. One position may help during one contraction, an alternative position during another: there are no hard-and-fast rules. You may find you need the support of your husband or partner, or your midwife, in order to get into a position that works for you.

During actual delivery most women find themselves in a semi-reclining position, although it is possible to deliver squatting, kneeling or even standing. Squatting has been demonstrated to increase the overall outlet for delivery by 28 per cent compared to lying down, although it may make the baby shoot out too quickly. It may also be, however, that at the end of a demanding labour your legs feel quite shaky and you need to be in a semi-sitting position in order to feel strong enough to bear down.

It is most unlikely that you will be expected to deliver actually lying down; it is generally accepted that this isn't helpful, as the main blood vessels of the mother's body are under the full weight of the abdomen, and may make her feel faint.

Postnatal Depression

See **Depression**

Posture

Your posture is an important factor in avoiding some of the minor aches and pains associated with advancing pregnancy. The combination of extra weight focused at the front of your body, plus the 'softening' effects of the hormone progesterone on your supporting ligaments, puts your back in particular at risk.

When standing and sitting, check that your posture is good: tummy tucked in, pelvis tilted forward, shoulders down and relaxed with your upper back straight. When sitting, place a small cushion or rolled-up towel in the small of your back to support the curved space rather than letting it sag.

One particularly good antenatal exercise is pelvic tilting, which helps keep the abdominal muscles toned and the back strong. This exercise can be done lying down, sitting or standing, but practise it lying down first so that you can judge how well you are doing it:

- *Lie on your back with your knees bent and feet flat on the floor;*

- *Place a small cushion under your head so that your neck is comfortable and you feel relaxed;*
- *Tighten the muscles of your tummy and bottom, pressing the small of your back into the floor;*
- *Hold for a count of five while breathing normally;*
- *Repeat five times and relax.*

While you are exercising antenatally it is a good idea to include pelvic floor exercises in your routine.

The Alexander Technique was designed to correct bad postural habits, and can be extremely useful during pregnancy. A qualified Alexander Technique teacher is essential for this and can be consulted either in order to avoid problems or once you are already experiencing backache and headaches which you feel may be linked to poor posture.

If you are participating in an antenatal yoga class, or have been practising yoga before becoming pregnant, you will find numerous yoga positions helpful for alleviating postural strain. Your yoga teacher should be familiar with the special needs of pregnancy; if not, he or she may be able to recommend someone with greater expertise in this area.

See also **Alexander Technique, Backache, Pelvic Floor Exercises, Yoga**

Pre-conceptual Care

There is a lot of relevant evidence to suggest that if both mother and father are in good health, then the chances of a positive outcome from conception and pregnancy – a healthy baby – are improved. Certainly the quality of a father's sperm can be adversely affected by excessive smoking and drinking, for example, and a mother's ability to conceive may be affected if she is either excessively over- or underweight.

If a pregnancy is planned, this allows time to consider any nutritional deficiencies and come off the contraceptive pill, etc. Folic acid supplements are recommended both before conception and during the first few months of pregnancy, for example.

However, very few pregnancies are planned with such well-thought out precision and, generally speaking, a baby will get what he or she needs even if it is to the detriment of the mother's health. There is no doubt that the first three months after conception, when development of all the major organs and body systems occur, is a crucial time, *but* the baby's survival tactic is to take, unconditionally, from its mother. It is usually only when there is trouble with conception and the baby's development, either through infertility, miscarriage or congenital abnormalities, that emphasis becomes specifically focused on pre-conceptual care. There is an association for pre-conceptual care, Foresight, which may be worth contacting if you need further information (*see Useful Addresses*).

See also **Folic Acid**, **Antenatal Care**

Pre-eclampsia

Pre-eclampsia is also known as pregnancy-induced hypertension, or PIH. The cause of this increase in blood-pressure during pregnancy is unknown, but it affects between 5 and 20 per cent of pregnant women, being seen most commonly during the last 8 weeks of pregnancy.

The reason you will have your blood-pressure taken and a urine test performed at every antenatal visit is that the three main signs of PIH are:

1   *a rise in blood-pressure so that it is significantly higher than on a previous visit;*
2   *protein showing up in a urine test;*

3   *swelling, not only of the feet and ankles but more*
     generally, and where if gentle finger-tip pressure is
     applied briefly the indentation remains.

If PIH is diagnosed, the treatment is bed rest, which should allow things to settle down and avoid the problems escalating into eclampsia. Bed rest usually means staying in hospital because it is almost impossible for a woman to rest adequately enough at home without full-time support and, to avoid the necessity of a premature delivery, rest is essential. The aim of treatment is to keep the pregnancy going until 38 weeks, closely monitoring both mother and baby, then inducing labour. If eclampsia develops, a caesarean section may be needed immediately.

Although there are many complementary therapies and remedies you can try to help relax and restore yourself, pre-eclampsia needs careful supervision and medical management. No alternative practitioner would recommend that you treat this condition without the full medical support you need to ensure the health of you and your baby. This condition is potentially too serious, and must always benefit from clinical management, although aromatherapy massage, homoeopathic remedies and even shiatsu and acupuncture can all have a place in assisting you through what may be a difficult time prior to the birth of your baby.

The good news is that the signs of PIH disappear within 48 to 72 hours of delivery of the baby, and cause no further complications.

See also **Eclampsia**

Pregnancy Testing

The quickest, most efficient way of confirming whether or not you are pregnant is to buy and use a home pregnancy test. These tests are as good as anything your doctor, pharmacy or local hospital can provide – the tests they use work in exactly the same way – and the results are immediate. Modern tests, as long as they are within the 'use by' date, are reliable and can be used as soon as you have missed your period.

Your doctor is unlikely to provide a free urine pregnancy test, and is more likely to ask you to return when you have missed two periods and your pregnancy can be confirmed with an internal examination.

Premature Birth

Officially this is a birth that occurs before the 37th week of pregnancy; it is usually referred to as pre-term. Term (or full-term) is considered to be between 38 and 42 weeks.

Presentation

Presentation describes which part of the baby is facing the womb's 'exit' (the cervix) prior to or at the beginning of labour. Usually the baby is head-down (or cephalic), with the top of the head (or vertex) presenting and the chin well tucked into the chest. This is the optimum position for delivery, as the narrowest dimension of the head is coming first and the baby's face is protected as it comes out.

This normal presentation can also be described in one of six ways, giving an indication of where the back of the baby's head is during his or her descent down the birth canal (you may see these terms on your antenatal chart): LOA/left occipito-anterior (15 per cent of babies are born in this position), ROA/right occipito-anterior (10 per cent), LOL/left occipito-lateral (40 per cent), ROL/right occipito-lateral (24 per cent), LOP/left occipito-posterior (3 per cent) or ROP/right occipito-posterior (8 per cent).

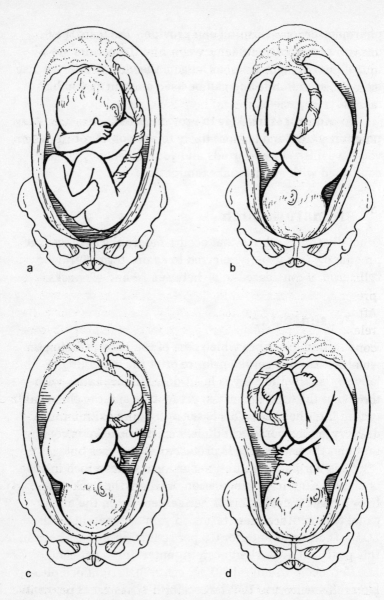

Presentation: a) Breech; b) Left occipito-anterior (LOA); c) Right occipito-anterior (ROA); d) Left occipito-posterior (LOP)

However, sometimes babies present brow or face first, or as a breech or shoulder presentation. These can pose quite serious complications; each presentation is of significance to the midwife delivering, allowing her to assess what type of special help is necessary.

Compare **Anterior Position, Breech Presentation, Brow Presentation, Face Presentation, Occipito-Anterior Position**

Pre-term

See **Premature Birth**

Progesterone

This is perhaps the most important female sex hormone in pregnancy, essential for the continuing life in the womb. After ovulation, progesterone is produced by the ovary that released the egg; then, if the egg is fertilized, progesterone continues to be secreted until the placenta has developed enough to take over its production.

Progesterone also influences the development of the breasts during pregnancy in preparation for producing milk after the birth. It has an impact on ligaments and muscles throughout the body as well, essentially to allow the suppleness and expansion necessary for giving birth.
This also accounts for some of the problems which may be experienced during pregnancy – backache, constipation and low blood-pressure, for example.

See also **Hormones**

Prolactin

After the delivery of the placenta, which has been responsible for the production of a number of key hormones such as oestrogen and progesterone, the levels of these hormones in the body fall rapidly. The sudden drop in oestrogen stimulates the pituitary gland to secrete the hormone prolactin, and this stimulates the production of milk in the breasts. During breastfeeding the levels of prolactin remain high and the activity of the ovaries is suppressed. If you don't breastfeed, it takes between 14 and 21 days for the effects of prolactin to subside, and ovulation to occur again.

See also **Breastfeeding, Natural Family Planning**

Prolapse

If the pelvic floor is weakened by prolonged labour, numerous pregnancies and/or no restorative pelvic floor exercises, the pelvic organs can – over time – begin to descend from their original position. This could affect the womb, bladder or rectum. Prolapse is less common than it used to be, partly because of the reduction in the number of pregnancies most women experience, better management of labour and birth, and more attention given to the importance of pelvic floor exercises before and after birth.

See also **Pelvic Floor Exercises**

Psychoprophylaxis

This is a method of preparation for labour and birth which teaches you to relax during the pain of contractions, thus reducing their impact. Part of this preparation is understanding the process of labour and the part contractions play. By anticipating the pain and learning a series of breathing exercises to use during the ebb and flow of a contraction it is possible to stay very focused and in control of your own response. In this way the experience of the pain is modified.

If psychoprophylaxis is going to be useful during labour, it requires extensive practice beforehand with an experienced teacher. The National Childbirth Trust in the UK, and Lamaze teachers, are your best resources (*see Useful Addresses*).

See also **Lamaze Method, Natural Childbirth**

Ptyalism

This is a rare side-effect of pregnancy which can, for some women, mean an excessive production of saliva. More common is a subtle change in the sense of taste, which many women experience. Some excess salivation is common during the early months of pregnancy if you are also experiencing a degree of nausea and vomiting.

Pudendal Block

The pudendal nerve supplies feeling to the vagina, perineum and vulva. A pudendal block is an injection of local anaesthetic, given prior to some forms of assisted delivery, in order to block feeling in this area.

Compare **Epidural**

Puerperal Psychosis

This refers to psychosis which occurs during the time immediately following childbirth, and which has in fact been triggered by the pregnancy and birth. It is a serious form of postnatal depression and needs sympathetic support and treatment.

Compare **Depression**

Q q

Quickening

This is an old-fashioned but very descriptive term for the first movements of a baby felt by his or her mother. It is a fluttering feeling low down in the abdomen, usually felt between 18 and 20 weeks with a first baby and between 16 and 18 weeks in subsequent pregnancies. You may not recognize the feeling at first, thinking it may be intestinal wind, but it soon becomes apparent that these first faint movements are indeed the reassuring sign that your baby is alive and well.

R r

Raspberry Leaf Tea

Of all the herbal teas, raspberry leaf deserves special mention because of its particular usefulness during pregnancy. Primarily it is recommended to tone the uterus in preparation for labour and birth. It is also recommended as a drink during labour, and for two to three weeks afterwards to encourage the uterine muscles to contract and return to normal. A suggested dosage is between 1 and 3 cups of raspberry leaf tea a day (made with 1 teaspoon of tea infused in boiling water). If you have trouble obtaining raspberry leaf tea, Neal's Yard and other mail-order suppliers can help (*see Useful Addresses*).

It is also recommended during early pregnancy as an aid to morning sickness; as a gargle for a sore throat; for gum disease (its antibacterial properties are beneficial here).

See also **Gingivitis, Morning Sickness**

Reflexology

Reflexology involves massage and manipulation of the feet, based on the premise that different areas of the feet correspond to different areas of the body. Through reflexology massage of the foot it is possible to treat ailments in other areas of the body, and even to detect problem areas or disorders that have occurred in the past, or may arise in the future.

In practice the right foot relates to the right side of the body, and the left foot to the left side. The theory behind reflexology is that reflex points in the foot are linked by energy lines, or meridians, to distant areas of the body. In this idea it is similar to acupuncture.

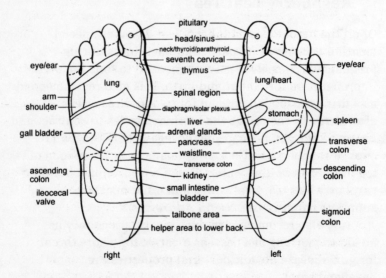

Reflexology points on the feet

Like the majority of alternative therapies, reflexology is holistic in approach. The principle behind treatment is to do with rebalancing the body's energies, unblocking them and restoring smooth channels of communication. To this end it has an important role to play not just in the treatment of disorders, but in promoting positive health, reducing stress and aiding relaxation. Reflexology cannot actually cure illness, but it can stimulate the body's own healing resources and dramatically reduce pain.

Reflexology is very useful for the following:

- *morning sickness;*
- *constipation;*
- *piles;*
- *indigestion and heartburn;*
- *swollen ankles (but not the swelling of pre-eclampsia);*
- *anxiety and insomnia, depression;*
- *pain in labour;*
- *to stimulate contractions – but only during labour;*
- *to stimulate milk production.*

Reflexology has much to offer during pregnancy and afterwards. It does, however, require the benefit of an experienced and skilled practitioner, especially for use during pregnancy. The effects of reflexology can be quite powerful and its use is not advised for a number of disorders including ectopic pregnancy, threatened miscarriage, placenta praevia, infections (especially where there is a fever), and pre-eclampsia.

To find a reflexologist, ask your midwife or doctor if they know of one locally, or contact the Association of Reflexologists (*see Useful Addresses*).

Compare **Acupuncture**, **Shiatsu**

Registering the Birth

In the UK, this has to be done within six weeks of your baby's birth (within three weeks in Scotland). You will need to visit your local registrar of births, marriages and deaths in order to do this, unless the registrar has made a hospital visit. Births have to be registered in the district in which they occur. There is a financial penalty to be paid if a birth isn't registered within the allotted time.

If you are married to your baby's father, you can go alone to register the birth and put the father's name on the birth certificate. If you and your baby's father aren't married, you will either have to go together to register the birth jointly, or the father will need to complete a statutory declaration (available from the Registrar) confirming that he is the father.

The hospital, or your community midwife if it was a home delivery, will have already notified the registrar of your baby's birth (this has to be done within 36 hours of the birth). But it is up to you, the parents, to register the birth and obtain a birth certificate. You will need a birth certificate for your baby in order to obtain an NHS number and register with a GP, apply for Child Benefit, or place your baby on your passport, for example.

A short birth certificate is issued free of charge and states the name and sex of the baby, and the date and place of birth. A full birth certificate, which also states the names, place of birth and occupations of each parent, is available for a small fee.

Relaxation

Many people find relaxing fully very difficult, and find that their rest – and sleep – suffer as a consequence. During pregnancy the muscles of your body are having to adapt to different stresses and strains, and muscle tension can easily result. Identifying muscle tension, then consciously relaxing it, is the first step in overall relaxation. It is a skill worth learning, especially as you get bigger towards the end of your pregnancy. Sleep may be less easy to come by as you become uncomfortable in bed, or need to get up several times in order to pee, but if you can gently doze and relax you will at least be able to rest your body somewhat.

Relaxation exercises should form part of any gentle exercise routine you practise during your pregnancy. Relaxation is also incorporated into the breathing exercises you may be learning in preparation for labour. In order to practise any form of relaxation, make sure you are in a comfortable position with your back well supported. Any relaxation skills you learn now will stand you in good stead during the early, stressful days of parenthood, and in the years to come.

Try the following:

- *Lie or sit comfortably, with your back well-supported, resting your head on a small cushion;*
- *Starting with your facial muscles, consciously screw them tight to a count of five, then relax;*
- *Repeat this with the muscles of your neck and shoulders, remembering to breathe gently in and out as you do so;*
- *Continue down your body through each main group of muscles, until you have consciously relaxed your whole body;*
- *Keep an eye on your breathing – deliberately breathe out slowly, let the in-breath take care of itself.*

You may want to combine relaxation exercises with listening to your favourite music, or while you prepare for a period of meditation. While relaxation exercises feel a little strange at first, you will soon become used to the process and find that this enforced practice becomes easier, and you will relax more quickly as you become more experienced.

During labour, breathing and relaxation exercises can help assist in dealing with the pain of contractions and resting in between.

See also **Breathing Exercises**, **Meditation**, **Posture**, **Psychoprophylaxis**

Relaxin

This is one of the pregnancy hormones, designed to relax the pelvic girdle and soften the cervix, and is at its peak level between weeks 38 and 42 of pregnancy. Although its primary purpose appears to be to assist the body during labour and birth, its general presence during pregnancy also affects the ligaments and muscles of the body, making them potentially more vulnerable to damage.

See also **Hormones**, **Progesterone**

Rhesus Factor

If a mother's blood group is Rhesus negative and a father's blood group is Rhesus positive, the baby's blood group may well be Rhesus positive too. This causes no problem during a first pregnancy, but during birth there will be some exchange between the mother's and the baby's blood as the placenta separates away from the womb during the third stage of labour, causing the mother's blood to produce antibodies to Rhesus positive blood. During a subsequent pregnancy, if the baby is again Rhesus positive, the mother's antibodies will consider the baby's blood a 'foreign body' and attempt to break it down. If this happens, haemolytic jaundice occurs and the baby's haemoglobin levels will be low, perhaps requiring a blood transfusion at birth. However, this is avoided by treatment following a first delivery.

All mothers have their blood group tested in pregnancy and, if they are Rhesus negative, they are closely monitored. At the birth of their first baby they are given an injection of 'Anti D' to prevent their blood from forming antibodies. (Anti D also needs to be given if there has been a miscarriage, bleeding in pregnancy or amniocentesis.) By taking this precaution, subsequent pregnancies will be protected and no haemolytic jaundice should occur. What used to be quite a problem is now, with effective antenatal care, a minor one that is easily treated.

See also **Antibodies**, **Passive Immunity**

Rubella

The current immunization programme for children in the UK includes a triple vaccine at one year for measles, mumps and Rubella. This is part of an attempt to wipe out Rubella, or German measles, because of the damage it can do to unborn babies if their mothers contract the illness during the first three months of pregnancy.

German measles in itself is a minor illness, causing a small rash and general ill-health for a short period. Diagnosis is often missed but the virus can cross the placenta and cause miscarriage, stillbirth, congenital defects affecting the heart, sight or hearing, and mental retardation. The incidence of multiple defects is directly related to the time at which the disease was contracted, with a 50–60 per cent chance if contracted during the first month of pregnancy.

Thankfully, because of the immunization programme and screening of pregnant mothers, congenital defects caused by the Rubella virus are becoming increasingly rare. A blood test, either prior to conception or antenatally, will demonstrate whether the mother has immunity to Rubella. Ask your midwife or doctor if you are concerned.

Sacrum

Your sacrum forms the back wall of your pelvis and consists of five vertebrae fused together, followed by the coccyx. There is no movement between the five fused vertebrae, but some movement during labour at the coccyx, allowing the pelvic outlet to increase by up to 30 per cent.

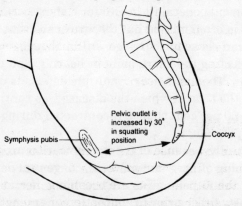

Pelvic outlet is increased by 30° in squatting position

Symphysis pubis

Coccyx

Lying on your back presses the coccyx towards the symphysis pubis, narrowing the pelvic outlet and reducing room for delivery

Saliva

See **Ptyalism**

Salmonella

Salmonella is a bacteria particularly associated with eggs and poultry, which can cause gastro-enteritis. Because your immune system is mildly suppressed by being pregnant you may be more susceptible generally to infections, including salmonella. While there is no effect on your unborn baby, if you do become infected with salmonella it can make you very sick with diarrhoea and vomiting, so it's best avoided.

Avoid raw and partially cooked eggs. While shop-bought mayonnaise is fine because the eggs used in it have been pasteurized, home-made mayonnaise is risky unless made with pasteurized egg products. Make sure that any poultry you use is stored on the bottom shelf of your fridge (where no juices can drop onto other foods), the temperature properly regulated. Take particular care when the weather is hot and fridges become overcrowded. Don't let raw poultry contaminate other foods or cooking surfaces, and cook thoroughly to ensure that any bacteria present are destroyed. Always wash your hands carefully before and after preparing poultry.

See also **Immune System**

Screening

There are a number of routine screening tests that are offered during pregnancy and which form part of general antenatal care. For example, routine blood tests include screening for low haemoglobin levels, because anaemia in pregnancy is best corrected with iron supplements before it causes a problem.

It is possible to screen for a wide number of problems and congenital abnormalities, but in some instances the risk of the screening process, for example the risk of miscarriage associated with amniocentesis, may be greater than the risk of your baby having a problem.

Whenever any screening over and above routine tests is offered, you will need to consider carefully what the tests involve and what the implications of diagnosis are. This needs to be discussed with your midwife and doctor beforehand. There may be, for example, an assumption made that you want to proceed with screening for Down's Syndrome because you would choose to have a termination if your baby was affected, when this is not in fact the case.

Antenatal screening includes the routine offer of ultrasound scanning, AFP blood test, and the Triple test (also a blood test). While there are merits to all forms of testing, you need to be sure that these merits exist for you; if for any reason you don't wish to have these tests, you are at liberty to refuse them.

See also **Alpha Fetoprotein (AFP) Test**, **Amniocentesis**, **Antenatal Testing**, **Triple Test**, **Ultrasound**

Second Stage of Labour

See **Labour**

Shared Care

This is the term for antenatal care that is split between your hospital and your community health centre, even though your baby is due to be born in hospital. You may see your midwife and obstetrically trained GP for most of your care, with a couple of key hospital visits.

Shiatsu

Shiatsu is a Japanese word meaning 'finger pressure'.
In much the same way that reflexology and acupuncture
work to free the flow of energy along energy channels (or
meridians) in the body, shiatsu uses finger-tip pressure
at key points on the body to either stimulate the flow of
energy or sedate it, in order to produce a beneficial effect.
Because shiatsu, like other alternative therapies, is holistic
in approach, a shiatsu therapist takes a full case history
and bases any diagnosis on both your physical and
emotional state.

Shiatsu is especially beneficial during pregnancy
because not only can it alleviate many symptoms and minor
problems, it also promotes positive health, enabling you to
avoid some ailments and deal better with others. In the
hands of a qualified practitioner, shiatsu is perfectly safe
for use during pregnancy. Shiatsu can help enormously
with the following complaints:

* *morning sickness;*
* *indigestion and heartburn;*
* *Carpal tunnel syndrome;*
* *muscular cramps;*
* *piles;*
* *swollen legs and ankles;*
* *backache;*
* *insomnia;*
* *headaches;*
* *breathlessness;*
* *tiredness.*

In addition, shiatsu can be of value during labour because it
can help induce and accelerate labour, increase the strength
of weak contractions, and also provide a degree of pain

relief in both the first and second stage of labour. Ideally your shiatsu therapist would be available to stay with you during labour and delivery. Alternatively he or she could advise your husband, partner or friend about which pressure points should be stimulated during this time.

Postnatally shiatsu is useful for improving the production of breastmilk, renewing depleted energy levels and counteracting chronic tiredness, and helping to alleviate postnatal depression. Shiatsu can also help your newborn baby, particularly with colic and sleeplessness.

Finding a well-qualified and experienced shiatsu practitioner is possible through The Shiatsu Society in the UK (*see Useful Addresses*), or you could ask your midwife or doctor to recommend someone locally.

Compare **Acupressure**, **Acupuncture**, **Reflexology**

Shirodkar Stitch

This is a stitch used to keep the cervix closed during pregnancy in cases of cervical incompetence.

See also **Cervical Incompetence**

Show

This is a description of the mucus discharge that appears from the vagina at the beginning of labour. It is usually slightly blood-stained and may even look pink in colour, and can appear as quite a large clot of mucus. This 'cervical plug' is also known as the operculum, and it is designed to form a barrier at the cervix between the womb and the vagina. The show may occur at any time during the first stage of labour (or even a day or two before labour begins), or may not be noticed at all, especially if it coincides with the waters breaking.

Signs and Symptoms of Pregnancy

Many women say that they 'knew' they were pregnant before they missed a period, but for most women a missed period is often the first sign. In addition there may be other symptoms, such as:

- *swollen, tender breasts;*
- *feelings of nausea and/or vomiting;*
- *changed sense of smell and/or taste;*
- *overwhelming fatigue;*
- *an increased need to pass water;*
- *darkening of the nipples and areola.*

For some women, any change is unspecific but very definite. Every woman is different, though if you have been pregnant before you are likely to follow the same pattern of early signs.

Skin

During pregnancy, increased activity of the melanin-stimulating hormone causes an increase in skin pigmentation. Your skin will probably tan more easily, but you may also be susceptible to uneven patches of pigmentation, especially on the face. This is sometimes referred to as chloasma and, although it does fade, you may be left with quite distinct patches of pigmentation on your face. Avoid full sunlight during pregnancy to protect against this, and use a moisturizer with sun protection factor in it, and apply sun cream with a high sun protection factor (10 or more) when you are actually out in the sunshine.

You will also notice, particularly if this is your first pregnancy, that your nipples darken quite dramatically. This is in preparation for breastfeeding, and they won't ever quite return to their original colour again. You will probably develop a brown line, the linea nigra, running from your navel to your pubic area, but that will eventually fade after birth.

Some women suffer badly from skin irritations and itching during pregnancy, or find that the skin on their body and especially on their enlarging abdomen becomes quite dry and flaky. Use lots of body lotion to keep your skin supple.

There are a number of homoeopathic remedies that may help with skin complaints during pregnancy. You can try *Calcarea sulphurica* or *Silica* if you have an outbreak of spots; *Sulphur* for itchy, dry skin; and *Sepia* for patchy areas of pigmentation on the face. As with any alternative therapy, you will benefit most from assessment, diagnosis and treatment from a qualified practitioner (*see Useful Addresses*).

You may also find that you feel much hotter when you are pregnant, and sweat much more. This is the combined effect of the pregnancy hormone progesterone plus increased blood volume and increased dilation of the blood vessels. Wear loose, cotton clothing in layers that can be removed if you feel too hot.

See also **Homoeopathy**, **Itching**

Sleep

Some people say that the inability to get a good night's sleep before your baby is born serves a purpose in preparing you for all those sleepless nights you can anticipate afterwards! However, whatever the cause, there is actually quite a lot you can do to improve your sleep.

If at all possible, identify what it is that is creating your sleeplessness. If you are anxious and worried about the impending birth and how you are going to manage, talk it through with your midwife, husband, partner or friends. Try to address what problems you can; as for those you can't, find some way to put them out of your mind. On occasions like this, meditation can be useful.

If you are physically uncomfortable in bed, you may find it easier to sleep in a semi-sitting position or propped up on pillows. If you are troubled by heartburn and find it keeps you awake at night, there are a number of alternative therapies you can try: homoeopathy, shiatsu, reflexology. The same applies for a number of minor, physical complaints which somehow seem much worse at 3 a.m.

If you have been suffering from backache, consult an osteopath. Shiatsu can also be beneficial, as can hypnotherapy.

You may find as your pregnancy progresses that you are doing very little in the way of physical activity. Some form of daily, gentle exercise – walking, stretching, swimming, yoga – will actually boost your energy levels *and* help you sleep better at night. Fresh air and exercise will serve both you and your baby well. Practise your breathing exercises, posture and relaxation as part of any exercise routine, however short.

If insomnia is becoming a real problem even though you have identified and tried to remedy any specific causes, you may have to devise an insomnia-beating regime:

- *Allow yourself enough time to 'wind down' at the end of the day;*
- *Avoid drinking coffee at all (and any other caffeine-fueled drinks, such as colas);*
- *Take a warm bath before bed, adding essential oil of* Camomile *to the water, or* Lavender *if you are in the last three months of pregnancy;*
- *If there is someone who can give you a body massage, use* Camomile *oil or* Marjoram, *or a blend of the two;*

- *Drink a cup of camomile or valerian tea;*
- *Use a hop- or herb-filled pillow to sleep on;*
- *Use a selection of pillows to support your back, legs and tummy in order to get comfortable in bed;*
- *If you still find sleep elusive, try not to get panicky about it but use the time to rest, relax and perhaps practise some meditation skills.*

During the first few weeks after your baby is born, you will have to rest and recuperate, especially if the birth was difficult, if you needed a caesarean, or if you are trying to get breastfeeding well established. Try not to get overtired or overwrought. Make sure you have some time during the day to rest. Housework and other chores can wait; when the baby naps (however briefly), have a lie-down yourself. Visitors should take second place to the needs of you and your family, so restrict their visits if necessary or excuse yourself in order to take a break. Visitors should be told they will be even more welcome if they bring a meal with them (this isn't the time to be entertaining masses of people)!

As soon as your baby becomes more settled and breastfeeding begins to show some sort of emerging pattern, he or she will probably follow some sort of sleeping routine, perhaps even for as long as four hours at a time. This may not occur at the optimum time for you, but as soon as it starts to happen take heart: you now have a core sleep pattern you can build on, so encourage it. After a bit you may be able to delay its start or extend it marginally. You should also try to let your baby go to sleep occasionally without being held or fed. One of the greatest gifts you can give your baby is the ability to go to sleep on his or her own, but this can't be gently learned if you always wait until your baby has passed out on the breast before you put him or her into bed. Even if you choose to have your baby in bed with you initially at night for night feeding, allowing day-time sleeps to follow some sort of routine in a cot or pram will begin to introduce the possibility of independent sleep. This may not seem a priority immediately, but you are trying to develop habits now that will pay dividends later, without having to make dramatic separations in a year's time when you are desperate for an unbroken patch of sleep.

If your delivery was long or difficult and your baby seems very jittery or colicky, then it is well worth consulting a cranial osteopath with experience in treating newborns and children. The change in a baby's behaviour can be quite dramatic when successfully treated. Shiatsu, homoeopathy and also reflexology also have their place in treating unsettled babies, so consider these options sooner rather than later if you think they might help your baby. Everyone feels happier and more able to cope with life when they have had enough sleep, and this includes your baby.

Compare **Breathing Exercises**, **Cranial Osteopathy**, **Homoeopathy**, **Hypnotherapy**, **Meditation**, **Osteopathy**, **Posture**, **Reflexology**, **Relaxation**, **Shiatsu**, **Yoga**

See also **Heartburn**, **Insomnia**

Smoking

If you smoke when you are pregnant you are forcing your unborn baby to tolerate a reduced oxygen and food supply, which will affect his or her growth in the womb. If babies and children live in a smoky atmosphere they are more likely to have coughs, colds and ear infections, and eventually to smoke themselves – they will, in fact, already be passive smokers, thereby running the risk of various lung diseases such as asthma and even cancer.

These are the facts, and if you do smoke you will already know that you shouldn't, not just for your baby's sake but also for your own. Give up as soon as you can, using all the help you can lay your hands on. Your health centre may run a quit-smoking clinic which is worth attending, and may help you work out why you smoke and what your individual 'triggers' are in wanting a cigarette, as well as supporting you in your efforts to stop. A number of alternative therapies have also proved successful in helping smokers kick the habit, including acupuncture, hypnotherapy, shiatsu massage and reflexology. Relaxation and breathing exercises may help you through periods when you feel desperate for a cigarette. If motivation and willpower have been lacking in the past, it may be that your pregnancy itself provides you with the impetus to succeed this time. It is certainly worth a try. Contact the organization Quit (*see Useful Addresses*) for further help, advice and support.

See also **Acupuncture**, **Breathing Exercises**, **Hypnotherapy**, **Reflexology**, **Relaxation**, **Shiatsu**

Special Care Baby Unit (SCBU)

Many maternity units have a special care baby unit, or a number of special care beds available. These are designed for pre-term or low birthweight babies, or babies born with some sort of physical disorder. The unit provides expert nursing and medical care, plus the sort of equipment needed to monitor life, essential for very sick babies. Your baby will be cared for in a see-through incubator where the environment can be kept at an even temperature and the nurses can see your baby at all times without disturbing him or her.

Most babies in special care are normal, healthy babies who just need to stay in an environment that more closely resembles the womb until some of their body systems mature, notably their ability to breathe independently. You will be able to touch your baby, and although he or she may be too little and weak to breastfeed, you will be able to express your milk to nourish your baby and establish a supply in readiness for feeding your baby yourself in due course.

If, during your antenatal care it becomes apparent that your baby may be at some sort of risk or may need special care at birth, it will probably be arranged for you to be booked into a maternity unit that has this facility, because not everywhere has. If your baby is born unexpectedly early, or with specific difficulties at birth, he or she may need to be transferred to another hospital which can look after him or her best. You would, of course, expect to go to the same hospital with your baby, and even if you are able to go home but your baby isn't you will be able to stay with your baby and start building that lifelong relationship in spite of the fact that he or she needs extra-special care at the moment.

Spina Bifida

Spina Bifida is a defect in the development of the spinal cord during the first 12 weeks. The AFP test screens for Spina Bifida risk, which can be checked by ultrasound scanning. Spina Bifida is relatively rare, with only around 400 babies a year born in the UK with severe disability. There is some variation in the degree to which babies are affected. In some it is very slight, resulting only in mild paralysis.

You can reduce your risk of Spina Bifida by ensuring that your diet before pregnancy and during the first three months is balanced and contains a good supply of folic acid.

If you want to know more about Spina Bifida, contact the Association for Spina Bifida and Hydrocephalus (*see Useful Addresses*).

See also **Alpha Fetoprotein (AFP) Test, Diet, Folic Acid**

Stillbirth

To lose a baby at birth, or to deliver a baby who has already died, is a devastating experience for any parent. A stillborn baby is one born after 24 weeks of pregnancy, prior to which time the loss is considered a miscarriage.

A stillborn baby's birth has to be notified and registered as a stillbirth, and will require a certificate of stillbirth issued by the doctor. The baby will need to be buried or cremated and, while parents can arrange this, the hospital can also do it on their behalf. Unlike the case with other instances of a death in the family, if you are receiving benefit you cannot be given a death grant for a stillbirth.

If the reason for the stillbirth was known, this information can sometimes be helpful in the grieving process necessary for parents to come to terms with their baby's death. Sometimes, however, no apparent cause is ever found. The Stillbirth and Neonatal Death Society (SANDS) may be a useful resource for further information and support (*see Useful Addresses*).

Stitches

If you had a vaginal tear or episiotomy during the birth of your baby, this will have been repaired with stitches. It is usual for the stitches to dissolve and drop out over a 7- to 10-day period, so don't be surprised to find a short length of thread in the bath. Often the perineal area and the stitches feel very sore for the first few days, so you will need to sit down gently on something soft – using a rubber ring is helpful as it keeps the pressure off the stitched area. It isn't actually the stitches that hurt, but the reason they were needed – the torn or cut area around the vaginal opening. As long as there is no infection during the healing process, the soreness should subside within 5 days or so.

Keep the area clean and dry, soaking in a warm bath once a day. Use a hair-dryer (on its lowest setting) to dry the area rather than rubbing it dry with a towel, although be careful the skin doesn't become too dry. If peeing makes you sore, try running clean, warm water over the perineal area while sitting on the lavatory. Adding a little *Camomile* or *Lavender* oil to the warm water may be soothing and is mildly antiseptic. If the swelling is very painful initially, try holding an ice pack or small packet of frozen peas wrapped in a clean cloth over the area (the packet of peas can be refrozen several times for this use, but *don't* expect to be able to eat them later on!).

Don't avoid a bowel movement if you need to have one, as this might lead to constipation later on. Press a pad of clean lavatory paper over your stitches while you open your bowels, to reduce the strain. Wash your perineal area afterwards by running clean, warm water over it as described above, after gently wiping your bottom from front to back.

See also **Pelvic Floor Exercises**

Stretch Marks

Some women get stretch marks and others don't, and there is not much you can do about them if you are going to get them. The stretch occurs in the collagen level of the skin, and is thought to be linked in some way to the production of cortico-steroids during pregnancy. Whether you get them or not is largely a matter of heredity.

Stretch marks can appear on the abdomen, thighs, breasts and buttocks; initially they resemble deep reddish-purple marks. Within six months of giving birth they will have faded to almost imperceptible white streaks, which will only show up slightly.

Although you can't prevent stretch marks entirely, you can keep your skin supple and your circulation active with regular, gentle exercise such as walking or swimming. Daily massage after the first three months of pregnancy, using a rich base oil such as avocado, peach nut kernel or jojoba, to which wheatgerm and essential oil of *Mandarin* have been added, keeps the skin particularly supple and may help to reduce stretch marks.

One homoeopathic remedy that is sometimes recommended is *Calcarea fluorica*. Excessive weight gain will exacerbate stretch marks, but dieting during pregnancy is inappropriate, and in any case won't prevent them.

Symptoms of Pregnancy

See Signs and Symptoms of Pregnancy

Syntometrine

When the placenta is delivered during the third stage of labour, following the birth of your baby, Syntocinon or Syntometrine are routinely given to reduce the risk of excessive blood loss. Syntocinon is a combination of two drugs: synthetic oxytocin, which acts like naturally occurring oxytocin, ensuring strong enough contractions of the womb to expel the placenta; and ergometrine, which ensures that the contractions close the cervix.

It is usual for Syntometrine or Syntocinon to be given, by injection, after the delivery of the first shoulder of the baby, thereby allowing around 7 minutes for the delivery of the placenta, almost immediately after the birth of the baby, before the cervix closes. If administered in this way the umbilical cord will need to be cut immediately rather than leaving it until it has finished pulsating. Because of this, it is the policy in some maternity units to wait for 30 minutes after the birth before giving Syntometrine or Syntocinon. This gives more time for a less rushed third stage.

There is of course a choice about whether or not you receive Syntometrine or Syntocinon to assist you in delivering the placenta. The occasions when it is most likely to be unnecessary are if you have had a completely drug-free, 'natural' labour and delivery, when your third stage follows this same pattern. If you have had an epidural for pain relief, for example, this may mean that delivery of the placenta isn't straightforward and that you will need help in order to complete the third stage successfully.

As ever, you need to discuss your particular circumstances and requirements with your midwife.

See also **Third Stage**

Tt

T'ai Chi

Unless you already practise T'ai chi, then beginning to learn when pregnant may not be the best time, although you will probably be able to find a teacher who is more than happy to take you on.

T'ai chi originated as a martial art, but because it improves stamina and flexibility and enhances positive health it has become popular as a form of exercise. The exercises take the form of a set routine of postures and movements which link harmoniously together to affect all parts of the body including the internal organs. The slow body movements, mental concentration and breathing are synchronized to stimulate the flow of energy, or 'chi', within the body. It is a sort of physically active meditation and has a beneficial effect not only on physical but also mental and emotional health.

For the reasons described above, T'ai chi has enormous benefits during pregnancy, although some of the postures may need to be adapted to your pregnant shape. T'ai chi also requires consistent and reflective practice, which may be hard to fit in if your daily routine is already somewhat hectic.

Further information in the UK can be requested from the British Council for Chinese Martial Arts (*see Useful Addresses*).

See also **Relaxation**

Taste

Many women find that when they are pregnant their sense of taste changes subtly. This may include having a constant metallic taste in the mouth, or increased salivation, a craving for eating strange things, or a sudden aversion to foods that you once liked. These changes will resolve themselves after the baby is born.

See also **Pica**, **Ptyalism**

Teeth

You are eligible for free dental care during your pregnancy and until your baby is a year old. Your teeth are slightly at risk during pregnancy because of the effect of the hormone oestrogen, which can make your gums spongy and more liable to infection. It is this that needs keeping an eye on, rather than an increased risk of cavities. You may need to pay special attention to the condition of your gums, visiting the oral hygienist and taking more time over gently cleaning your teeth after each meal. It used to be said that you lost a tooth for each baby you had, but that certainly doesn't need to be the case!

See also **Gingivitis**, **Gums (Bleeding)**

TENS (Transcutaneous Electrical Nerve Stimulation)

By placing electrodes at a number of sites on your lower back and exposing the nerves in the skin of your back to a brief electrical current, you can also affect those nerves in the spinal cord which transmit the pain message from your womb to your brain during labour. This has the effect of either reducing or blocking the sensation of pain from the contractions. There is no effect on the baby, and TENS may provide enough pain relief to get you through labour, or mean that less additional pain relief is required.

It is an option to be considered, but you need to find out whether or not you will be able to use it, or even if you can tolerate the sensation on your skin, by having a practice run. Don't wait until you are in the middle of labour to find out you don't like it. Talk to your midwife and to any mothers you know who have used it about its ease and effectiveness. Bear in mind, however, that your experience – although it may be similar – will be different from anyone else's. In addition, many hospitals do not yet supply TENS, so you may have to hire your own equipment (*see Useful Addresses*).

See also **Pain Relief**

Thalassaemia

Thalassaemia is a form of anaemia that occurs because the red blood cells are a distorted shape and cannot carry enough haemoglobin. It is a hereditary disorder occurring mostly among people of Mediterranean origin. A pregnant mother with thalassaemia will need careful monitoring throughout to ensure that her health and the health of her baby remain good. Folic acid supplements are usually given because this helps the bone marrow, which is very active in replacing the short-lived red blood cells.

Thick Skin

You may find that this something you need to develop in pregnancy! Once your bump is visible, you seem to become public property. When I was pregnant I had a complete stranger come up to me in a restaurant and ask if he could feel my bump and, to my amazement, I let him. More intrusive are those individuals who make unwanted comments and give unwanted advice. This can range from 'Aren't you getting fat?' to 'You won't want to work after your baby's born' to 'Make sure they don't give you Syntometrine.' Worst still, some comments aren't even well-meaning and others are thinly-disguised old wives' tales or plain horror stories. Ignore them, even if this means not seeing a certain relative or friend while you are pregnant. Turn to the people whose opinions and experience you value and trust. Alternatively, you can practise your assertiveness training and tell anyone who tries to lecture you that you are not interested. In any event, be warned and try to spend time only with those who reinforce the positive aspects of impending parenthood.

See also **Anxiety**, **Emotions**

Third Stage

This is the third stage of labour, when the placenta is delivered. While you may not notice much of what is happening at this stage, having safely delivered and therefore being totally wrapped up in your new baby, your midwife has to make sure that the remaining contents of the womb – the placenta and membranes – are fully expelled. Her priority is to ensure there is no excessive bleeding or remnants left behind that could cause a subsequent infection.

It is easy to forget the third stage, and how you would like it managed. So talk to your midwife about different approaches and what is possible. For example, if you don't want the umbilical cord cut until it has stopped pulsating, you need to know that administering Syntometrine needs to be delayed. Giving this injection as your baby's shoulders are born limits the time before the placenta must be delivered, and this requires the cord to be cut immediately at birth. Syntometrine can still be given after the cord has been cut, if it is needed to assist the delivery of the placenta.

See also **Birth**, **Labour**, **Syntometrine**

Thrush

This extremely irritating fungal infection of the vulva and vagina, caused by the fungus *Candida albicans*. It is very common during pregnancy because of both the change in your hormonal make-up and the decrease in immunity. *Candida albicans* is present in the gut in between 25 and 50 per cent of the population, where it causes no problems unless there is a change in its environment allowing it to flourish.

While conventional treatments in the form of antifungal pessaries and creams are usually effective, to reduce your susceptibility or to avoid chronic thrush there are a number of steps you can take:

- *reduce your intake of sweet, starchy and refined foods;*
- *eat lots of fresh fruit and vegetables, live yoghurt (check the label to make sure it contains acidophilus, the live yoghurt culture), garlic;*
- *try adding powdered acidophilus, available from health food shops, to your food;*
- *drink lots of water and herb teas;*
- *wear only cotton underwear, avoid tights, and wash pants out in mild soap, not detergent, rinsing well without fabric softener;*

- *go without wearing any pants when it's practical;*
- *wash and dry your vulva carefully after peeing and making love: sit on the lavatory and pour warm, clean water over your genitals;*
- *use a condom and lots of lubricating jelly while any infection is clearing up: avoid penetrative intercourse if you are very itchy and sore;*
- *don't add scented oils to your bath water, or use any form of vaginal deodorant;*
- *apply live yoghurt to your vulva; you can even insert a mini-tampon or sterilized natural sponge which has been dipped in live yoghurt into your vagina;*
- *you may be able to get tea-tree oil pessaries from a health store; these are antibacterial and antiviral as well as antifungal.*

Even if you are taking these preventative measures, or treating yourself, you should mention any irritation or infection to your midwife or doctor. You may well benefit from a medical diagnosis and conventional treatment as well.

If you use *Canesten*, available without prescription from your pharmacist, ask your partner to use it as well, to prevent recurrent cross-infection.

See also **Antibiotics**

Tiredness

While this can be a symptom of lack of sleep, it can also be a sign of other problems with which you may need help and treatment, for example anaemia. It may also be emotional in origin as well as physical: chronic tiredness with no apparent cause may be a result of depression. In early pregnancy (during the first three months), tiredness can be overwhelming for no apparent reason. It does pass, but you may have to reconcile yourself to early nights for a while.

Very often a symptom as intangible as tiredness, while being common in pregnancy, can be difficult to treat. Bear in mind that your body is accommodating both a new life and enormous physical and emotional upheaval. Even though this is perfectly natural, the adjustments you are having to make are very demanding on your energy. It is very often on occasions like these that alternative therapies come into their own, not just because of their holistic approach in rebalancing the body and treating disorders but also in actively promoting positive health.

If persistent tiredness is spoiling your pregnancy, look for any specific reasons and treat those, but also look to alternative therapies such as reflexology, shiatsu, homoeopathy or acupuncture to supplement a positive programme of good nutrition, rest and gentle exercise. It is important not to allow yourself to become chronically tired before your baby is born, because you will need lots of energy for the birth and afterwards.

Compare **Insomnia**
See also **Anaemia, Sleep**

Tissue Salts

See **Biochemic Tissue Salts**

Toxaemia

This means, literally, poisoning of the blood by toxins. It was previously thought to be the cause of pre-eclampsia, which was sometimes referred to as toxaemia of pregnancy.
See also **Pre-eclampsia**

Toxoplasmosis

Toxoplasma is a parasite found in cat faeces and raw meat. If infected with it, it can cause flu-like symptoms but no other more serious problems – unless you are pregnant. The parasite can severely affect your unborn child, causing a number of problems including brain damage, blindness and stillbirth.

Avoid the possibility of toxoplasmosis by taking the following precautions:

- *never eat raw or undercooked meat or meat products, and wash your hands thoroughly after handling uncooked meats;*
- *always carefully wash uncooked fruit and vegetables;*
- *don't eat unpasteurized goat's milk cheese or drink unpasteurized goat's milk;*
- *if you handle cats or kittens, wash your hands thoroughly afterwards;*
- *if you have to change a cat litter tray, wear gloves and wash your hands thoroughly afterwards, though best of all would be to have someone else change the litter for you;*
- *when gardening, wear gloves and wash your hands thoroughly afterwards.*

By the age of 30, three out of 10 people will have been infected with toxoplasmosis without knowing it and will be immune to subsequent infections. Without a blood test you won't know whether or not you are immune, but you can ask for this blood test before you become pregnant. It will show whether you are immune or not; if you are not, you will need to take the precautions described above.

The same blood test can also show if you have the infection. If the test is positive, and you are pregnant, you will need to be treated with antibiotics – this will reduce the risk of infection to your baby by 60 to 70 per cent. If you need further information about toxoplasmosis, contact the Toxoplasmosis Trust (*see Useful Addresses*).

Transition

Between the first and second stage of labour there is a phase where the hormonal message telling the cervix to dilate changes to one telling the womb to push the baby out. If the cervix is fully dilated when this occurs, transition from one stage to the other follows smoothly and, in fact, you may not notice it particularly. But if the cervix is still not fully dilated before the urge to push begins, there can be a certain amount of hormonal confusion which can be difficult to deal with. Very often, if this happens, women find themselves having to concentrate hard to avoid becoming overwhelmed, and don't welcome any offers of support or advice. This is the notorious time for women to tell their husbands, partners, midwife and anyone else within earshot what they think of them. And not all of it will be complimentary!

If you have a difficult transition, bear in mind that it heralds the end of the first stage and that your baby will be born quite soon. However overwhelming it seems, rely on your instincts about what position to adopt, and focus on what your body is telling you. If you have an urge to push before your cervix is fully dilated, try getting onto all fours or in a knee-to-chest position. Also try blowing out on every other breath while trying not to push, until the midwife gives you the go-ahead.

If you and your husband or partner have discussed this phase, it may be that he can be helpful with supporting you and encouraging you without being put off if you reject his suggestions. Distraction tactics may have their place now: try to maintain eye contact with your partner, or perhaps listen to some music or try to sing or just concentrate (albeit difficult) on something else!

See also **Birth, Labour, Third Stage**

Transverse Lie

If the baby is lying across the womb rather than head-down, and continues to do so up to labour, then the lie of the baby is referred to as transverse. If this is the case at the beginning of labour, the baby is found to be a shoulder presentation, which would make vaginal delivery impossible and a caesarean section unavoidable.

Transverse lie and shoulder presentation occurs in about 1 in 250 births, usually in women who have already had more than one baby. If this problem is suspected towards the end of pregnancy, an ultrasound scan can confirm the baby's position and avoid discovering this after labour has started.

See also **Anterior Position, Breech Presentation, Brow Presentation, Face Presentation, Unstable Lie**

Trial of Labour

This is more accurately referred to as a trial of vaginal delivery. In some cases, where vaginal delivery is not certain, it is possible to allow a trial of labour. This can only happen in a well-equipped maternity unit with the necessary staff available should it be essential to perform a caesarean section. A trial of vaginal delivery is also only possible where the mother and her unborn baby are fit and healthy and there are no other potential problems.

A trial of vaginal delivery would be considered when a degree of cephalopelvic disproportion is suspected (where it is uncertain whether the head will pass through the pelvic bones adequately). Should it become apparent

that the baby's head is stuck, a caesarean section
will be performed.

See also **Caesarean Section, Cephalopelvic
Disproportion, Labour**

Trimesters

Pregnancy, considered to be a nine-month period, is
divided up into three sections of three months each. These
three-month sections are referred to as trimesters. So the
first trimester is the first three-month period, the second
is months 4 through 6 of the pregnancy, and the third
trimester the last three months.

See also **Fetal Development**

Triple Test

This is a blood test that can detect whether or not a woman
has an increased risk of her baby having either Spina Bifida
or Down's Syndrome. There is also now a Triple-Plus test,
which tests for yet another substance in the mother's blood
which can indicate whether or not there is an increased risk
of Down's Syndrome. The Triple-Plus test can be done at 13
weeks. If you would like more information about this, and
where the test can be done privately if necessary, contact
the Down's Syndrome Screening Service (*see Useful
Addresses*), which publishes a booklet entitled *Screening
for Down's Syndrome: A Patient's Guide.*

Compare **Bart's Test**
See also **Down's Syndrome**

Twins

See **Multiple Pregnancy**

Uu

Ultrasound Scan

It is customary in the UK for all pregnant women to have
at least one ultrasound scan during their pregnancy, usually
at around 16 to 18 weeks, but sometimes earlier. This is
usually done to confirm your dates, and in conjunction with
blood tests for assessing any risk of Spina Bifida and
Down's Syndrome; it is also useful for diagnosis of multiple
pregnancy. While it also plays a major role in reassuring
mothers that all is well with their baby, it should not be
forgotten that the scan is also a diagnostic tool and can
sometimes reveal problems in the developing baby.

Ultrasound scans reflect high-pitched sound waves
back from internal organs as echoes. These can be
electronically reproduced on a screen as a recognizable
image of your baby, and can also provide you with a picture
you can keep. The ultrasound operator can then 'hold' an
image on the screen and measure the length of the baby's
thigh to confirm his or her maturity; it's also possible to
check the major organs, number of fingers and toes, etc.
An experienced operator could probably see what sex your

baby is, especially on a scan done later in your pregnancy. He or she won't mention this or tell you unless you ask and he or she is sure. Some hospitals have a blanket policy of never revealing the sex of a baby to the parents at all.

The ultrasound scan is also extremely valuable in seeing where the placenta is placed. Antenatal diagnosis of placenta praevia has made an enormous difference in the safe managing of this type of pregnancy and delivery. If at 16 to 18 weeks the placenta is seen to be low-lying, a subsequent scan in the last three months can show whether or not is has 'moved up', as it often does.

Ultrasound scanning has also made the use of amniocentesis much safer. Being able to 'see' into the womb, and exactly where the baby and placenta are situated, is very helpful in a skilled procedure like this.

Although the long-term safety of ultrasound scanning has not been established, it has now been in routine use for 20 years, and its benefits seem to far outweigh any known negative effects.

Compare **Alpha Fetoprotein (AFP) Test,
Amniocentesis, Nuchal Translucency Scan, Triple Test**
See also **Placenta Praevia**

Umbilical Cord

The umbilical cord is your baby's lifeline, his or her link via the placenta to all the nutrients and oxygen he or she needs for healthy growth in the womb. The cord also transports carbon dioxide and waste products away. It consists of two umbilical arteries and one umbilical vein, and its total length is on average around 50 cm (20 inches).

After birth the cord is clamped in two places and then cut between the two clamps, usually after the baby has begun breathing independently. Your midwife will check on the cord stump each day, and advise you on its care. She will probably remove the clamp after a day or so and tie a piece of tape securely around the stump, which needs to be kept clean and dry, and shouldn't be covered by the baby's nappy. Between the sixth and 10th day after birth, the remaining piece of cord has usually withered and blackened and dropped off.

See also **Placenta**, **Syntometrine**, **Third Stage**

Unstable Lie

This describes the changing position of the baby in the womb, and is only noted as such if changes occur between antenatal visits after 36 weeks. Ideally during these last few weeks the baby adopts a head-down position, ready for labour and delivery, even if the head isn't engaged. An unstable lie is noted and will need to be assessed if it continues up to the beginning of labour. If there is a breech or shoulder presentation, the midwife will have to decide whether a trial of vaginal labour is advisable or if the obstetrician should be consulted. A home birth would probably have to be transferred to hospital in case a caesarean section proves necessary.

Compare **Transverse Lie**
See also **Breech Presentation**, **Engagement**,
Trial of Labour

Urine Testing

You will have your urine tested routinely at every antenatal visit because it is a useful way of checking for a number of problems which occasionally arise in pregnancy.

The presence of protein or glucose or ketones may need further investigation. Protein could indicate one of three things: contamination of your sample, a possible urine infection (unfortunately common during pregnancy) or, occasionally, pre-eclampsia. Glucose may show up as a trace because you had just eaten a meal with a high sugar content before taking the sample; or it might indicate diabetes. If this were considered a possibility, you would probably be asked to take a Glucose Tolerance Test. Ketones in your urine could also mean diabetes, though they can also indicate that you need to eat something (that is, they reveal that your blood sugar level is low). In the absence of available carbohydrate, your body utilizes fats to produce energy: ketones are a by-product of this process.

See also **Glucose Tolerance Test, Ketones, Pre-eclampsia**

Uterus

See **Womb**

Vv

Vaccination

See **Immunization**

Vacuum Extraction

Applying a cap to the baby's head and using suction to keep it there, the head can be gently pulled down the birth canal in order to assist delivery. It takes about 10 to 15 minutes to set up, but can be used before the cervix is fully dilated. When correctly positioned it can help the baby flex his or her neck and turn the head for easier delivery. If the mother is particularly tired at the end of a long first stage, or the contractions are growing less strong, vacuum extraction (also called Ventouse) can be helpful. It can't, however, be used in an emergency where there is any urgent need to deliver the baby, as it takes too long.

After a vacuum extraction your baby's head will probably show signs of swelling and bruising, but this causes no long-term harm and quickly subsides.

Compare **Forceps**

Vagina

This is the passage from the cervix at the bottom of the womb to the outside of the body, and is positioned below the clitoris and urethra, and above the anus. It forms part of the birth canal, and stretches to allow the birth of the baby. If a tear occurs, or an episiotomy is needed, this will occur at the bottom of the vagina. Following the birth, pelvic floor exercises help heal, tone and firm the area.

See also **Pelvic Floor Exercises**

Varicose Veins

Unfortunately the pregnancy hormone progesterone relaxes the muscular walls of the veins, makes the valves inefficient and makes circulation sluggish. If you have a family history of varicose veins, this may make you more prone to them during pregnancy. If your work involves standing for long periods of time, this may increase your risk also. Varicose veins can occur in the legs, the anus and, very rarely, in the vulva.

To avoid exacerbating any risk of varicose veins in your legs make sure you get enough gentle exercise during your pregnancy. Walking is good as this will exercise your calf muscles and help your circulation. Put your feet up as often as you can – the rest will do you good! If you have to stand for any length of time, try to keep flexing your calf muscles (this will also help if you feel faint). When sitting, make sure your legs aren't crossed and elevate your feet on a low stool. Exercise your legs and ankles by rotating your feet while sitting, as this will also exercise your calf muscles. Support tights may be helpful too. If you have varicose veins that become painful during pregnancy, try sleeping with the foot of the bed raised by about 15 cm (6 inches). Witch hazel compresses applied to the veins may help reduce swelling and inflammation. Increase your dietary intake of garlic, which is always good for improving circulation. The addition of essential oil of lemon to a warm bath may also be soothing. Don't massage affected veins.

Take whatever preventative measures you can to relieve the discomfort of varicose veins. They will improve once your baby has been delivered and your hormones settle down again.

See also **Haemorrhoids**

Ventouse

See **Vacuum Extraction**

Vernix

Vernix caseosa is the white, greasy covering over the baby's skin while in the womb. It appears at around 30 to 32 weeks, and is most evident between weeks 36 and 37, and usually evident at birth. It forms a protective barrier against the amniotic fluid of the womb and protects the baby's skin from any friction.

Vitamin A

Vitamin A in large quantities has been associated with some birth defects. However. you are unlikely to be eating it in large enough amounts, under normal circumstances, for this to be a problem. Don't take vitamin supplements that include vitamin A, and check with your doctor about any vitamin supplements you may consider taking. It is also suggested that you *don't* eat liver or other liver products while you are pregnant, because liver has been found to contain high levels of vitamin A.

See also **Vitamins**

Vitamin K

It is usual for babies in the UK to be given a dose of vitamin K after birth, because it is an essential factor in the blood's ability to clot efficiently. Babies are given it because their own ability to synthesize vitamin K in the gut is inefficient for the first few days after birth.

Breastfed babies get a good supply of vitamin K from their mother's colostrum first of all, and then from breastmilk itself. It is not considered necessary by all maternity units for babies to have vitamin K, and it is preferable for it to be given orally rather than by injection. So discuss this with your midwife. It is often considered most advisable for pre-term babies, and for those whose delivery was particularly difficult.

Vitamins

Vitamins are essential for health. If you are eating nutritiously there should be no need for additional vitamins during pregnancy. Your body can store vitamins A, D and B_{12}, and, taken in excess, vitamins A, C, D and B_6 can be toxic, so it's better not to take vitamin supplements during pregnancy unless advised to do so by your doctor.

See also **Diet**, **Minerals**

Ww

Water Birth

There is now quite extensive evidence to suggest that immersion in warm water for the first stage of labour provides extremely good pain relief. Many maternity units in the UK now have birthing pools available, so this may be an option you'd like to consider. However, this will only be possible if you meet certain criteria, which include:

- *no known problems or risk factors;*
- *size of baby is compatible with your ability to deliver safely;*
- *you must be at least 38 weeks pregnant at time of labour;*
- *the baby must be head-down;*
- *if your waters have broken, there must be no sign of meconium signalling that the baby is in distress;*
- *your midwife is satisfied with your baby's heart rate on admission.*

Research has shown that in warm water the cervix dilates at 2.5 cm (1 inch) an hour as opposed to 1 cm (half an inch), so the duration of the first stage is reduced. However, it is more difficult for a midwife to monitor your progress, so there may be occasions when you will be asked to leave the pool. If for any reason your midwife is concerned about you or your baby's safety, you will also be asked to leave the pool. Agreeing to a water birth is dependent on agreement between yourself and your midwife, and you have to understand what is safe and sensible.

Your choice of pain relief if you are in the water will be limited. Gas and air is fine, but using pethidine, TENS or having an epidural isn't possible.

If you are considering a water birth in your own home, there are some quite important practical considerations to bear in mind. You will need to hire the pool itself, and for a period of weeks as you won't know exactly when your baby will arrive. You have to be sure that the midwife attending your birth is confident about water birth, familiar with safety guidelines and knows how to manage an emergency should it occur. Water birth pools hold 100 gallons of water, and one gallon weighs about 4.5 kg (10 lb). So if you are planning to have your birth pool in an upstairs bedroom, you had better be sure your floor can take the weight! You also need to check that your domestic water tank holds enough water to fill your birth pool (most domestic tanks hold between 40 and 70 gallons).

Having considered all these important points, if you want to find out more contact the Active Birth Centre (*see Useful Addresses*) who can supply you with information about water births and where you can hire birthing pools.

See also **Birth Plan, Meconium, Odent (Dr Michel)**

Weight Gain

Average weight gain during pregnancy is around 10 to 12 kg (22 to 26 lb). You gain around 2.5 kg (5.5 lb) per week during the first 20 weeks, and then only about 0.5 kg (1 lb) per week until your baby is born.

The average distribution of weight gain is as follows:

- *baby: 3.4 kg (7.5 lb);*
- *placenta: 0.7 kg (1.5 lb);*
- *amniotic fluid: 1 kg (2.2 lb);*
- *increase in womb: 1 kg (2.2 lb);*
- *blood volume: 1.4 kg (3 lb);*
- *breasts: 0.5 kg (1 lb);*
- *fat: 3.4 kg (7.5 lb).*

Bear in mind that these figures are only average, and that if your baby turns out to be 4 kg (9 lb), your weight gain could be expected to be above this. Less emphasis is paid now on keeping weight gain to a minimum than on a healthy, happy pregnancy which incorporates a well-balanced, nutritious diet. Pregnancy is not the time to diet.

You will lose around 10 kg (20 lb) in weight within the first two weeks following the birth, including the weight of your baby. Within three to four months you should find that you are back to your pre-pregnancy weight, and if you breastfeed your baby you could find that you return to your pre-pregnant weight reasonably quickly. This is because the fat stores laid down during pregnancy are designed to be used up in the process of milk production.

Whooping Cough

You will be offered immunization for your baby for whooping cough (also known as pertussis) in conjunction with immunization for diphtheria, tetanus and polio. These injections are given in three stages when your baby is 3 months, 4 months and 5 months old.

Your baby won't have any of your immunity to whooping cough, because the antibodies to this disease cannot cross the placenta. While there has been some publicity over the years about damage caused by the whooping cough vaccine, statistically the risks associated with whooping cough in young babies outweigh the risks associated with the vaccine. If you are unsure about the benefits of immunization, talk to your health visitor, who should be up to date on all the latest information, or contact Informed Parent (*see Useful Addresses*)

In addition, a homoeopath might be able to advise you on a constitutional remedy for your baby, to promote his or her resistance to whooping cough whether or not you decide to go ahead with immunization. But bear in mind that this is no substitute for immunization.

See also **Homoeopathy**, **Immunization**

Womb

The womb, also known as the uterus, is a pear-shaped, muscular organ that is about 7.5 cm (3 in) long and 5 cm (2 in) at its widest part when you are not pregnant. It is divided into two main parts: the body of the womb consists of the top two-thirds, and the cervix or neck of the womb is the lower third. The lining of the womb is called the endometrium; it is this that responds to hormonal changes in your menstrual cycle. The endometrium either comes away at the end of each cycle to form your period, or develops to nurture a growing fetus if an egg is fertilized.

The muscular properties of the womb respond to the hormone oestrogen to grow and expand to contain your growing baby. Growth of the muscles of the womb occurs for the first 20 weeks, after which progesterone relaxes these same muscles, allowing them to stretch.

After the birth the womb returns to its pre-pregnancy size by a process referred to as involution, which takes about six to eight weeks. Involution is greatly assisted by the hormone stimulated by breastfeeding, oxytocin.

See also **Involution, Menstrual Cycle, Oxytocin**

Work

You are entitled to paid time off work for antenatal visits while you are pregnant, and can continue working for as long as you feel comfortable doing so. You can, however, start your maternity leave and receive maternity benefit from 11 weeks before your expected date of delivery.

As long as you fulfil certain criteria, you are also entitled not to be dismissed from work because of your pregnancy, and to return to your old job after the baby is born.

Your employers should have all the details relevant, so discuss your plans with them. In addition, in the UK, the Maternity Alliance (*see Useful Addresses*) can give you up-to-date information.

See also **Benefits, Maternity Rights**

Xx

X-Chromosome

Whether or not your baby will be a boy or a girl depends on the male sperm, which will either carry the X-chromosome or the Y-chromosome. The egg to be fertilized carries only the X-chromosome. If your egg is fertilized by an X-chromosome from the male, you will have a girl (XX), and if fertilized by a Y-chromosome, you will have a boy (XY). The deciding factor in the sex of a child is the male sperm, so you have a 50/50 chance of having one or the other. However, there are some circumstances that are thought to be more favourable to the conception of one sex or the other, although nothing is foolproof. The only time where the sex of your unborn baby is really relevant is when your family has a history of hereditary disease which is linked to the sex chromosome – for example haemophilia – but this requires specialist care and counselling.

X-Rays

Generally, any sort of X-ray should be avoided in pregnancy, especially during the first three months when rapid growth and development of the major organs is taking place. This is because there is some risk that X-rays can harm the development of the baby's cells. Whenever you have an X-ray when you are not pregnant, you will be asked for the date of your 'last menstrual period', which is a quick check to see whether or not you may be in the first stages of pregnancy. The use of lead aprons is customary too, as an added precaution. Even if you are having a routine X-ray at the dentist, although the risk is small, your dentist should check too.

Later in pregnancy the use of X-rays may be necessary to check the size of your pelvic cavity, prior to birth, for example. You can be reassured that, if an X-ray during pregnancy is necessary for some reason, it will be at a time when the benefits outweigh the risks.

Y y

Y-Chromosome

See X-Chromosome

Yoga

If you already practise yoga it will be a good exercise to continue with during pregnancy, with the necessary modifications as you get bigger. Talk to your instructor about how much is sensible to do; if unsure, he or she will probably be able to refer you to someone with more expertise. As long as your yoga teacher is experienced and properly qualified, you should be fine.

For those wishing to find some form of gentle exercise during pregnancy, specially designed yoga classes for pregnant women are an excellent form of antenatal exercise. The combination of stretching, relaxation and gentle exercise is particularly suitable. Finding a yoga class or teacher who is experienced in organizing classes for pregnant women may be possible through your midwife, local branch of the National

Childbirth Trust or the British Wheel of Yoga (*see Useful Addresses*).

Yoga is wonderfully helpful in teaching you to focus attention on your posture throughout pregnancy. It encourages strength and suppleness, and correct breathing. In addition, breathing exercises and meditation are especially useful for reducing muscular and emotional tension and promoting relaxation and positive health. Many of the yoga poses, adapted to your pregnant state, have therapeutic properties. A number of pregnancy ailments can also be alleviated by yoga, including constipation, heartburn, morning sickness, backache, and the pain of labour.

See also **Breathing Exercises**, **Meditation**, **Posture**, **Relaxation**

Zz

Zinc

This is a trace mineral essential to human development.
It is thought to be necessary to assist the egg in implanting
in the womb.

Zinc deficiency is uncommon and, although there is
a larger amount present in cow's milk, the availability of
zinc in human breastmilk is greater. Good sources of zinc
include red meat, pulses, wholegrains and bananas. It is
worth noting that taking iron supplements can inhibit zinc
absorption. If you are prescribed iron supplements, ensure
that your diet includes an adequate source of zinc.

Compare **Folic Acid**, **Minerals**
See also **Implantation**

Zone Therapy

See **Reflexology**

Zygote

This is the first stage of the fertilized egg, prior to cell division and implantation in the lining of the womb.
Compare **Fetal Development**

USEFUL ADDRESSES

Active Birth

ACTIVE BIRTH CENTRE
26 Bickerton Road
London N19
0171–561 9006

AIMS (ASSOCIATION FOR THE IMPROVEMENT OF MATERNITY SERVICES)
40 Kingswood Avenue
London NW6 6LS
0181–960 5585

BIRTHWORKS
Unit 4E
Brent Mill Trading Estate
South Brent
Devon TQ10 9YT
01364 72802

INDEPENDENT MIDWIVES ASSOCIATION
Nightingale Cottage
Shamblehurst Lane
Botley
Southampton SO32 2BY
01703 694429

INFORMED CHOICE
PO Box 669
Bristol BS99 5FG
Recorded message/answer-phone to order information leaflets: 0891 210400
provides information leaflets from MIDIRS (Midwives Information and Research Service) on topics such as ultrasound, support in labour, monitoring, alcohol, positions in labour

MATERNITY ALLIANCE
14 Britannia Street
London WC1 9JP
0171–837 1265

MEET-A-MUM ASSOCIATION
53 Malden Avenue
London SE25 4HS
0181–656 7318

MULTIPLE BIRTHS FOUNDATION
Queen Charlotte's and
Chelsea Hospital
Goldhawk Road
London W6 0XG
0181–740 3519

NATIONAL CHILDBIRTH TRUST
Alexander House
Oldham Terrace
Acton
London W3 6NH
0181–992 8637

SOCIETY TO SUPPORT HOME CONFINEMENT
Lydgate
Wolsingham
Co Durham DL13 3HA
01388 528044

TAMBA (TWINS AND MULTIPLE BIRTH ASSOCIATION)
PO Box 30
Little Sutton
South Wirral L66 1TH
01732 86800

Breastfeeding

ASSOCIATION OF BREASTFEEDING MOTHERS
26 Hornsham Close
London SE26 4PH
0181–778 4769

LA LECHE LEAGUE
Box BM 3434
London WC1N 3XX
0171–242 1278

Support Groups

APEC (ACTION ON PRE-ECLAMPSIA)
31–33 College Road
Harrow
Middlesex HA1 1EJ
01923 266778

ASSOCIATION FOR SPINA BIFIDA AND HYDROCEPHALUS
ASBAH House
42 Park Road
Peterborough
Cambridgeshire PE1 2UQ
01733 555988

BLISS (SUPPORT FOR PREMATURE AND SPECIAL CARE BABIES)
17–21 Emerald Street
London WC1N 3QL
0171–831 9393

CAESAREAN SUPPORT NETWORK
2 Hurst Park Drive
Huyton
Liverpool L36 1TF
0151–480 1184

CERVICAL STITCH NETWORK
'Fairfield'
Wolverton Road
Norton Lindsey
Warwickshire CV35 8LA
01926 843223

CHILD BEREAVEMENT TRUST
11 Millside
Riverdale
Bourne End
Buckinghamshire SL8 5EB
01494 765001

DOWN'S SYNDROME ASSOCIATION
155 Mitcham Road
London SW17 9PG
0181–682 4001

THE INFORMED PARENT
19 Woodlands Road
Harrow
Middlesex HA1 2RT
for information about immunization

MISCARRIAGE ASSOCIATION
c/o Clayton Hospital
Northgate
Wakefield
West Yorks WF1 3JS
01924 200799

NATIONAL COUNCIL FOR ONE PARENT FAMILIES
255 Kentish Town Road
London NW5 2LZ
0171–267 1361

SAFTA (SUPPORT AFTER TERMINATION FOR ABNORMALITY)
73–75 Charlotte Street
London W1P 1LB
0171–631 0280

SANDS (STILLBIRTH AND NEONATAL DEATH SOCIETY)
28 Portland Place
London W1N 4DE
0171–436 7940

SCOPE
12 Park Crescent
London W1N 4EQ
0171–636 5020
National freephone helpline
0800 626216 (Mon–Fri 9
a.m.–11 p.m.; Sat–Sun 2–6
p.m.)

TOXOPLASMOSIS SOCIETY
Room 26
61–71 Collier Street
London N1 9BE
0171–713 0599

Staying Healthy

**AVERT: NATIONAL AIDS
HELPLINE**
Freephone 0800 567 123

**BRITISH DIABETIC
ASSOCIATION**
10 Queen Anne Street
London W1M 9LD
0171–323 1531

**BRITISH DIETETIC
ASSOCIATION**
7th floor
Elizabeth House
22 Suffolk Street
Queensway
Birmingham B1 1LS
0121–643 5483

BRITISH WHEEL OF YOGA
1 Hamilton Place
Boston Road
Sleaford
Lincolnshire NG34 7ES
01529 306851

CONTINENCE FOUNDATION
2 Doughty Street
London WC1N 2PH
0171–213 0050

DEPARTMENT OF HEALTH
79 Whitehall
London SW1A 2NS
0171–210 4850
Health Information Service
freephone 0800 665544
(Mon–Fri 10 a.m.–5 p.m.)

**EATING IN PREGNANCY
HELPLINE**
0114 242 4084 (Mon–Fri and
24-hr answerphone)

**FAMILY HEALTH SERVICES
ASSOCIATION (FHSA)**
*see your local telephone
directory*

**FAMILY PLANNING
ASSOCIATION**
27–35 Mortimer Street
London W1N 3HT
0171–636 7866

FORESIGHT
Association for the Promotion
of Pre-conceptual Care
28 The Paddock
Godalming
Surrey GU7 1XD
01483 427839

HERPES ASSOCIATION
41 North Road
London N7 9DD
0171–609 9061

POSITIVELY WOMEN
5 Sebastian Street
London EC1V 0HE
0171–490 5515
*support for women who are
HIV-positive*

QUIT
Victory House
170 Tottenham Court Road
London W1P 0HA
0171–487 3000
*for information on giving up
smoking*

VEGAN SOCIETY
7 Battle Road
St Leonards-on-Sea
East Sussex TN37 7AA
01424 427393

VEGETARIAN SOCIETY
Parkdale
Dunham Road
Altrincham
Cheshire WA14 4QG
0161–928 0793

**YOGA FOR HEALTH
FOUNDATION**
Ickwell Bury
Biggleswade
Bedfordshire
01767 627271

Counselling and Psychotherapy

**ASSOCIATION FOR POSTNATAL
ILLNESS**
25 Jerdan Place
London SW6 1BE
0171–386 0868

**BRITISH ASSOCIATION FOR
COUNSELLING**
1 Regent Place
Rugby
Warwickshire CV21 2PJ
01788 578328

RELATE (MARRIAGE GUIDANCE)
Herbert Gray College
Little Church Street
Rugby
Warwickshire CV21 3AP
01788 573241

Complementary Therapies

AROMATHERAPY ORGANISATIONS COUNCIL
01858 434242

ASSOCIATION OF REFLEXOLOGISTS
27 Old Gloucester Street
London WC1 3XX
Offices: 01892 512612
National number: 0990 673320
send SAE for register of members

ASSOCIATION OF SYSTEMIC KINESIOLOGY
39 Browns Road
Surbiton
Surrey KT5 8ST
0181–399 3215

BACH CENTRE
Mount Vernon
Sotwell
Wallingford
Oxfordshire OX10 0PZ
01491 39489

BRITISH ASSOCIATION FOR AUTOGENIC TRAINING AND THERAPY
101 Harley Street
London W1N 1DF

BRITISH CHIROPRACTIC ASSOCIATION
Premier House
Greycoat Place
London SW1P 1SB
0171–222 8866

BRITISH COMPLEMENTARY MEDICINE ASSOCIATION
St Charles Hospital
Exmoor Street
London W10 6DZ
0181–964 1205

BRITISH COUNCIL OF CHINESE MARTIAL ARTS
46 Oaston Road
Nuneaton
Warwickshire CV11 6JZ
01203 394642
for information on T'ai Chi

**BRITISH HOLISTIC MEDICAL
ASSOCIATION**
St Marylebone Parish Church
Marylebone Road
London NW1 5LT
0171–262 5299

**BRITISH HOMOEOPATHIC
ASSOCIATION**
27a Devonshire Street
London W1N 7RJ
0171–935 2163

**BRITISH HYPNOTHERAPY
ASSOCIATION**
1 Wythburn Place
London W1H 5WL
0171–262 8852/723 4443

**BRITISH SCHOOL OF
OSTEOPATHY**
1–4 Suffolk Street
London SW1Y 4HG
0171–930 9254

BRITISH SHIATSU COUNCIL
121 Sheen Road
Richmond
Surrey TW9 1YJ
0181–852 1080

**BRITISH SOCIETY FOR
NUTRITIONAL MEDICINE**
PO Box 3AP
London W1A 3AP
0171–436 8532

**THE COUNCIL FOR
ACUPUNCTURE**
179 Gloucester Place
London NW1 6DX
0171–724 5756

**COUNCIL FOR
COMPLEMENTARY AND
ALTERNATIVE MEDICINE**
179 Gloucester Place
London NW1 6DX
0171–724 9103

**GENERAL COUNCIL AND
REGISTER OF NATUROPATHS**
6 Netherhall Gardens
London NW3 5RR
0171–435 8728

**GENERAL COUNCIL AND
REGISTER OF OSTEOPATHS**
56 London Street
Reading
Berkshire RG1 4SG
01734 576585

**NATIONAL INSTITUTE OF
MEDICAL HERBALISTS**
56 Longbrook Street
Exeter EX4 6AH
01392 426022

**NATIONAL REGISTER OF
HYPNOTHERAPISTS**
12 Cross Street
Nelson
Lancashire
01282 699378

**OSTEOPATHIC INFORMATION
CENTRE**
37 Soho Square
London W1V 5DG
0171–439 7177

**REGISTER OF TRADITIONAL
CHINESE MEDICINE**
19 Trinity Road
London N2 8JJ
0181–883 8431

SHIATSU SOCIETY
14 Oakdene Road
Redhill
Surrey RH1 6BT

SOCIETY OF HOMOEOPATHS
2 Artizan Road
Northampton NN1 4HU
01604 21400

**SOCIETY OF TEACHERS OF
ALEXANDER TECHNIQUE**
London House
266 Fulham Road
London SW10 9EL
0171–351 0828

Suppliers

AINSWORTH PHARMACY
38 New Cavendish Street
London W1M 7LH
0171–935 5330
*homoeopathic remedies
available by mail-order*

HELIOS PHARMACY
97 Camden Road
Tunbridge Wells
Kent TN1 2QR
01892 536393
*homoeopathic remedies by
mail-order*

MEDCARE LTD
39 Ashness Road
London SW11 6RY
0171–228 2577
*TENS suppliers (also check
with your midwife or
antenatal teacher for
advice)*

NEAL'S YARD REMEDIES
15 Neal's Yard
London WC2H 9DP
0171–379 7222
mail-order service available
on 0181–379 0705

OBTENS
Obstetric TENS Hire
17 Theresa Avenue
Bishopston
Bristol BS7 9ER
01272 429221

SHIRLEY PRICE
Essentia House
Upper Bond Street
Hinckley
Leicestershire LE10 1RS
01455 615436
aromatherapy oils

TISSERAND OILS
Newtown Road
Hove
Sussex BN3 7BA
01273 325666

Australia

ASSOCIATION OF MASSAGE
THERAPISTS
18a Spit Road
Mosman NSW 2088
969 8445

AUSTRALASIAN COLLEGE OF
NATURAL THERAPIES
620 Harris Street
Ultimo NSW 2007
(02) 212 6699

AUSTRALIAN ACADEMY OF
OSTEOPATHY
7th floor
235 Macquarie Street
Sydney NSW 2000
233 1655

AUSTRALIAN FEDERATION OF
HOMOEOPATHS
21 Bulah Close
Berowra Heights NSW 2082
(02) 456 3602

AUSTRALIAN NATURAL
THERAPISTS ASSOCIATION LTD
PO Box 522
Sutherland NSW 2232
(02) 521 2063

NATIONAL HERBALISTS
ASSOCIATION OF AUSTRALIA
14/249 Kingsgrove Road
Kingsgrove NSW 2208
502 2938

USA

**AMERICAN CHIROPRACTIC
ASSOCIATION**
1701 Clarendon Blvd
Arlington, VA 24203
703/276–8800

**AMERICAN OSTEOPATHIC
ASSOCIATION**
142 E. Ontario Street
Chicago, IL 60611
312/280–5800

**CALIFORNIA SCHOOL OF
HERBAL STUDIES**
P.O. Box 39
Forestville, CA 95436
707/887–7457

**DR. EDWARD BACH HEALING
SOCIETY**
644 Merrick Road
Lynbrook, NY 11563
516/593–2206

FLOWER ESSENCE SOCIETY
P.O. Box 1769
Nevada City, CA 95959
916/265–9163

**INTERNATIONAL ASSOCIATION
FOR CHILDBIRTH AT HOME**
P.O. Box 430
Glendale, CA 91209
213/663–4996

**LA LECHE LEAGUE
INTERNATIONAL**
9616 Minneapolis Avenue
P.O. Box 1209
Franklin Park, IL 60131–8209
708/455–7730

**NATIONAL CENTER FOR
HOMEOPATHY**
801 N. Fairfax Street
Alexandria, VA 22314
703/548–7790

**NATIONAL ORGANIZATION FOR
WOMEN**
1000 16th Street N.W.
Suite 700
Washington, DC 20036
202/331–0066

**NATIONAL RESOURCE CENTER
ON WOMEN AND AIDS**
2000 P. Street N.W.
Suite 508
Washington, DC 20036
202/872–1770

FURTHER READING

Janet Balaskas, *Active Birth* (Thorsons)
The Body Shop, *Mamatoto: A Celebration of Birth* (Virago)
Gordon Bourne, *Pregnancy* (Pan)
Miranda Castro, *Homoeopathy for Mother and Baby* (Papermac)
Susan Curtis and Romy Fraser, *Natural Healing for Women* (Pandora)
Caroline Flint, *Sensitive Midwifery* (Butterworth Heinemann)
Dr Anna Flynn and Melissa Brooks, *A Manual of Natural Family Planning* (Thorsons)
Sheila Kitzinger, *Pregnancy and Childbirth* (Michael Joseph)
Anna Knopfler, *Diabetes and Pregnancy* (Vermilion)
Nancy Durrell McKenna, *Birth* (Bloomsbury)
Peter Moore, *Born Too Early* (Thorsons)
Dr Michel Odent, *Birth Reborn* (Souvenir)
Renfrew, Fisher, Arms, *Bestfeeding: Getting Breastfeeding Right for You* (Celestial Arts)
Barbara Katz Rothman, *The Tentative Pregnancy* (Pandora)
Denise Tiran and Sue Mack, *Complementary Therapies for Pregnancy and Birth* (Balliere Tindall)
Nicky Wesson, *Alternative Maternity* (Vermilion)
–, *Home Birth* (Vermilion)